Ascend AI Processor Architecture and Programming

Ascend AI Processor Architecture and Programming

Principles and Applications of CANN

Xiaoyao Liang

*Supervisor and Academic Leader, Department of Computer Science and Engineering,
Shanghai Jiaotong University, Shanghai, China*

ELSEVIER

Elsevier
Radarweg 29, PO Box 211, 1000 AE Amsterdam, Netherlands
The Boulevard, Langford Lane, Kidlington, Oxford OX5 1GB, United Kingdom
50 Hampshire Street, 5th Floor, Cambridge, MA 02139, United States

Notices
Knowledge and best practice in this field are constantly changing. As new research and experience broaden our understanding, changes in research methods, professional practices, or medical treatment may become necessary.

Practitioners and researchers must always rely on their own experience and knowledge in evaluating and using any information, methods, compounds, or experiments described herein. In using such information or methods they should be mindful of their own safety and the safety of others, including parties for whom they have a professional responsibility.

To the fullest extent of the law, neither the Publisher nor the authors, contributors, or editors, assume any liability for any injury and/or damage to persons or property as a matter of products liability, negligence or otherwise, or from any use or operation of any methods, products, instructions, or ideas contained in the material herein.

Library of Congress Cataloging-in-Publication Data
A catalog record for this book is available from the Library of Congress

British Library Cataloguing-in-Publication Data
A catalogue record for this book is available from the British Library

ISBN: 978-0-12-823488-4

For information on all Elsevier publications
visit our website at https://www.elsevier.com/books-and-journals

Publisher: Glyn Jones
Editorial Project Manager: Naomi Robertson
Project Manager: Selvaraj Raviraj
Cover designer: Christian J. Bilbow

Typeset by SPi Global, India

Contents

About the Author

Xiaoyao Liang is a professor, PhD supervisor, and academic leader in the Department of Computer Science and Engineering, Shanghai Jiaotong University. He graduated from Harvard University, United States, and has worked in many companies such as Nvidia and Intel. His research directions include computer architecture, integrated circuit design, general graphics processor, and artificial intelligence processor architecture. He has published more than 80 papers, including for international top academic conferences ISCA, HPCA, MICRO, ISSCC, DAC, ICCAD, etc., among which two papers were selected as the annual best paper of computer architecture (IEEE MICRO TOP PICKS).

Preface

With the recent success of deep learning in the field of artificial intelligence, from CPUs to GPUs, to various application-specific processors, we are embracing another golden age of computer architecture evolution. However, the research and development cycle of processor chips ranges from a few years to a dozen years. To be successful in this new trend of the computer industry, the most important aspects include the perseverance and spirit of the craftsman.

When Huawei invited me to write a reference book for their Ascend AI processors, I accepted their request without any hesitation, due to the high recognition of Huawei as a hardware technology company and the sincerity of its employees in ensuring they are at the forefront of revolutionary technologies.

Huawei's launch of the AI processor for artificial intelligence computing offers much more computing power and significantly less power consumption. It brings greater possibilities for a wide range of deep learning applications. A famous Chinese proverb says "the journey of a thousand miles begins with a single step." The Ascend AI processor still has a long way to go. For a high-end processor, the development of the ecosystem and the acceptance by program developers play very important roles, which is critical to the success of this product. The purpose of writing this book is to primarily demystify the Ascend AI processor to the world through exploring its inner design concept. From both the software and hardware perspective, this text introduces good development practices for the Ascend AI processor platforms. Rome was not built in one day. If creating an ecosystem is a journey of a thousand miles, this book is the first step in this journey.

This book can be used as a selective textbook in the field of artificial intelligence processor design. Since the target readers are mainly engineers, we have limited the complexity of abstract formulas, theorems, and theoretical derivations as much as possible. The reader only needs to possess basic mathematical knowledge and programming skills, and there are no course prerequisites. The ideal audience for this book is R&D personnel who require large-scale deep learning calculations in the field of artificial intelligence, computer science, electronics, biomedicine, physics, chemistry, or financial statistics. The book, therefore, provides a comprehensive and effective reference to companies and developers of AI processors.

This book is divided into six chapters. The content includes basic theory of neural networks, computer processor design, open-source neural network architectures, Ascend AI processor hardware and software architecture, programming theory and methods, as well as use-case presentations, etc. By introducing both the theory and practical experiences, we hope to assist readers in understanding the DaVinci architecture used by the AI processor and master its specific programming and usage methods. Through this process, readers will be capable of creating their own artificial intelligence applications.

Many thanks to Xiaolei Wang, Zishan Jiang, and Xing Li for their great contributions to the writing of this book. They have injected great energy into sorting references, text editing, and testing of all the sample code in this book. Without their full commitment, it would not have been possible to complete this book successfully.

Thanks to Ziyuan Chen and several others for carefully editing and modifying the illustrations in this book as well as making the content clearer. After their feedback, the interpretation of images and concepts is more specific and clear.

Thanks to Huawei for the resources and support provided during the writing of this book.

Thanks to the support of Mr. Dongliang Sheng and Ms. Zhifang Zhong from Tsinghua University Press for their careful and meticulous efforts. Their involvement has guaranteed the quality of this book.

There are inevitable omissions and errors in the book, and readers are recommended to provide feedback, as appropriate.

## CHAPTER 1

Theoretical basis

1.1 Brief history of artificial intelligence

When the development of a skill reaches the peak, it can reflect highly anthropomorphic intelligence. From Ancient China's Master Yan's ability to sing and dance, to Ancient Arabic Jazari's automatic puppets (as shown in Fig. 1.1), the relentless pursuit of intelligence never ends. Human beings hope to give wisdom and thought to machines, which can be used to liberate productive forces, facilitate people's lives, and promote social development. From ancient myths to science fiction, and now to modern science and technology, they all demonstrate the human desire for intelligence. The birth of artificial intelligence (AI) was a slow and long process, whereas the improvement of AI is keeping pace with the development of human knowledge and even transcending human wisdom in some aspects. In the early days, the development of Formal Reasoning provided a research direction for the mechanization of human intelligence.

In the mid-17th century, Gottfried Wilhelm Leibniz, Rene Descartes, and Thomas Hobbes (Fig. 1.2) devoted themselves to the systematic study of rational thinking. These studies led to the emergence of the formal symbol system that became the beacon of AI research. By the 20th century, the contributions of Bertrand Arthur William Russell, Alfred North Whitehead, and Kurt Godel in the field of mathematical logic provided a theoretical basis for the mechanization of mathematical reasoning. The creation of the Turing Machine provided supporting evidence of machine thought from the view of semiotics. In the engineering domain, from Charles Babbage's original idea of "Instrumental Analysis" to the large ENIAC decoding machine serving in World War II, we have witnessed the realization of the theories of Alan Turing and John von Neumann (see Fig. 1.3), which has accelerated the development of AI.

1.1.1 Birth of AI

In the mid-20th century, scientists from different fields made a series of preparations for the birth of AI, including Shannon's information theory, Turing's computational theory, and the development of Neurology.

In 1950, Turing published the paper *Computing Machinery and Intelligence*. In this paper, the famous Turing test was proposed: If a machine can answer any questions to it, using the same words that an ordinary person would, then we may call that machine intelligent.

Ascend AI Processor Architecture and Programming. https://doi.org/10.1016/B978-0-12-823488-4.00001-1

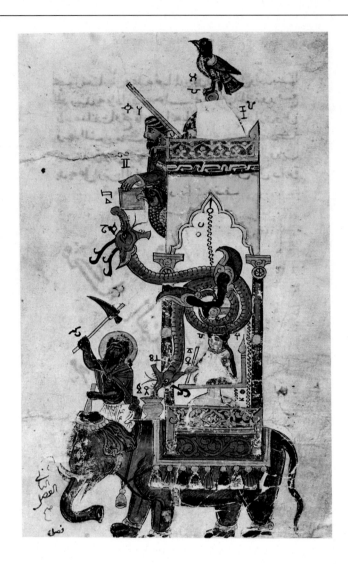

Fig. 1.1
Jazari's automatic elephant clock. *Picture from: https://commons.wikimedia.org/wiki/File:Al-jazari_
elephant_clock.png.*

The proposal of the Turing test is of great significance to the development of AI in more recent times. In 1951, the 24-year-old Marvin Minsky, as well as Dean Edmonds, built the Stochastic Neural Analog Reinforcement Calculator. Minsky continued to work in the field of AI, playing a huge role in promoting the development of AI, which contributed to his winning of Turing Award. In 1955, a program called Logic Theorist was introduced and subsequently refined. The ingenious method proved 38 of 52 theorems in the Principles of Mathematics. With this work, the authors Allen Newell and Herbert Simon opened a new methodology for intelligent machines.

Fig. 1.2

Leibniz, Descartes, Hobbes (from left to right). *Leibniz photo source: https://commons.wikimedia.org/wiki/File:Gottfried_Wilhelm_Leibniz.jpg; Descartes photo source: https://en.wikipedia.org/wiki/Ren%C3%A9_Descartes; Hobbes photo source: https://commons.wikimedia.org/wiki/File:Thomas_Hobbes_(portrait).jpg.*

Fig. 1.3

Turing and Von Neumann (from left to right). *Turing photo source: https://upload.wikimedia.org/wikipedia/commons/thumb/a/a1/Alan_Turing_Aged_16.jpg/220px-Alan_Turing_Aged_16.jpg; Von Neumann photo source: https://commons.wikimedia.org/wiki/File:JohnvonNeumann-LosAlamos.jpg.*

A year later, 10 participants at the Dartmouth Conference, including McCarthy, Shannon, and Nathan Rochester, argued that "any aspect of learning or intelligence should be accurately described so that people can build a machine to simulate it." In that moment, AI entered the world with its mission clearly defined, opening up a brand new world of science.

1.1.2 Set sail

After the Dartmouth Conference, AI developments proceeded akin to a volcanic eruption. The conference started a wave of activity that swept across the globe. Through these developments, significant progress was achieved. Computers were shown to succeed at more advanced tasks, such as solving algebraic problems, geometric proofs, and certain problems in the field of language processing. These advances made researchers enthusiastic and confident about the improvement of AI, and attracted a large amount of funds to the research field.

In 1958, Herbert Gelernter implemented a geometric theorem-roving machine based on a search algorithm. Newell and Simon extended the application of search-based reasoning through a "General Problem Solver" program. At the same time, search-based reasoning was applied to decision-making, such as STRIPS, a Stanford University robotic system. In the field of natural language, Ross Quillian developed the first Semantic Web. Subsequently, Joseph Weizenbaum created the first dialogue robot, ELIZA. ELIZA was sufficiently lifelike that it could be mistaken for a human being when communicating with a person. The advent of ELIZA marked a great milestone in AI. In June 1963, MIT received funding from the United States Agency for Advanced Research Projects (ARPA) to commercialize the MAC (The Project on Mathematics and Computation) project. Minsky and McCarthy were major participants in the project. The MAC project played an important role in the history of AI and also in the development of computer science, giving birth to the famous MIT Computer Science and Artificial Intelligence Laboratory.

In this period, people came to expect the rapid acceleration of AI developments. As Minsky predicted in 1970: "in three to eight years we will have a machine with average human intelligence." However, the development of AI still required the lengthy process of continuous improvement and maturity, which meant that progress would be slowly moving forward.

1.1.3 Encounter bottlenecks

In the early 1970s, the development of AI gradually slowed down. At that time, the best AI programs could only solve problems in constrained environments, which was difficult to meet the needs of real-world applications. This result arose because AI research had met a bottleneck that was difficult to break through. In terms of computing power, the memory size and processor speed of computers at that time were insufficient for actual AI requirements, which need high-performance computing resources. An obvious example was that in natural language research, only a small vocabulary containing less than 20 words could be processed. Computational complexity was another concern. Richard Karp proved in 1972 that the time complexity of many problems is proportional to the power of input size, which implies that AI is almost impossible in problems that might lead to an exponential explosion. In the fields of natural language and machine vision, a large amount of external cognitive information is needed as the basis for recognition. Researchers found that the construction of AI databases is very difficult even if the target is to reach the level of a child's cognition. For computers, the ability to deal with mathematical problems such as theorem proving and geometry is much stronger than the ability to deal with tasks that seem extremely simple to humans, such as object recognition. This unexpected challenge made researchers almost want to quit their studies in these areas.

As a result of these factors, government agencies gradually lost patience with the prospects of AI and began to shift funding to other projects. At the same time, AI gradually faded out of people's vision.

1.1.4 Moving on again

After several years at a low ebb, the emergence of "expert systems," along with the resurgence of neural network, led AI on its way again to becoming a hot spot once again. Edward Feigenbaum led the development of a program that could solve specific domain problems according to a set of specific logical rules. Afterward, the MYCIN system, which could diagnose blood infectious diseases, increased the influence of AI in specific fields. In 1980, the XCON (eXpert CONfigurer) expert setup program was famous for saving customers 40 million dollars and brought huge commercial value to the application of automatically selecting computer components that met customers' needs. XCON also greatly increased researchers' interests in developing expert systems. In 1981, Japan increased funding to $850 million for the Fifth Generation Computer Project, with the goal of realizing solutions for human-computer interaction, machine translation, image recognition, and automatic reasoning. Britain poured 350 million pounds into the Alvey project, and the United States increased its funding for AI as well. In 1982, John Hopfield's neural network changed the way machines process information. In 1986, David Rumelhart applied the back-propagation algorithm to neural networks and formed a general training method. This wave of technological innovation promoted the continuous development of AI.

However, good times did not last long, and the winter of AI arrived quietly once again. The limited applications of expert systems represented by the XCON program as well as the high maintenance costs made it gradually lose its original competitiveness in the market. When the initial enthusiasm for the fifth generation project did not yield the expected returns, R&D funds were gradually exhausted. Researchers' enthusiasm also waned. For a while, AI was controversial and plunged into a cold winter.

1.1.5 Dawn rise

After years of tempering expectations while still adhering to the pursuit of the mystery of human intelligence, AI continued moving forward. AI also added vitality to other fields in the development process, such as statistical theory and optimization theory. At the same time, integration with other disciplines brought technological revolutions in data mining, image recognition, and robotics. On May 11, 1997, after IBM's Dark Blue Computer System defeated human world champion Kasparov in chess, AI was brought back to the world stage.

At the same time, the rapid development of hardware also facilitated the realization of AI. For example, the Tesla V100 processor of NVIDIA can now process 10 trillion floating-point operations per second, which better meets people's demand for computing performance. In 2011, Google Brain used distributed frameworks and large-scale neural networks for training; it learned to recognize the concept of "cat" from YouTube videos without any prior knowledge. In 2016, Google's AlphaGo defeated world champion Lee Sedol in the field of Go, shocking the world. In 2017, AlphaGo's improved version again outperformed Ke Jie, the world's number one professional Go player. This series of achievements indicated that AI had reached a new peak, causing the proliferation of AI to more fields. References for AI history can be found via [1] and references therein.

1.2 Introduction to deep learning

1.2.1 History

In order to enable computers to understand the knowledge of humans, it is necessary to construct a multilayer network composed of simple concepts to define complex objects. After the network is trained iteratively, it can capture the characteristics of this object. This method is generally called deep learning (DL). The development of the Internet has produced a huge amount of data, which provides greater opportunities for the development of DL. This rapid increase in data volumes has made AI a very hot research topic nowadays, and deep neural networks are the current superstar. Multiple layers of neurons constitute a neural network, where the network depth corresponds to the number of layers. The more layers a network has, the stronger the ability it has to represent information. The complexity of machine learning will also be increased by the depth of a neural network.

In 1943, mathematician Walter Pitts and psychologist Warren McCulloch first proposed the artificial neural network (ANN) and modeled neurons in the ANN mathematically and theoretically. This seminal work opened up research on ANNs. In 1949, psychologist Donald Olding Hebb provided a mathematical model of neurons and introduced the learning rules of ANNs for the first time. In 1957, Frank Rosenblatt proposed a neural Perceptron using the Hebb learning rule or least square method to train parameters. Rosenblatt implemented the first Perceptron model Mark 1 in hardware. In 1974, Paul Werbos proposed a back-propagation algorithm to train neural networks. Geoffrey Hinton and others extended this algorithm to multilayer deep neural networks. In 1982, the earliest recurrent neural network (RNN), a Hopfield network, was proposed by Hopfield. In 1984, Fukushima Bangyan proposed the original model of a convolutional neural network (CNN), Neocognitron.

In 1990, Yoshua Bengio proposed a probabilistic model to process sequential data, which combined a neural network with a hidden Markov model for the first time and was applied to handwritten digit recognition. In 1997, Jurgen Schmidhuber and others proposed the Long Short-Term Memory (LSTM), which made RNNs develop rapidly in the field of machine translation. In 1998, Yann LeCun put forward the theory of the CNN. In 2006, the DL pioneer Hinton and his students proposed a method for dimension reduction and layer-by-layer pretraining which was published in Science. This work eliminated the difficulty of network training and enabled deep networks to solve specific problems. In 2019, these three pioneers, Hinton, LeCun, and Bengio won the Turing Award for their great contributions in the field of DL and their far-reaching significance to the development of AI today. More references on the history of DL can be found in Ref. [2] and references therein.

1.2.2 Applications

After years of development, DL has shown great value in applications, and has attracted attention from both industry and academia. DL has made significant progress in image, speech, natural language processing, and big data [2].

In 2009, Microsoft and Hinton collaborated to integrate Hidden Markov Models into DL to develop commercial speech recognition and simultaneous translation systems.

In 2012, AlexNet led in the World ImageNet Large Scale Visual Recognition Challenge (ILSVRC) by a wide margin. Jeff Dean of Google and Andrew Ng of Stanford University used 160,000 CPUs to build a deep neural network, which showed amazing results in image and speech recognition. The combination of DL with reinforcement learning improved the performance of reinforcement learning algorithms, enabling DeepMind's reinforcement learning system to learn to play Atari games independently and even outperform human players.

Driven by high commercial profits, there are many frameworks suitable for DL, such as Caffe, TensorFlow, PyTorch, and Mindspore, which have helped to promote the application of DL to various fields. Since the 1980s, DL has continuously absorbed the knowledge of neuroscience, statistics, and applied mathematics, promoted its rapid development, and extended its antennae to practical problems in more fields. At the same time, it has enabled computers to continuously obtain higher recognition accuracy and prediction ability.

1.2.3 Future challenges

The development of DL benefits from advances in data, modeling, and computing hardware. With the development of the Internet and information technology, massive amounts of data can be used by computers, which is an advantage that was not available before. Research on deep neural networks has promoted the rapid development of neural network models, enabling these models to complete increasingly complex processing tasks in a wider range of fields. The rapid development of semiconductor processors and computer technology has provided fast and energy-efficient computing resources for neural network models and data, such as CPUs, GPUs, TPUs, and Huawei's latest Ascend AI processor. But the factors that promote development can often cause restrictions because of their own limitations. The same situation is true of the relationship between DL and factors such as data quantity, network models, and computing hardware.

In terms of data, the labeling of large amounts of data poses a great challenge to DL. DL requires large quantities of data to train a neural network so that it can solve practical problems. However, raw data cannot be used directly for training; it needs to be labeled manually firstly. Because the amount of data needed for training is very large and the type of data is complex, some data also requires experts in specific fields to assign labels. As such, manual labeling is time-consuming and expensive, which can be an unaffordable burden for research institutes or companies engaged in DL. To address this challenge, researchers intend to find a new type of algorithm that can study and train unlabeled data. One such example is dual learning, but the road ahead in this research direction is long and still needs a lot of effort and time.

More complex models are required if we want to attain higher accuracy. Specifically, for a neural network, it needs more layers and more parameters. This complexity will result in the increase of storage for model parameters and the requirement for computing power. However, in recent years, the demand for DL on mobile devices is also growing and the resources on mobiles are typically insufficient to satisfy the computing requirements. In order to resolve the contradiction between limited resources and high computing requirements, we need to lighten the model, while simultaneously ensuring that the accuracy of the model is not significantly affected. As a result, many methods have been introduced to lighten models, such as pruning, distillation, weight sharing, and low-precision quantization. Considerable progress has been made. However, new methods need to be studied continuously to break through limitations of models.

In the development of any technology, it is difficult to break away from the constraint of realization costs, which is the same for DL. At present, although computing hardware resources for DL are abundant, due to the complexity of the network models and the huge amount of data, model training is often still carried out on limited hardware resources. In such situations, model training can still take a long time, making it difficult to meet the timelines of product research and development. In order to address this challenge, we have adopted the method of expanding hardware computing platforms in exchange for training time. However, such hardware is expensive and cannot be expanded infinitely, so the time-efficiency improvement brought by huge expenditure is limited. At the same time, by building a powerful computing platform and developing a cost-effective strategy to shorten the computing time of the model, the beneficiaries are merely limited to giants such as Google, Alibaba, and other large companies. In order to solve this problem, researchers are searching for more efficient algorithms which can accelerate the computing of neural networks. This direction also requires extensive and lengthy research.

Many methods in DL still require solid theoretical support, such as convergence of bifurcation algorithms. DL has always been regarded as a black box or alchemy. Most of the conclusions about DL come from experience and a lack of theoretical proof. DL lacks strict and logical evidence, and does not comply well with the existing theoretical system of thinking. Some scholars believe that DL can be used as one of the many ways to achieve AI, but it cannot be expected to become a universal key for solving all AI problems. At present, DL has strong applicability to static tasks, such as image recognition and speech recognition, but for dynamic tasks (such as autonomous driving and financial trading) it is still weak and short of meeting requirements.

In short, there is no doubt that DL has achieved great success in many fields in modern society. However, due to the numerous challenges in the development of data modeling, computing hardware, and theory, DL still has a long way to go. For more references on DL, please refer to Ref. [3].

1.3 Neural network theory

A well-known proverb states: "There are a thousand Hamlets in a thousand people's eyes." In a similar fashion, scholars in different fields have different understandings of neural networks. Biologists may associate the connection to the human brain neural network. Mathematicians may infer the mathematical principles behind neural networks. DL engineers may think about how to adjust the network structure and parameters. From the point of view of computer science, it is a fundamental problem to study the computational architecture and implementation of neural networks.

ANNs, also referred to as neural networks, are an important machine learning (ML) technology. It is an interdisciplinary subject between machine learning and neural networks. Scientists mathematically model the most basic cells, neurons, and construct ANNs by collecting these neurons in a certain hierarchical relationship. These collections of neurons can learn from the outside world and adjust their internal structure through learning and training in order to solve various complex problems. The ANN is based on the biological neuron mathematical model, M-P neuron, which was used in the perceptron, and subsequently the multilayer perceptron (MLP). Finally, the more complete CNN model has been developed and is now in wide use.

1.3.1 Neuron model

The most basic unit in a biological neural network is a neuron, and its structure is shown in Fig. 1.4. In the original mechanism of biological neural networks, each neuron has multiple dendrites, one axon, and one cell body. The dendrites are short and multibranched, with one axon that is long. Functionally, dendrites are used to introduce nerve impulses transmitted by other neurons, while axons are used to transmit nerve impulses to other neurons. When a nerve impulse introduced by a dendritic or cellular body excites a neuron, the neuron transmits excitability to other neurons through the axon.

In the 1940s, American psychologist Warren McCulloch and mathematician Walter Pitts proposed the M-P neuron model based on the structure and working principle of biological neurons [4]. The mathematical model is shown in Fig. 1.5. The M-P neuron model, which was named after its coinventors, contains multiple inputs that correspond to dendrites, and the multiple dendrites are used to sense nerve impulses. More formally, this design is equivalent to the input signal X_i transmitted by n other neurons via an axon per neuron. In biological neurons, nerve impulses enter the cell body through complex biological effects, which is equivalent to the weighted summation and output of these signals in the M-P neuron model through the role of weights W_i. These weights are termed connection weights. A dendrite receives a nerve impulse transmitted by a synapse, which is equivalent to multiplying the input signal with the weight to get an output $x_i w_i$. Biological cells will feel the excitation of a nerve impulse transmitted by multiple synapses. The excitatory response in biological cells is then transmitted to other neurons through axons. This behavior is imitated in the M-P model, as the input signal of M-P neurons is processed with a neuron threshold b. Subsequently, the neuron output is

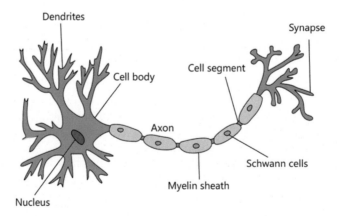

Fig. 1.4

Biological neuron structure. *Picture (original) source: https://commons.wikimedia.org/wiki/File:Neuron_ Hand-tuned.svg, available under the Creative Commons Attribution-Share Alike 3.0 Unported license, Copyright ©2009, Quasar Jarosz at English Wikipedia.*

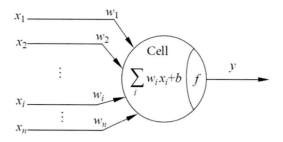

Fig. 1.5
M-P neuron model.

generated for the next M-P neuron by applying an activation function. Therefore, the working principle of M-P neurons abstracts the biological neurons mathematically, and can be reconstructed and computed manually.

The schematic diagram of the M-P neuron model is shown in Fig. 1.5, where $x_1, x_2, \ldots x_n$ denotes input signals from n neurons, respectively. Further, $w_1, w_2, \ldots w_n$ denote the weights of the connections between n neurons and the current neuron, b denotes the bias threshold, y denotes the output of the current neuron, and f denotes the activation function. Putting everything together, the mathematical expression for the whole neuron is

$$y = f\left(\sum_{i=1}^{n} w_i x_i + b\right) \tag{1.1}$$

The function of formula (1.1) is to simulate the working mechanism of biological neurons: The neuron receives multiple input signals, weighted summation is performed, and a threshold is added. When the threshold b in formula (1.1) is negative, adding b is equivalent to subtracting the positive threshold. The output control is carried out through the activation function, which shows the process of neuron computation and processing. If multiple inputs are represented as a vector $\boldsymbol{x} = [x_1, x_2, \ldots, x_n]^T$, and multiple connection weights are represented as a vector $\boldsymbol{w} = [w_1, w_2, \ldots, w_n]$, then the output of the neuron becomes $y = f(\boldsymbol{x} \cdot \boldsymbol{w} + b)$. In detail, first perform vector multiplication on input signal vector and connection weight vector, and add bias value, then pass it through the activation function to obtain the final output.

Activation functions are used to simulate the excitation of cells and signal transduction in biological neurons. Analysis of biological nerve signal transmission mechanisms found that there are only two states of nerve cells: the first is to achieve the excited state of nerve cells and to open the nerve impulse transmission; the second is a failure to make the nerve cells excited, which does not produce nerve impulses. In M-P neurons, the control function that activates this optimal output is a step function, as shown in Fig. 1.6, which maps the difference between the weighted summation value and the threshold to 1 or 0. If the difference is greater than or

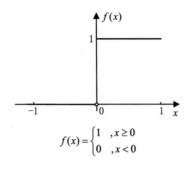

$$f(x) = \begin{cases} 1 & ,x \geq 0 \\ 0 & ,x < 0 \end{cases}$$

Fig. 1.6
Step function.

equal to zero, the output is 1, corresponding to the excited state of the biological cell; if the difference is less than zero, the output is 0. This design corresponds to the inhibition state of biological cells.

The M-P neuron model is the first mathematical model to characterize biological neurons. This model simulates the working mechanism of biological neurons, lifts the mysterious veil of biological neural systems, lays a foundation for the development of subsequent neural networks, and has a far-reaching importance in the establishment of the atomic structure of neural networks.

1.3.2 Perceptron

The structure of the perceptron is shown in Fig. 1.7. It is an ANN model based on the M-P neuron model [5]. The perceptron is a description of a network of neurons consisting of two levels: The first layer is the input layer, which consists of $m+1$ inputs, $x_0, x_1,..., x_m$.

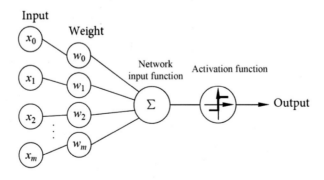

Fig. 1.7
Perceptron structure.

These neurons only receive signals and do not do any processing. The second layer is the output layer, which consists of an input function and an activation function of $m+1$ weights $w_0, w_1,\ldots, w_m$. The network input function can be expressed as a weighted summation. The activation function is different from the M-P neuron. The perceptron uses the antisymmetric symbol function, as shown in Eq. (1.2). When the input is greater than or equal to 0, the output is $+1$. When the input is less than 0, the output takes a value of -1. Generally, the perceptron is a network with multiple inputs and a single output.

$$f(\mathrm{x}) = \begin{cases} +1, & x \geq 0 \\ -1, & x < 0 \end{cases} \tag{1.2}$$

The basic mathematical principles of the perceptron and the M-P neuron model are the same, and they inherit the neuron model $y=f(x\cdot w+b)$. At the same time, since the perceptron divides the positive and negative examples of the training set into two parts and can be used to classify input data, the perceptron is a binary classifier. A perceptron is akin to how a person learns to recognize an object. For example, when a teacher instructs a student to recognize an apple, the teacher first shows a positive example by taking out an apple and telling the student, "This is an apple." Subsequently, the teacher shows a counterexample by taking out a banana and telling the student, "This is not an apple." Following these initial examples, the teacher may continue to show another example by taking out a slightly different apple and telling the students, "This is also an apple." After a long period of training, the students finally learn to judge what an apple is, and thus know how to distinguish between apples and nonapples. This skill of "recognizing apples" is a trained model of perceptron. The emergence of the perceptron directly finds a preliminary direction for the application of neurons. The perceptron based on the M-P neuron model is a practical, simple ANN, which can solve straightforward binary linear classification problems. As shown in Fig. 1.8, two kinds of objects are classified by a linear method. The perceptron can find the dashed lines between $(x_1,0)$ and $(0,x_2)$ points in Fig. 1.8, and correctly distinguish between $+$ and $-$ objects. At the same time, the task of perceptron can be transferred, and it can be retrained by the Hebb learning rule or least-squares method. By adjusting the weights of the perceptron network without changing the network structure, the same perceptron can have the function of solving different binary classification problems.

In addition, it is particularly important that the perceptron also has hardware achievability. The first perceptron model, Mark1, implemented on the hardware, brought the neural network from theory to application. Because of the potential value of the perceptron, it immediately attracted the attention of many researchers.

Unfortunately, perceptrons are limited to linear binary classification. For example, a perceptron cannot solve simple XOR problems. The XOR operation is shown in Fig. 1.9, with $+$ for 1 and $-$ for 0. Four logical rules are required for the XOR function: (1) 0 XOR 0 $= -$, corresponds to the lower left corner in the coordinate system; (2) 0 XOR 1 $= +$, corresponds to the upper left

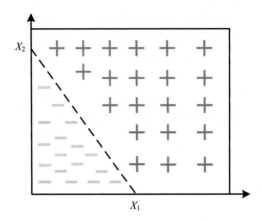

Fig. 1.8
Binary linear classification problem.

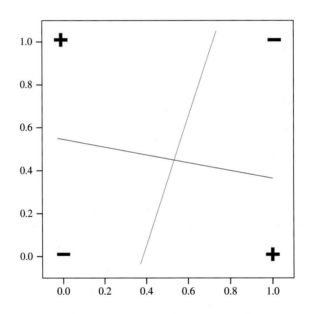

Fig. 1.9
XOR operation (XOR problem cannot be solved by linear classification).

corner in the coordinate system; (3) 1 XOR 0=+, corresponds to the lower right corner in the coordinate system; (4) 1 XOR 1=−, corresponds to the upper right corner in the coordinate system. These four rules produce two results of + and −. If you want to classify these outputs by a linear classifier, the perceptron will not be able to find a line in the coordinate system that can separate the + and − attributes into the two distinct areas. Therefore, the application of the perceptron is extremely limited, making it necessary to find new ways to solve more complex classification problems.

1.3.3 Multilayer perceptron

1.3.3.1 Working principle

The perceptron can only deal with linear classification problems, and the output results are limited to 0 and 1. In order to solve more complex problems based on the traditional perceptron structure, such as multiclass classification problems, the structure of multiple hidden layers is used instead of a single layer. This deep structure is called multilayer perceptron (MLP), also known as a fully connected neural network (FCNN) [2]. MLPs are the earliest examples of DL feedforward neural networks. An MLP can classify an input into multiple categories. In an MLP, data can only flow in one direction, from the input layer, through the hidden layer, to the output layer, and does not form any cycles or loops within the network.

The input nodes in the MLP constitute the input layer, which receives data from the outside, but does not process the data. These nodes merely pass the data directly to the hidden nodes. Hidden layers are composed of several hidden nodes. Hidden nodes do not receive external data; they only receive data from input nodes, compute, and pass their results to output nodes. An MLP can have no hidden layers or it can have multiple hidden layers, but it must contain an input layer and an output layer. Output nodes form the output layer, which receives data from the upper layer (either the input layer or the hidden layer), computes, and passes the results to the external system. Hidden nodes and output nodes can be equivalent to neurons because they have similar computational processing functions. The perceptron can be regarded as the simplest MLP. It has no hidden layer, but has multiple inputs and one output. It can only classify input data into simple linear-classifiable categories.

An MLP with two hidden layers is shown in Fig. 1.10. The structure is "Input Layer → Hidden Layer 1 → Hidden Layer 2 → Output Layer." Fully connected data transmission is used between each layer, that is, each layer of neurons is connected to each neuron in the upper layer. In Fig. 1.10, neurons in Hidden Layer 1 process the input data to generate the output of neurons. For example, neuron 1 receives input to produce an output. There are four neurons in Hidden Layer 1, so there are four output results. These four outputs are processed by the neurons in Hidden Layer 2, with a total of three outputs. Following the same procedure, an MLP produces the final output. Therefore, the final output of the whole MLP can be regarded as the result of nested computation of multilayer neurons.

From a computational point of view, due to the one-way flow of feedforward network data, the MLP is essentially a nested call of the perceptron model, that is, the input data vector undergoes multiple perceptrons (e.g., formula (1.1)) in repeated processing in order to get the output. At present, there are many neurons in each layer of an MLP, whose input is vector x and output is vector y. The weight of each neuron is a vector w, and the weight vector w of multiple neurons constitutes a weight matrix W. Similarly, multiple biases of a layer of neurons constitute a biased vector b. Therefore, the fully connected computation model of multiple

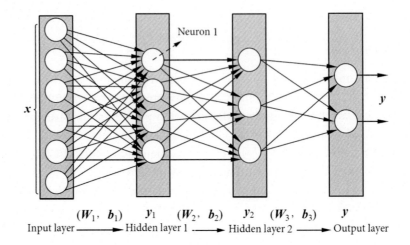

Fig. 1.10
Multilayer perceptron with two hidden layers.

neurons in one layer can be expressed by formula (1.3). After multiplying the input vector x and the weight matrix, the bias vector can be added. The output vector y can be obtained by processing the activation function f, which completes the computation of multiple neurons in one layer of the network.

$$y = f(x \cdot W + b) \tag{1.3}$$

In Fig. 1.10, the vector x and the vector y are used to represent the input data and output data of the MLP, respectively. The terms W_1, W_2, W_3 are used to represent the weight matrices of the connection weights between the neurons of different layers, while b_1, b_2, b_3 represent the offset vectors of the different layers, and the vectors y_1, y_2 represent the calculated output of hidden layer 1 and hidden layer 2, respectively. When the input vector enters hidden layer 1 from the input layer, the weight matrix W_1, and the offset vector b_1, will have been applied. After the computation of the fully connected model, the output vector y_1 is used as the input vector of the hidden layer 2. This process is continued through the entire fully connected network. Finally, the result y of the MLP is obtained through the output layer. This process is typical for a fully connected network.

1.3.3.2 Computational complexity

MLPs overcome the disadvantage that perceptrons cannot discriminate linearly nonseparable data. Accordingly, MLPs can solve nonlinear classification problems (e.g., the XOR problem). At the same time, with the increase in layers, any function can be approximated by MLP in finite intervals, which makes it widely used in speech and image recognition. However, when people begin to think that this kind of neural network can solve almost all problems, the limitations of MLP begin to appear. Since the MLP is fully connected and has a large number of parameters, the training time is very long and the computation is heavy. At the same time, the model can easily fall into the locally optimal solutions, which leads to difficulties with the optimization process of the MLP.

To illustrate the computational complexity of MLP, a simple MLP can be selected for demonstration purposes. As shown in Fig. 1.11, the structure for the network is "input layer → hidden layer → output layer" for a total of three layers. In this case, the input layer has 700 inputs and the hidden layer consists of 400 neurons, which are fully connected to the input layer. Each of these 400 neurons has 700 connections, and each connection has a weight. Therefore, the connection weight matrix of the hidden layer and the input layer is 700×400, while the neurons of each hidden layer also have an offset, so the offset vector of the hidden layer is 400. Next, in this example, assume the output layer has 10 outputs. Since the output layer and the hidden layer are also fully connected, the weight matrix between the output layer and the hidden layer is 400×10, and the offset vector of the output layer is 10. Therefore, the total number of weights of the entire MLP is $700 \times 400 + 400 \times 10 = 284,000$, and the total number of offsets is $400 + 10 = 410$. A weight of a neuron needs to be multiplied with the input data, so the entire MLP must perform 284,000 multiplication operations. At the same time, during the weighted summation, addition operations are required

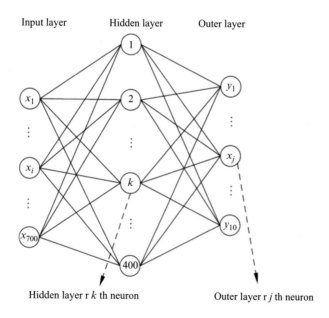

Fig. 1.11
Multilayer perceptron computation diagram.

(which are less complex than multiplication). The total number of additions is equal to the number of multiplications, that is, $(700 - 1) \times 400 + 400 + (400 - 1) \times 10 + 10 = 284,000$.

In this simple example, even though the MLP with only one hidden layer is used to solve the 10-class classification problem of 700 inputs, the parameters multiplication and addition have reached nearly 300,000, respectively. This amount of computation and parameters is very large. When considering that a standard image may have a size of roughly 1000×1000 pixels, it is clear that 700 inputs is very small. With a more typical image, its pixel size could be on the order of 1 million, and 1000 nodes could be used as output for 1000 classes. So even if the whole MLP contains only one hidden layer of 100 nodes in one layer, the number of parameters are easily over 100 million. Even by the power of today's mainstream computers, the amount of computation and parameters are considerable.

In addition, for image recognition tasks, each pixel is closely related to its surrounding pixels, while the correlation with distant pixels is relatively small. However, MLPs can only take input in the form of vectors, so the image of a two-dimensional matrix must be converted into vectors prior to being fed into the network for computation and processing. In other words, the input of this vector causes all the pixels in the image to be treated equally, without incorporating the position-related information between the pixels in the image. Consequently, many connections have little effect on feature extraction. At the same time, too many parameters and computations negatively affect the computational performance of predictions and applications.

With the addition of more layers of the MLP, the stronger the representation ability it has. However, it is very difficult to train an MLP with a large number of layers by the commonly used gradient descent method. The number of layers directly affects the parameters and computation. Generally speaking, gradients are difficult to transmit over three layers, so it is impossible to get a deep MLP. Due to the problem of high computational load with MLP s, researchers continued to search for more efficient neural network algorithms.

1.3.4 Convolutional neural network

Since the MLP is built in the form of a fully connected feedforward network, there are too many parameters, which leads to limitations such as long training time and difficulty in network tuning. At the same time, due to its fully connected form, the network deals with global features of the image, which makes it difficult to capture the rich local features. These limitations forced researchers to seek new network structures. In this scenario, multilayer neural networks emerged. Multilayer neural networks overcome the limitations of MLPs, and the CNN is representative of various multilayer neural networks [2].

The CNN is based on a neuron model and connects thousands of neurons through a hierarchical structure by following certain rules. From the perspective of computer science, the essence of CNNs is always a recursive call of the M-P neuron model.

The earliest CNN was LeNet5, which was published by LeCun in 1998, in the paper *LeNet5-Gradient-Based Learning Applied to Document Recognition.* However, CNNs were not popularized until 2012, when AlexNet (8-layer CNN) won the championship with a top-5 error rate of 15.3% in the ILSVRC competition classification challenge. The CNN prompted an upsurge of neural network studies, driven by an accuracy in the ILSVRC competition that was far higher than second place. AlexNet became a foundation of deep neural networks and reignited interest in DL.

Despite their longer history, CNNs were not particularly popular until 2012. One of the factors that sparked interest in CNNs in 2012 was the progress of heterogeneous computing that enabled people to use the power of a large number of GPUs for network training. Further, there was simultaneously an explosive growth in data availability for network training. On the other hand, the increasing depth of neural networks was well handled, as certain solutions and techniques were proposed to enable stable training of deep convolution neural networks. At present, common deep neural networks, such as AlexNet, VGG, GoogleNet, and LeNet, are all CNNs.

The CNN has made many improvements upon MLPs. It introduces new features such as local connections, weight sharing, and pooling. These techniques largely solve the inherent flaws of the perceptron. At the same time, the CNN has strong feature extraction and recognition ability, so it is widely used in the image recognition field. Common applications include object detection, image classification, and pathological image diagnosis.

1.3.4.1 Introduction to network architecture

CNNs require three processes: build the network architecture, train the network, and perform inference. For a specific application, a hierarchical architecture of CNNs, including an input layer, convolution layers, pooling layers, fully connected layers, and output layer, are required. By flexibly arranging or reusing these layers, a wide variety of CNNs can be generated. After defining the CNN structure, a large amount of data is needed to train the network to obtain optimal weights of the network. After training is complete, the model of the optimal network structure is obtained and can be used to infer new data and perform tests or predictions. In fact, the ultimate goal of CNNs is to provide an end-to-end learning model for specific applications. This learning model completes the task for a specific application, such as feature extraction and recognition/classification.

As shown in Fig. 1.12, the LeNet5 network structure is the most classic CNN [6]. The LeNet5 network consists of one input layer, two convolution layers, two pooling layers, two fully connected layers, and one output layer. The network structure is "Input Layer → Convolution Layer 1 → Pool Layer 1 → Convolution Layer 2 → Pooling layer 2 → Fully connected layer 1 → Fully connected layer 2 → Output layer." The data is fed to the input layer, passes through the convolution layers, the pooling layers, and the fully connected layers, and finally to the

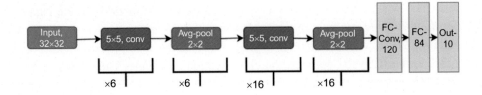

Fig. 1.12

Architecture of LeNet5. *Adapted from the paper: Y. LeCun, L. Bottou, Y. Bengio, et al., Gradient-based learning applied to document recognition, Proc. IEEE 86(11) (1998) 2278–2324.*

output layer. The data flows in one direction. Therefore, LeNet5 is also a typical feedforward neural network, and later CNN architectures are developed on this basis. Each functional layer (such as convolutional layer, pooling layer, etc.) has an Input Feature Map and an Output Feature Map. All input feature maps of the same functional layer have the same size, and all output feature maps of the same functional layer have the same size. However, the size and number of the input and output feature maps for the same functional layer may vary, depending on the properties of the functional layer itself.

Like traditional image processing, the input image data needs to be preprocessed before it is sent to the input layer, so that the data obtained in the input layer can meet the format requirements of the CNN. In general, the input image data is also referred to as an input feature map, and may be a three-dimensional 8-bit integer data in RGB format. For example, with input image data of size $224 \times 224 \times 3$, the data format is $[224, 224, 3]$. The first 224 is the image width; the second 224 is the image height, and the number of pixels in the whole image is the height multiplied by the width, i.e., 224×224. The final dimension, 3, indicates the number of channels of the input feature map, such as R, G, and B. There are totally three color channels. Therefore, the dimensions of an input feature map consist of width, height, and number of channels.

The neural network generally averages the input data, so that the mean value of the sample data is adjusted to zero. In addition, in order to facilitate the learning of a CNN, the input data is also normalized to a specific range, such as $[-1.0, 1.0]$. Thus, the actual input to the network may be represented as a single-precision, floating-point number. Sometimes, in order to adapt to the requirements of the neural network, the size of the input data is also adjusted to a specified size. For example, the data could be reduced to a constant size by principal component analysis (PCA) [7]. In short, the input layer is used to prepare the data so that it can be easily processed by the CNN. Once the input data is processed, it is then processed by the convolutional layers, the pooling layers, etc., and finally the result is computed by the fully connected layers and the output layer.

1.3.4.2 Convolutional layer

The input layer conveys data to the convolutional layer and is then processed by the convolutional layer. As the core layer in the neural network, the convolutional layer can enhance the feature information and filter out useless information. The convolution layer extracts key features from the input feature map through multiple convolution operations, and generates an output feature map. The convolutional layer usually convolves the image by two-dimensional convolution, and performs convolutions upon a set of neighborhood pixels centered on each pixel. Each neuron performs the weighted summation of neighborhoods of each pixel and outputs the result. The offset is added to adjust the range of the final result. This final result is called the feature value. The output feature values of a number of neurons in the convolutional layer constitute a feature map.

The weighted summation in the convolution process uses a convolution kernel, which is also called a filter. A single convolution kernel is usually a three-dimensional matrix and needs to be described by three parameters, width, height, and depth. The depth is the same as the number of channels of the input feature data. The convolution kernel depth shown in Fig. 1.13 is three. Different convolution kernels extract different features. As some convolution kernels are sensitive to color information, and some convolution kernels are sensitive to shape information, a CNN can contain multiple convolution kernels to model multiple features.

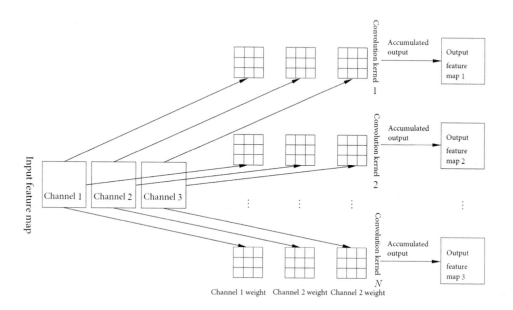

Fig. 1.13
Computational logic of the convolutional layer.

The value of the convolution kernel is stored in the form of a two-dimensional weight matrix, which is represented by width and height. The number of weight matrices in a convolution kernel is consistent with the depth of the convolution kernel, which is equal to the number of channels in the input feature map. The distance at which the convolution kernel slides at a time on the feature map is called the step size. The convolution kernel weights generally use a matrix of size 1×1, 3×3, or 7×7, and the weight of each convolution kernel is shared by all convolution windows on the input feature map. Sizes of convolution kernels are the same in one layer, but they can be distinct in different layers. In Fig. 1.14, the size of all convolution kernels in the first layer is unified to 3×3.

The portion of the original input feature map (or the first input feature map) corresponding to a convolution window is called the receptive field. The receptive field is a rectangular area on the original input feature map. Because there may be multiple convolutional layers in the network, the convolution window size and the receptive field size of the same input feature map may be different. But the convolution window of the first layer is generally of the same size as the receptive field. The receptive field is represented by two parameters, height and width. The height and width of the convolution window are consistent with the height and width of the convolution kernel of the same layer. As shown in Fig. 1.14, the 3×3 convolution kernel on the first convolutional layer has a receptive field size of 3×3 on the input image. Similarly, the 2×2 size convolution kernel in the second convolution layer corresponds to a convolution window size of 2×2 on the output feature map of the first layer, but this actually corresponds to a receptive field size of 5×5 on the original image.

Neurons cannot perceive all the information of the input feature map; they can only act on the receptive field of the original input feature map through the convolution kernel at each

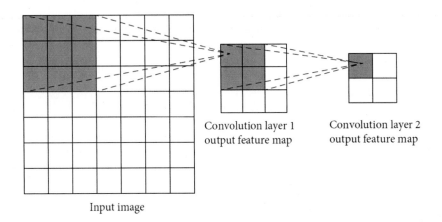

Convolution layer 1
output feature map

Convolution layer 2
output feature map

Input image

Fig. 1.14
Schematic map of receptive fields.

layer. Thus, the larger the receptive field, the larger the area of the convolution kernel acting on the original image. When the convolution kernel slides horizontally and vertically with a specific step size on the input feature map, at each step the weight matrix will be multiplied by the corresponding elements in the corresponding input feature map, and finally the output feature values can be obtained by deducting the offset. When the convolution kernel traverses all the positions of the input feature map, it generates a two-dimensional output feature map. Usually, the output feature maps of all channels corresponding to the same convolution kernel are added to form the final output feature map for the convolution kernel. Multiple convolution kernels generate multiple output feature maps, which are provided as input for the next layer.

After the convolution operation, each feature value in the output feature map needs to be activated by the activation function. Because the step function is discontinuous and not smooth, it is difficult to train. In practice, we normally use sigmoid, tanh and ReLU (Rectified Linear Unit), to approximate the step function. The activation function filters the output feature values to ensure the effective transmission of information. At the same time, the activation function is usually nonlinear, while the convolution is linear. That is to say, in the convolutional layer, neurons only have a linear processing function, because the linear combination of linear functions remains linear, no matter how deep a neural network is used. Without a nonlinear activation function, a purely linear deep neural network is equivalent to a shallow network. The activation function introduces nonlinear factors into a neural network, which enhances the ability of DL to fit nonlinear features.

Properties of the convolution layer

As seen from MLPs, the number of weights has a great influence on the computation complexity and storage size of the model during training and inference. CNNs adopt local connection and weight sharing to reduce the storage space of the network model and improve the computing performance.

(1) Local connection

Full connections are adopted in MLPs, meaning that almost the whole image is processed by each neuron. As shown in Fig. 1.15, neuron 1 acts on all the pixels of the input image and has a weight in connection with each pixel. Thus, a single neuron generates many weights, as well as many neurons, resulting in a huge number of parameters. The convolution neural network adopts the sparse connection, which makes each neuron in the convolution layer only process the data in the receptive field of the input feature map. This is another advantage of the convolution neural network.

In Fig. 1.15, Neuron 1, Neuron 2, Neuron 3, and Neuron 4 only affect the pixels of a small area, which makes the weight parameters of the whole area decrease sharply. The theoretical basis of using a local connection in CNNs is that in a feature map, each pixel is closely related to its adjacent pixels, while the correlation between distant pixels is weak.

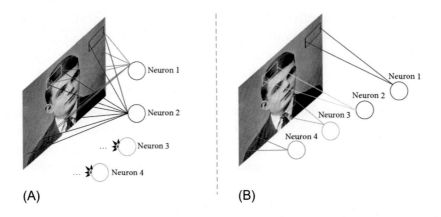

Fig. 1.15

Comparison of full connection and local connection. (A) Fully connected. (B) Locally connected. *Turing photo source: https://upload.wikimedia.org/wikipedia/commons/thumb/a/a1/Alan_Turing_Aged_16. jpg/220px-Alan_Turing_Aged_16.jpg.*

Therefore, the influence of the distant pixels on the extraction of output features is shielded, and it also reduces the number of network model parameters.

(2) Weight sharing

Different feature values on the output feature map are generated by different neurons in the convolutional layer. Different neurons in the same convolutional layer use the same convolution kernel, so there is weight sharing between these neurons. Weight sharing greatly reduces the number of parameters in the CNN. As shown in Fig. 1.16, if weight sharing is not used, Neurons 1, Neurons 2, Neurons 3, and Neurons 4 on the same convolutional layer have different weights, corresponding to Weight 1, Weight 2, Weight 3, and Weight 4. In the weight sharing mode, the four neurons share the same weight of 1, directly reducing the total weight of this neuron to 1/4 of the weight-independent model, which greatly reduces the number of parameters in the neural network.

The reason why weight sharing has little influence on the output feature map is that each image has inherent features, and these inherent features will be near identical in every part of the image. Therefore, using the same feature extraction method for different parts of the image, or even convolution with the same weights, can be effective in obtaining the features. The loss of information provided by the features is small, which ensures the integrity of the image features, while significantly reducing the number of weights. Therefore, no matter how many neurons there are in the convolution layer, for each image, only a set of weights needs to be trained. In this way, the time required for training parameters is greatly reduced. However, sometimes weight sharing also fails, for example, if the input image has a central structure and the goal is to extract different features from

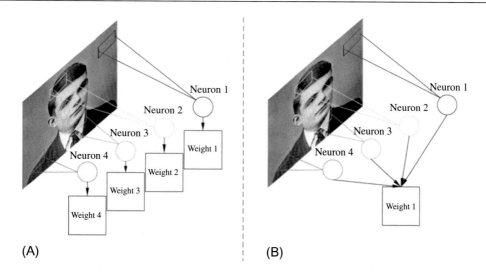

Fig. 1.16

Weight sharing. (A) Weight-independent. (B) Weight-sharing. *Turing photo source: https://upload. wikimedia.org/wikipedia/commons/thumb/a/a1/Alan_Turing_Aged_16.jpg/220px-Alan_Turing_Aged_16.jpg.*

different positions of the image by convolution. In this case, the corresponding neurons of different image positions may need different weights.

Implementation of the convolutional layer

(1) Direct convolution

There are several ways to implement a convolutional layer. The most straightforward way is direct convolution. Direct convolution is computed based on the inherent property of the convolutional layer, and the input feature map needs to be padded before computation. One of the benefits of zero padding is that the input feature map can be consistent with the size of the output feature map after the convolutional layer is processed. At the same time, zero padding can protect the edge information of the input feature map, so that it is effectively protected during convolution. If the input feature map is not padded, the input data will decrease in size during convolution, causing loss of information at the edge. Therefore, zero padding is a common preprocessing method before convolutional layers. The weight matrix of the convolution kernel slides over the input feature map after zero padding. At each position in the input feature map, a submatrix, matching the size of the convolutional kernel, is multiplied by the corresponding elements (also called a "dot product"). Here, this submatrix is called the input feature submatrix, and the number of input feature submatrices in one input feature map is the same as the number of elements in the output feature map.

X

1	1	1	1	2
1	1	1	2	1
0	0	2	1	2
0	0	0	1	2
1	2	1	1	1

W_1

1	0	1
0	0	-1
0	0	-1

b_1 0

W_2

-1	0	0
-1	0	0
-1	1	-1

b_2 1

Fig. 1.17
Input data of the convolution.

As mentioned later in this book, most CNN accelerators are designed using direct convolution computations. For example, the Tensor Processing Unit (TPU) proposed by Google uses the computation method of the systolic array. This computation method utilizes input and output feature map parallelism and weight parallelism, and maximizes the reuse of the weight and input data in the architecture design, which can reduce the bandwidth requirement of the computing unit and achieve high computational parallelism. Specifically, as shown in Fig. 1.17, for an input feature map matrix X having only one channel, its size is 5×5. There are two convolution kernels, where convolution kernel 1 has weight W_1, and all elements in the b_1 offset are 0; convolution kernel 2 has a weight of W_2, and all elements in the b_2 offset are 1. The weights of the kernels are shown in the 3×3 matrices, the step size of the convolution kernels is 2, and the padding size at the boundary is 1.

As shown in Fig. 1.18, when convolution is performed, the input feature matrix X is first padded with zeros. Since the size of the zero padding is 1, the feature matrix is extended outward by one pixel to obtain the matrix X_p. In the process of convolution, the weight W_1 acts on the initial position x_1 of the X_p matrix, and the dot product between the input feature submatrix X_1 in X_p and W_1 is computed. The result of this dot product forms the first element of the output feature matrix Y_1 after the bias b_1 is added. The result is -2, as computed by: $0 \times 1 + 0 \times 0 + 0 \times 1 + 0 \times 0 + 1 \times 0 + 1 \times (-1) + 0 \times 0 + 1 \times 0 + 1 \times (-1)$ $+0 = -2$. After the first element of Y_1 is computed, the weight W_1 matrix slides the step size of the two elements to the right. At this time, the weight W_1 matrix overlaps with the input feature submatrix X_2 in the matrix X_p, and the dot product of the corresponding elements is performed. Then, after adding the offset, the value of the second element of the output feature matrix Y_1 is computed to be -3. Following this rule, the computation of all elements in the first row of the output feature matrix Y_1 is completed. When performing the element computation of the second row of the output feature matrix Y_1, it should be noted that the weight W_1 needs to slide the step size of two elements vertically downward from the position of the input feature submatrix X_1. The first element of

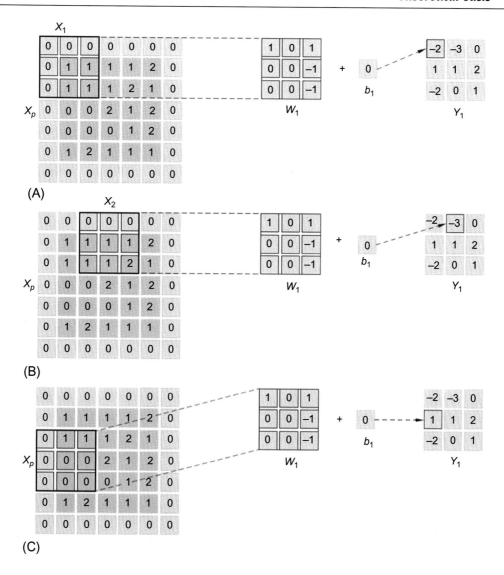

Fig. 1.18

Direct computation of convolution. (A) Output first element. (B) Row sliding computing. (C) Column sliding computing.

the second row is computed as 1, as shown in Fig. 1.18. The step size plays a role in both the lateral and longitudinal movements of the convolution kernel on the input feature map. Thus, after nine movements and dot products, all elements of the output feature map Y_1 are obtained. For convolution kernel 2, the output feature map Y_2 can be obtained using the same method.

So far, the convolution of the input feature map and the weight matrix is completed by the direct convolution method. In real applications, each convolution kernel has multiple channels, and the weight matrix of all channels needs to be used to convolve the corresponding channel of the input feature map. The results of all channels are accumulated as the final output feature map of the convolution kernel.

(2) Convolution by matrix multiplication

In addition to the direct convolution method described above, convolution can also be achieved by matrix multiplication, and this method is widely used in CPU, GPU, and other processors, including Huawei's Ascend AI processor.

This method first expands the input feature map and the convolution kernel weight matrix in the convolution layer by Img2Col (Image-to-Column), and then converts the dot product of the input feature submatrix and the weight matrix in the convolution into the matrix operation of the multiplication and addition of the row and column vectors, so that a large number of convolution computations in the convolutional layer can be converted into the parallelized matrix operations. Therefore, the processor only needs to efficiently implement matrix multiplication, and the convolution operation can be performed efficiently. Both CPU and GPU provide specialized Basic Linear Algebra Subprograms (BLAS) to efficiently perform vector and matrix operations.

The Img2Col function expands each input feature submatrix into a row (or a column) and generates a new input feature matrix whose number of rows is the same as the number of input feature submatrices. At the same time, the weight matrix in the convolution kernel is expanded into one column (which may also be one row), and the multiple weight matrices may be arranged in multiple columns. As shown in Fig. 1.19, the input feature map X_p is expanded into a new matrix X_{I2C} by Img2Col expansion. First, the input feature submatrix X_1 is expanded into the first row of X_{I2C}, and the input feature submatrix X_2 is expanded into the second row. Since there are nine input feature submatrices, all of which are expanded into nine rows, the final X_{I2C} matrix can be generated. Similarly, the weight matrices W_1 and W_2 of the two convolution kernels can be expanded into a matrix W_{I2C}, and the offset matrix b_{I2C} can be similarly processed. Next, the matrix multiplication operation is performed, and the first row of X_{I2C} and the first column of W_{I2C} are combined, yielding the first value of Y_{I2C} after adding the offset. The remaining elements of the output map matrix Y_{I2C} are obtained similarly.

The function of Img2Col is to facilitate the conversion of the convolution into matrix multiplication, so that the feature submatrices can be stored in continuous memory before matrix multiplication is performed. This reorganization reduces the number of memory accesses and thus reduces the overall time of the computation. In the case of direct convolution computation, since the input feature submatrices are stored in memory with overlapping but discontinuous addresses, it may be necessary to access the memory multiple times during the computation. These multiple memory accesses directly increase the data transfer time, which further affects the speed of convolution computation.

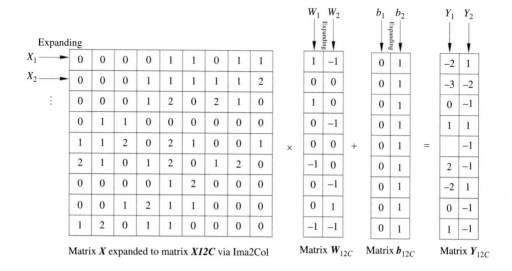

Fig. 1.19
Convolution by matrix multiplication.

Img2Col plays a vital role in facilitating the convolution computation, by converting the convolution computation into matrix multiplication.

When the offset value is constant in a convolution kernel, the computation of the offset can be further optimized. Specifically, the offset value and the weight matrix of the convolution kernel can be combined, and the coefficients are added to the input feature matrix. As a result of this optimization, the computation of matrix multiplication and bias accumulation is implemented at one time. As shown in Fig. 1.20, the coefficient matrix I is appended to the X_{I2C} matrix, where the I matrix is a 9×1 dimensional and all elements are set to unity The bias matrix b is also appended to the W_{I2C} matrix, where $b = [0\ 1]$. Then the computation is.

$$Y_{I2C}(X_{I2C} \cdot I) \cdot \binom{W_{I2C}}{b} = X_{I2C} \cdot W_{I2C} + b_{I2C} \tag{1.4}$$

From Eq. (1.4), the multiplication of the matrix $(X_{I2C}I)$ with $\binom{W_{I2C}}{b}$ is equivalent to the result of multiplication of (X_{I2C}) and (W_{I2C}) followed by the addition of b_{I2C}. By increasing the dimensions of the matrix, it is possible to perform computations using only matrix multiplications, saving computational resources on the hardware and simplifying the computation process.

It is worth mentioning that convolution in modern processors can also be achieved by other means such as fast Fourier transform (FFT) and the Winograd algorithm. These methods all reduce the computational complexity by transforming complex convolution

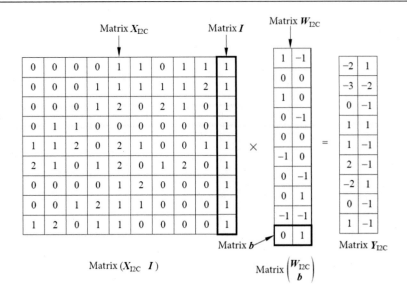

Fig. 1.20
Optimization of bias accumulation.

operations into simpler operations. The convolution in the cuDNN library provided by NVIDIA partially uses the Winograd algorithm. Generally, in the CNN, the parameter and number of operations in the convolutional layer account for the vast majority of the entire network. Accordingly, acceleration of the convolutional layers can greatly improve the computation speed of the overall network and the execution efficiency of the entire system.

1.3.4.3 Pooling layer

As the CNN continues to get deeper, the number of neurons increases, and enormous amounts of parameters need to be trained. In addition, the overfitting problem still exists, even after employing the abovementioned methods of weight sharing and local connections. The CNN innovatively adopts a downsampling strategy, which regularly inserts a pooling layer between adjacent convolutional layers, reducing the number of feature values (the output of neurons) following the pooling layer. With this approach, the main features are retained while the size of feature maps is reduced, resulting in a reduction in the total number of computations, and a reduced chance of overfitting.

The pooling layer typically uses a filter to extract representative features (e.g., maximum, average, etc.) for different locations. The pooling filter commonly uses two parameters: size F and step size S. The method of extracting features from the pooling filter is called a pooling function. The pooling function uses the overall statistical features of the output in the neighborhood of a location to replace the value of the output at that location. The commonly used pooling functions include the maximum pooling function, average pooling function, L2 normalization, and weighted average pooling function based on the distance from the center pixel. For example, the maximum pooling function gives the maximum value in the adjacent rectangular region.

After the convolution layer is performed, the output data is handed over to the pooling layer for processing. In the input feature map of the pooling layer, the pooling filter usually slides horizontally and vertically with a window size FxF and step size of S. At each position, the maximum or average value in the window of the input feature map is obtained and forms the output feature value. Consider the example shown in Fig. 1.21, where the pooling filter is a 2×2 matrix and the step size is 2. In this example, a 4×4 input feature map is the input of the pooling layer. Output feature map 1 is computed by the maximum pooling function and has a size of 2×2, while output feature map 2 is generated by the average pooling function. The size of the output feature map is 2×2, which indicates that the pooling layer directly reduces the number of feature values of the output feature map to 1/4 of the input feature map size. This process reduces the amount of data while retaining the main feature information.

When using different pooling functions, the pooling filter does a small amount of translation on the input feature map. However, most of the feature information will not change after the pooling function, which means that it effectively retains the majority of the feature information of the input. This characteristic is called local translation invariance. Local translation invariance is a very useful property, especially when it is concerned about whether a feature appears or not. For example, when deciding whether a face is included in an image, it is not necessary to know the exact location of the pixels of the eyes, but to know that

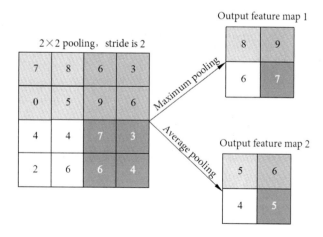

Fig. 1.21
Maximum pooling and average pooling.

one eye is on the left side of the face and the other eye is on the right side of the face. However, in some other applications, the specific location of features is very important. For example, if you want to find a corner where two edges intersect, you need to preserve the position of the edges to determine whether the two edges intersect. In this case, the pooling layer will cause damage to the output features.

In short, the pooling layer summarizes all the feature information centered on each position of the input feature map, which makes it reasonable that the output data of the pooling layer is less than the input data. This method reduces the input data to the next layer and improves the computational efficiency of the CNN. This reduction in size is particularly important when the next layer is the fully connected layer. In this case, the large-scale reduction of input data will not only improve the statistical efficiency, but also directly lead to a significant reduction in the number of parameters, thus reducing storage requirements and accelerating computation performance.

1.3.4.4 Fully connected layer

The data stream of a convolution neural network is processed by convolution layers and pooling layers for multiple iterations, which are then followed by fully connected layers. A fully connected layer is equivalent to an MLP, which performs classification upon input features. As shown in Fig. 1.22, the fully connected layer consists of 1×4096 neurons, each of which is fully connected to each neuron in the previous layer (often a pooling layer). After extracting the image features from the convolutional layers, the image features are classified by the fully connected layer, determining the class of the features. There are 1000 output classes in Fig. 1.22. After identifying the classes of the features, the probability of all classes is output through the output layer. For example, a fully connected layer will detect the features of a cat, such as a cat's ear, cat's tail, and so on. These data will be categorized as a cat, and finally the output layer will predict a large probability that the object is a cat.

1.3.4.5 Optimization and acceleration

The computation in convolution layers has five levels of parallelism: synaptic parallelism, neuron parallelism, input feature map parallelism, output feature map parallelism, and batch processing parallelism. These five parallelization methods make up the whole convolution process. The levels are sorted from low to high, and the amount of computing data for the various levels is graded from small to large. As the parallelization level rises, the requirement of computing resources becomes higher.

Consider the following example of a convolutional layer, in which the input image has N channels, the size of a single convolution kernel is $K \times K$, the number of convolution kernels is M, and the size of the output feature map is $S_O \times S_O$. Let us consider the manner in which the convolution layer is processed in order to understand how each parallelization level works.

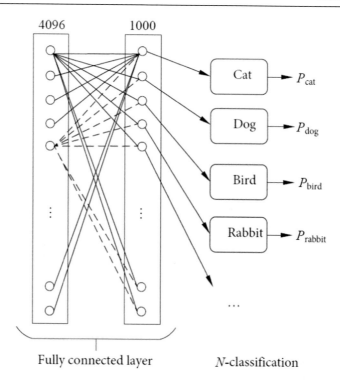

Fig. 1.22
Fully connected layer.

Synaptic parallelism

When the weight matrix in a convolution kernel is computed in a single convolution window of an input feature map, the weights are multiplied by the input feature values in the convolution window, and a total of K × K multiplication operations are performed. There is no data dependency in the process, so the multiplication operation in the same convolution window can be performed in parallel. A multiplication operation is similar to a synaptic signal of a neuron acting on a dendrite. Therefore, this type of parallel methods is called a synaptic parallel. For convolution kernels of size K × K, the maximum synaptic parallelism is also K × K. In addition, after multiplication gives the products, it is necessary to perform the accumulation output immediately. Assuming that the addition unit can be shared by multiple convolution kernels, the pipeline mechanism can be used, that is, when the multiplication step is performed in a weight matrix, the previous weight matrix can do the summation using the addition unit. Multiplication and addition by multiple weight matrices can be performed in parallel.

Neuron parallelism

When an input feature map is processed by a convolution neural network, a convolution kernel slides over the input feature map, causing the generation of multiple convolution windows. Each of the convolution windows has no data dependency upon the other and thus can be computed in parallel. The dot product operation of each convolution window can be performed by a single neuron, so that multiple neurons can perform parallel operations on multiple convolution windows. This parallel mode is called neuron parallelism.

If the size of a convolutional layer output feature map is $S_O \times S_O$, where each output feature value is computed by a convolution kernel in the corresponding convolution window, a total of $S_O \times S_O$ convolution windows are required. The computation can be performed simultaneously by $S_O \times S_O$ neurons in parallel, yielding parallelism in the convolutional layer of $S_O \times S_O$. At the same time, in this parallel mode, since the convolution kernel weights used in multiple convolution windows can be shared (they are actually the same set of weights), and the input feature values of multiple convolution windows overlap, part of the data is reusable. By fully exploiting this data reusability in convolution computations, it is possible to reduce the size of the on-chip cache and the number of data read and write operations. These improvements lead to reduced processor power consumption and improved performance.

Input feature map parallelism

A typical CNN processes a multichannel input image, such as an RGB image. The number of channels in a convolution kernel is generally equal to the number of channels in the image. After each channel of the input feature map enters the convolutional layer, it is two-dimensionally convolved with the corresponding channel of the weight matrix in a convolution kernel. Each channel of the weight matrix is convolved only with the corresponding channel of the input feature map. This operation yields a channel of the matrix of output features. However, the output feature matrix for the multiple channels must be aggregated in order to obtain the final output feature map, which is the result of the convolution kernel.

Since the multichannel weight matrices in a single convolution kernel are independent in the convolution process and the multichannel input feature maps are also independent, channel-level parallel processing can be performed. The parallel processing is called input feature map parallelism.

As an example, for an RGB image, the number of channels in the input feature map is three, and parallel convolution can be performed for the three channels of the weight matrix in the convolution kernel. Therefore, the maximum parallelism for an input image with N channels is N. In the input feature map parallel mode, the data of multiple two-dimensional convolution operations does not overlap and has no dependencies. Therefore, the hardware can perform parallel computation of the input feature map as long as it can provide sufficient bandwidth and computational power.

Output feature map parallelism

In a CNN, in order to extract multiple features of an image, such as shape contours and color textures, it is necessary to use a number of different convolution kernels to extract features. When the same image is set as input, multiple convolution kernels perform convolution computations on the same image and produce multiple output feature maps. The number of output feature maps and the number of convolution kernels are equal. Multiple convolution kernels are computationally independent and have no interdependencies. Therefore, the operations of multiple convolution kernels can be parallelized and independently derive the corresponding output feature maps. Such parallelism is called output feature map parallelism.

For computation of convolutional layers with M convolution kernels, the maximum degree of parallelism is M. In this parallel mode, the weight values of multiple convolution kernels do not coincide, but the input feature map data can be shared by all convolution kernels. Therefore, taking full advantage of the reusability of the input data can help achieve the best performance.

Batch parallelism

In the practical application of CNNs, in order to make full use of the bandwidth and computing power of the hardware, more than one image are processed at a time, which form a batch. If the number of images contained in a batch is P, the parallelism of the batch is P. The same CNN model uses the same convolution layer for different images processed in batches, so the network weights used by different images can be reused. The advantage of such large-scale image processing is that the on-chip cache resources can be fully utilized, and the weight data that has been transferred to the processor can be fully utilized, thus avoiding frequent memory accesses. These optimizations reduce the power consumption and delay of data transfer.

On the other hand, computing hardware can process multiple tasks in parallel, improving the utilization of hardware resources and the overall computing throughput. Task-level parallelism is also a way that CNNs can be accelerated, but compared with task-level parallelism, batch processing has higher requirements for hardware resources.

According to the actual situation, flexibly using the parallel methods of convolutional layers can efficiently accelerate the computation of a CNN. Considering the extreme case, since each of the parallel methods is performed at different levels, theoretically all parallel methods can be used simultaneously. Therefore, the theoretical maximum parallelism in a convolutional layer is the product of the parallelism exhibited by all parallel methods. As shown in Eq. (1.5), $K \times K$ is the synaptic parallelism, $S_O \times S_O$ is for the neuron parallelism, N is the input feature map parallelism, M is the output feature map parallelism, and the total number of input images in one batch is P. Achieving maximum parallelism is equivalent to all multiplications in the convolutional layers of all tasks being computed simultaneously.

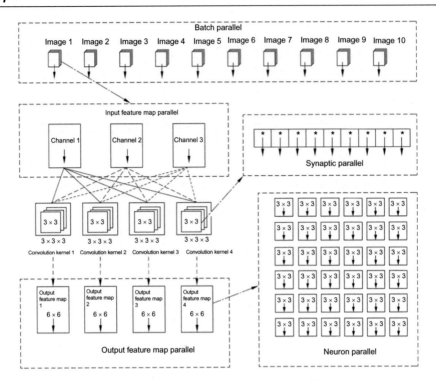

Fig. 1.23
Illustration of parallel mode.

$$\text{Maximum parallelism} = K \times K \times S_o \times S_o \times N \times M \times P \qquad (1.5)$$

For example, in Fig. 1.23, the number of channels of the input feature map is $N=3$, the width and height of the convolution kernel weight matrix are $K=3$, the number of convolution kernels is $M=4$, and the output feature map dimension is $S_O=6$. In the processing of the convolutional layer, synaptic parallelism is first performed; that is, a 3×3 parallel multiplication with a degree of parallelism of 9. Simultaneously with neuron parallelism, a 6×6 output feature map can be convolved by 6×6 neurons with a degree of parallelism of 36. When the input feature maps are parallelized, the three channels of the input feature maps are simultaneously convoluted with a parallelism of three. Finally, the output feature map can be computed in parallel. The four output feature maps are generated in parallel under the action of four convolution kernels with a parallelism of four. If a batch of 10 images is processed simultaneously, it is also possible to add a dimension with a parallelism of 10, so that the maximum parallelism of the convolutional layer is $3 \times 3 \times 6 \times 6 \times 3 \times 4 \times 10 = 38,880$. That is to say, 38,880 multiplication computations can be performed simultaneously, and the degree of parallelism is considerable.

However, in practice, the size of the input image, the number of convolution kernels, and the number of processed images are all large. As such, given the computing resources and architecture design of hardware, it is not possible to achieve the theoretical maximum parallelism during execution. This same argument can be made for types of operations other than convolution. The limitations of Amdahl's Law also apply to the acceleration ratio in real practice. At present, various accelerators on the market actually seek an optimal balance between the parallelisms of various dimensions based on specific application requirements.

1.3.5 Application example

AI has a wide range of applications in real life, and is commonly used in robotics, natural language processing, image recognition, and expert systems. A simple application example for beginners is handwritten number recognizing, which is equivalent to the "Hello World" program for beginners to learn programming. Handwritten numbers are widely used, and humans can understand handwritten numbers without difficulty, but for computers it is very challenging. In the early days, traditional methods were adopted. In order to program a computer to recognize handwritten numbers, it took a long time and the recognition accuracy was not high. While people were racking their brains regarding this problem, researchers found that it is easy to solve such problems through machine learning.

Turing Award winner LeCun first established a dataset known as MNIST (Modified NIST and MNIST) through the National Institute of Standards and Technology (NIST) handwritten digit library [8]. The MNIST dataset contains handwritten images of 70,000 Arabic numerals, as shown in Fig. 1.24. These digital images are grayscale and were collected from various places. The dataset is split such that 60,000 can be used as training data, and the remaining 10,000 are to be used as test data. The size of each picture is 28×28. Based on the MNIST dataset, researchers have proposed a variety of handwritten digit recognition networks, which have improved algorithm accuracy to a level comparable to humans.

The MNIST dataset only includes numbers from 0 to 9. The task is to arbitrarily select a picture with a number and let the computer recognize it. From another angle, the task can be considered as classifying the digital meaning of the picture into one of 0–9. Let us take a clear look at the process of digit recognition.

This case is realized by a LeNet network, a CNN proposed by LeCun. The LeNet network is also one of the earliest CNNs. As shown in Fig. 1.25, a simple digit recognition process includes the steps of loading a dataset, constructing a neural network structure, initializing, training, and testing. The training includes two substeps: validation and tuning.

Fig. 1.24

MNIST dataset examples. *Picture (original) from https://commons.wikimedia.org/wiki/File:MnistExamples. png, available under Creative Commons Attribution-Share Alike 4.0 International license. Copyright ©2017, Josef Steppan.*

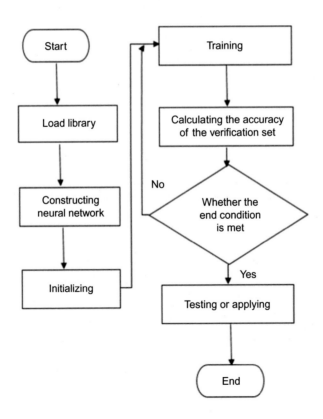

Fig. 1.25
Process of handwritten digit recognition.

1.3.5.1 Initial setup

In the initial setup stage, loading datasets, constructing neural network structures, and initializing operations are needed. Usually the MNIST dataset needs to be loaded first for training and testing. Next, we need to construct a neural network, defining the corresponding input layer, convolution layers, downsampling layers, fully connected layers, output layer, and the connections between them. Moreover, the input and output dimensions of each layer must be specified. These aspects of the network structure are considered as hyperparameters. Except the first layer, which needs to be clearly specified, the input and output sizes of the hidden and output layers can be automatically inferred. Specific hyperparameters include the size of the convolution kernels in the convolution layer, the step size of the downsampling layer, and the number of nodes in the fully connected layer.

If the digit recognition program is to be trained on GPU, it is often necessary to allocate the GPU device and reference the upper limit of the memory occupancy. The setting of these parameters with different GPU hardware configurations is very important in determining how to use the resources of the GPU efficiently. The GPU should be allocated as needed so as to make the best use of the memory. Finally, when initializing, we need to set the trainable parameters such as the convolution kernels of convolution layers, weights and biases of fully connected layers, and assign initial values to these parameters based on the specified initialization methods (such as Gaussian random initialization, constant initialization, etc.).

1.3.5.2 Training

In the training stage, the data from the training dataset is transferred to the neural network, and the neural network attempts to learn the patterns exemplifying each class. The trainable parameters of the model are consistently modified to make the neural network converge. At the same time, we consistently calculate the accuracy of the current model on the validation dataset and decide whether the model has reached the required accuracy or whether there has been any overfitting. Generally, the training should be stopped when the number of training steps specified in advance has been reached, when the model has converged, or when the target accuracy has been reached. It is also possible that the parameters of the neural network have converged to a local optimum rather than the global optimum.

1.3.5.3 Test

As shown in Fig. 1.26, when testing the trained and optimized neural network, handwritten digits 2 and 7 are, respectively, fed into the handwritten input layer. After the neural network receives the test data, it carries out automatic prediction, and outputs the probability of each digit as the label of the input data. If the corresponding number is recognized, it will be displayed by the system. As shown in Fig. 1.26, the input images show the numbers 2 and 7, and the results of the corresponding output layer are highlighted with white squares.

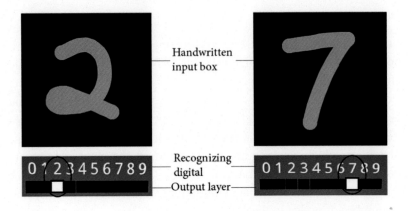

Fig. 1.26

Digital handwriting output sample. *Picture generated from http://scs.ryerson.ca/~aharley/vis/conv/flat.html.*

At present, handwritten digit recognition technology is quite mature and is mainly applied in the fields of large-scale data statistics, finance, taxation, and mail sorting systems. It greatly improves the recognition speed of digital numbers in specific businesses and has high application value.

References

[1] History of Artificial Intelligence, https://en.wikipedia.org/wiki/History_of_artificial_intelligence (Accessed 2020).
[2] Deep Learning, Wikipedia. https://en.wikipedia.org/wiki/Deep_learning (Accessed 2020).
[3] I. Goodfellow, Y. Bengio, A. Courville, Deep Learning, MIT Press, 2016.
[4] Artificial Neuron, Wikipedia. https://en.wikipedia.org/wiki/Artificial_neuron (Accessed 2020).
[5] Perceptron, Wikipedia. https://en.wikipedia.org/wiki/Perceptron (Accessed 2020).
[6] Y. LeCun, L. Bottou, Y. Bengio, P. Haffner, Gradient-based learning applied to document recognition, Proc. IEEE 86 (11) (1998) 2278–2324.
[7] Principal component analysis, Wikipedia. https://en.wikipedia.org/wiki/Principal_component_analysis (Accessed 2020).
[8] Y. LeCun, C. Cortes, C.J.C. Burges, The MNIST Database, http://yann.lecun.com/exdb/mnist/ (Accessed 2020).

## CHAPTER 2

Industry background

With the rapid development of deep learning, Nvidia continues to focus on its GPU processors and has launched the Volta [1] and Turing [2] architectures to continuously meet deep learning's requirements for huge computing power. Microsoft also uses FPGAs in its data centers instead of CPUs to complete computationally intensive tasks [3]. Google specifically designed the TPU processor for the deep neural network, marking the rise of the domain-specific architecture (DSA) [4]. In this environment, Huawei has also launched its self-developed Ascend AI processor, which aims to provide higher computing power and lower energy consumption for deep learning research, development, and deployment [5].

Over time, deep learning open-source software frameworks have become increasingly mature and provide efficient and convenient development platforms [6]. These frameworks allow researchers to focus on algorithm research while enjoying hardware acceleration without worrying about the implementation of specific details. The collaborative development of software and hardware has become a new trend in the deep learning field.

2.1 Current status of the neural network processors

2.1.1 CPU

In the process of computer development, central processing unit (CPU) plays an irreplaceable role. Early computer performance steadily improved year by year with Moore's Law [7] and met the needs of the market. A large part of this improvement was driven by the progress of underlying hardware technologies to accelerate the upper-layer application software. In recent years, physical bottlenecks such as heat dissipation and power consumption have made the growth of CPU performance slower than what is predicted by Moore's Law, indicating traditional CPU architectures are reaching their limits. As a result, the performance of serial programs operating under traditional CPU architectures cannot be significantly improved. This has led the industry to continuously search for new architectures and software frameworks for the post-Moore's law era.

As a result, multicore processors have emerged to meet the requirements of hardware speed requested by software. Intel's i7 series processors, based on the x86 instruction set, use four independent kernels to build an instruction parallel processor core, which improves the processor running speed to a certain extent. However, the number of kernels cannot be increased infinitely, and most traditional CPU programs are written in serial programming mode due to costs or difficulty of expressing them in a parallel form. As a result, a large number of programs cannot be accelerated.

In the trend of AI industry development, deep learning has become a hot spot. Its demand for computing power and memory bandwidth is becoming more and more intense. Traditional CPUs are insufficiently confronted with the huge demand for computing power required by deep learning. Since CPUs are facing great challenges in terms of both software and hardware, the industry must try to find new alternatives and develop new processors that can implement large-scale parallel computing suitable for deep learning. A revolution in the computer industry has come.

2.1.2 GPU

The GeForce GTX 280 graphics card launched by Nvidia in the early stage uses the graphics processing unit (GPU) composed of multicore streaming multiprocessors (SM). Each stream processor supports a multithread processing mode called single instruction multiple threading (SIMT). This large-scale hardware parallel solution brings breakthroughs in high throughput operations, especially floating-point computing performance. Compared with multicore CPU, GPU design does not start from the instruction control logic or expand the cache. Therefore, complex instructions and data access do not increase the delay. On the other hand, GPUs use a relatively simple storage model and data execution process, which relies on discovering the intrinsic data parallelism to improve throughput. This leads to greatly improved the performance of many modern data-intensive programs compared to CPUs. Due to its unique advantages, the GPU has gradually been adopted into the domain of supercomputing applications and has deeply changed the fields of automatic driving, biomolecular simulation, manufacturing, intelligent video analysis, real-time translation, and artificial intelligence through deep learning [8].

The architecture of GPUs is different from that of CPUs. CPUs focus on logic control in instruction execution while GPUs have a prominent advantage in the parallel computing of large-scale intensive data. To optimize a program, it is often necessary to use the respective capabilities of both CPUs and GPUs to perform collaborative processing. In this model, the CPU can flexibly process complex logical operations and hybrid computing of multiple data types while the GPU is needed to schedule rapid large-scale parallel computing. Generally, CPUs perform the serial part of the program well, whereas GPUs efficiently perform parallel processing of large-scale data.

To implement the collaborative computing paradigm, new software architectures can be used to program both CPUs and GPUs in a common unified framework. Nvidia proposes a compute unified device architecture (CUDA) framework to solve complex computing problems that apply to GPUs [9]. CUDA consists of a dedicated instruction set architecture and a parallel computing engine inside the GPU. It provides direct access to the GPU hardware so that the GPU does not rely on traditional graphics application programming interface. Instead, programmers can use C-like languages to directly program the GPU, which provides a powerful capability for modern computer systems in large-scale data-parallel computing.

In addition, because the C-like language is used as core language for GPU programming, CUDA allows programmers to quickly adapt to its programming environment. This facilitates the rapid development and verification of high-performance computing solutions by developers. Because CUDA implements a complete and universal solution on GPUs, it is widely used in many common computing fields such as science, business, and industry.

With the emergence and development of deep learning technology and given their outstanding performance in matrix computing and parallel computing, GPUs have been widely used as the first dedicated acceleration processors for deep learning algorithms and have become the core computing components applied to artificial intelligence (AI). Currently, GPUs are widely used in smart terminals and data centers, and take a leading role in deep learning training. GPUs have played an indispensable role in the AI field. As a result, Nvidia has introduced improved architectures featuring Tensor Cores and launched new-generation GPU products based on the Volta and Turing architectures in order to promote the continuous development of the deep learning hardware industry.

Nvidia recently proposed a GPU TU102 processor based on the Turing architecture [2]. It supports both general-purpose computing of the GPU and dedicated neural networks. The TU102 processor uses a 12 nm manufacturing process with areas exceeding 700 mm^2. A large number of tensor units are introduced inside the TU102 processor which supports multiple-precision operations such as FP32, FP16, INT32, INT8, and INT4. The processor's technical specifications that indicate the hardware computing capability are measured by the number of floating-point operations per second (Tera FLOPs per Second, TFLOPS) or the number of integer operations per second (Tera OPs per Second, TOPS).

In the GeForce RTX 2080 Ti using the TU102 processor, FP32 performance can reach 13.4 TFLOPS [10]. It can reach 13.4 TOPS on INT32, 26.9 TFLOPS on FP16, 107.6 TFLOPS on tensor FP16, 215.2 TOPS on INT8, and an astonishing 430.3 TOPS on INT4. Total power consumption of the system is less than 300 W.

The advantage of the Turing architecture is that the original general computing framework is retained, meanwhile allowing the CUDA framework to be used in neural network modules. This is good news for developers accustomed to CUDA programming. The core idea of Turing in processing convolutional neural networks is to convert convolution to matrix operations, and then use dedicated tensor processing units to perform these operations in parallel to accelerate the overall calculation. In essence, convolution in the tensor processing unit is accelerated using highly optimized matrix multiplication, thereby improving the neural network's performance. The Turing architecture controls the operation of the tensor unit by using a dedicated instruction.

2.1.3 TPU

With the rapid progress of AI, the demands for higher performance of processors that support deep learning algorithms are ever increasing. Despite high performance, GPUs suffer from high power consumption. The need for processors with higher performance and better efficiency has become more urgent. As early as 2006, Google has gradually developed new computing processors, known as application-specific integrated circuits (ASIC) [11], and applied them to neural networks. Recently, Google released the tensor processing unit (TPU) [4], an AI specific processor that supports the deep learning TensorFlow open-source framework.

The first-generation TPU adopts a 28 nm manufacturing technology with the power consumption of about 40 W and clock frequency of 700 MHz. To ensure that the TPU is compatible with existing hardware systems, Google designed the TPU as an independent accelerator and uses a SATA hard disk slot to insert the TPU into servers. In addition, the TPU communicates with the host through the PCIe Gen3x16 bus. The effective bandwidth can reach 12.5 GB/s.

The primary difference between GPU and TPU for floating-point calculations is that the TPU uses low precision INT8 integer number calculation. This minimizes the number of transistors required and greatly decreases power consumption while improving operation speed. In practice, this reduction of accuracy in calculations has little effect on the accuracy of deep learning applications. To further improve performance, TPUs use up to 24 MB on-chip memory and 6 MB accumulator memory to reduce access to off-chip main memory or RAM since these accesses are slow and power-hungry. In matrix multiplications and convolution operations, much of the data is reusable and can exploit data-locality. TPUs use the systolic array to optimize matrix multiplication and convolution operations, by fully exploiting data locality, reducing memory access frequencies, and reducing energy consumption. Compared with GPU's more flexible computing models, these improvements enable the TPU to produce higher computing power with lower power consumption.

The core concept of TPUs is to keep the computing unit running by optimizing the overall architecture and data supply, thus achieving extremely high throughput. A multilevel pipeline is used in TPU operation process with multiple multiplication instructions executed to reduce delay. Unlike traditional CPUs and GPUs, the systolic array structure adopted by TPU is especially suitable for large-scale convolution operations. During the calculation process, data flows through the operation array and when the systolic array is fully loaded, maximum performance can be achieved. In addition, bit-shift operations of the systolic array can make full use of data locality in convolution calculations, which greatly reduces power consumption by not repeatedly reading data.

TPUs efficiently accelerate the most common operations in the deep neural network by using large-scale systolic arrays and large amounts of on-chip storage. Currently, TPUs are used in the Google Street View Service, AlphaGo, Cloud TPU Platform, and Google Machine Learning Supercomputers.

2.1.4 FPGA

Field-programmable gate arrays (FPGAs) are developed as hardware prototype systems in electronics [12]. While GPUs and TPUs play important roles in the AI field, FPGAs enable developers familiar with hardware description languages to quickly implement AI algorithms and achieve considerable acceleration, thanks to their highly flexible hardware programmability, the parallelism of computing resources and relatively mature toolchains. FPGAs are now widely used in artificial intelligence after years of being in a "supporting role" and have brought a new architecture choice to the industry.

The first FPGA XC2064 was launched in 1985 by Xilinx who gradually developed a series of FPGA processors dedicated to flexible programmable electronic hardware systems. Due to the need for neural network computing power, FPGAs were first applied in the field of neural networks in 1994. With the evolution of modern deep learning algorithms into more difficult and complex directions, FPGAs began to show their unique network acceleration capabilities. FPGAs consist of programmable logic hardware units that can be dynamically programmed to achieve the logical functions required. This capability enables FPGA to be highly applicable to many domains and they are widely used. Optimized properly, FPGAs feature high performance and low power consumption. The flexible nature of FPGAs gives them an unparalleled advantage compared to other hardware with fixed capabilities.

A unique and distinctive feature of FPGAs is reconfigurability. This allows reprogramming and changing the hardware functionality, allowing multiple different hardware designs to be tested in order to achieve optimal performance. In this way, optimal solutions for neural networks in a specific application scenario can be obtained. Reconfigurability is categorized into static and dynamic. The former refers to the reconfiguration and reprogramming of hardware before hardware execution in order to adapt to system functions. The latter refers to hardware reconfiguration based on specific requirements during program execution.

Reconfigurability gives FPGAs advantages in deep neural networks, but it incurs some costs. For example, reprogramming may be slow and often unacceptable for real-time programs. In addition, FPGAs have a high cost. For large-scale use, the cost is higher than dedicated ASICs. The reconfigurability of FPGAs is based on hardware description languages (HDLs) and reconfiguring often requires using HDLs (such as Verilog and VHDL) for programming. These languages are more difficult and complex than high-level software programming languages and are not easily mastered by most programmers.

In June 2019, Xilinx launched its next-generation Versal series components [13]. It is an adaptive computing acceleration platform (ACAP) and a new heterogeneous computing device. With it as the most recent example, FPGAs have evolved from a basic programmable logic gate array to dynamically configurable domain-specific hardware. The Versal adopts 7 nm technology. It integrates programmable and dynamically configurable hardware for the first time, integrating a scalar engine, AI inference engine, and FPGA hardware programming engine for embedded computing. This gives it a flexible multifunction capability. In some applications, its computing performance and power efficiency exceed that of GPUs. Versal has high computing performance and low latency. It focuses on AI inference engines and benefits from its powerful and dynamic adaptability in automatic driving, data center, and 5G network communication.

2.1.5 Ascend AI processor

In this fierce competition within the AI field, Huawei has also begun to build a new architecture for deep learning. In 2018, Huawei launched the Ascend AI processor (as shown in Fig. 2.1) based on its own DaVinci architecture and began Huawei's AI journey.

Fig. 2.1
Huawei ascend AI processor.

Stemming from fundamental research in natural language processing, computer vision and automatic driving, the Ascend AI processor is dedicated to building a full-stack and all-scenario solution for both cloud and edge computing. Full-stack refers to technical aspects, including IP, processor, driver, compiler, and application algorithms. All-scenario refers to wide applicability, including public cloud, private cloud, edge computing, IoT industry terminals, and consumer devices.

To cooperate applications, an efficient operator library and highly automated neural network operator development tool were built called the Compute Architecture for Neural Network (CANN). Based on this full-stack and all-scenarios technology, Huawei uses these processors as the driving force to push AI development beyond limits in the future.

In October 2018, Ascend AI processor series products named 910 and 310 were launched. The computing density of the Ascend 910 processor is very large due to using advanced 7 nm manufacturing processes. The maximum power consumption is 350 W while FP16 computing power can reach 256 TFLOPS. The computing density of a single processor is higher than that of a Tesla V100 GPU from the same era. INT8 computing capability can reach 512 TOPS and 128 channel full HD video decoding (H.264/H.265) is supported. The Ascend 910 processor is mainly applied to the cloud and also provides powerful computing power for deep learning training algorithm. The Ascend 310 processor launched in the same period is a powerful artificial intelligence System on Chip (SoC) for mobile computing scenarios. The processor uses a 12-nm manufacturing process. Maximum power consumption is only 8 W with FP16 performance up to 8 TFLOPS, INT8 integer performance of 16 TOPS, and integrated 16-channel HD video decoder. The Ascend 310 processor is intended primarily for edge computing products and mobile devices.

In terms of design, the Ascend AI processor is intended to break the constraints of AI processors in power consumption, computing performance, and efficiency. The Ascend AI processor adopts Huawei's in-house hardware architecture and is tailored to the computing features of deep neural networks. Based on the high-performance 3D Cube computing unit, the Ascend AI processor greatly improves computing power per watt. Each matrix computing unit performs 4096 multiplications and additions in one instruction. In addition, the processor also supports a multidimensional computing mode including scalar, vector, and tensor, which exceeds the limits of other dedicated artificial intelligence processors and increases computing flexibility. Finally, many types of hybrid precision calculation are supported for training and inference.

The versatility of the DaVinci architecture is reflected in its excellent suitability for applications with widely varying requirements. The unified architecture has best-in-class power efficiency while supporting processors from fractions to hundreds of watts. Simultaneously, the streamlined development process improves software efficiency across development, deployment, and migration for a wide range of applications. Finally, the performance is unmatched, making it the natural choice for applications from cloud to mobile to edge computing.

The DaVinci architecture instruction set adopts a highly flexible CISC instruction set. It can cope with rapidly changing new algorithms and models that are common nowadays. The efficient computing-intensive CISC architecture contains special instructions that are dedicated to neural networks and help with developing new models in AI. In addition, they help developers to quickly deploy new services, implement online upgrades, and promote industry development. The Ascend AI processor uses a scenario-based perspective, systematic design, and built-in hardware accelerators for processing. A variety of I/O interfaces enables multiple combinations of Ascend AI-based acceleration card designs, which are flexible and scalable enough to cope with cloud and edge computing and meet the challenges of energy efficiency. This allows Ascend AI-based designs to enable powerful applications across all scenarios.

2.2 Neural network processor acceleration theory

2.2.1 GPU acceleration theory

2.2.1.1 GPU computing neural networks principles

Because computations in neural networks are easily parallelized, GPUs can be used to accelerate neural networks. The major ways to accelerate neural networks with GPUs are through parallelization and vectorization. One of the most common GPU-accelerated operations in neural networks is the general matrix multiply (GEMM) since for most neural networks the core computations can be expanded into matrix operations. Convolutional neural networks are one of the most commonly used neural networks, so we take it as an example to explain how they can be accelerated with GPUs.

Convolution is the core operation of the convolutional neural network. As shown in Fig. 2.2, the convolution is illustrated with a two-dimensional input. A convolution kernel slides with a specific step size through the input image. The value of each pixel on the output image is equal to the dot product between the convolution kernel and the corresponding data block from the input image. Since GPU instructions do not directly support convolutions, to implement the operation on a GPU, the input image or feature map and convolution kernel must be preprocessed. The preprocessing is called the Img2Col. As shown in Fig. 2.2, the input image or feature map F has a size of 3×3 and the number of channels is 2; the convolution kernels W and G have a size of 2×2, and the number of convolution kernels is 2. In order to facilitate the convolution operation, the weight of each convolution kernel is first reshaped into a vector, and then the two vectors from the two channels of each convolution kernel are concatenated into one vector. The vectors from W and G are stacked as rows and finally, the corresponding 2 two-channel convolution kernels are expanded into a 2×8 matrix.

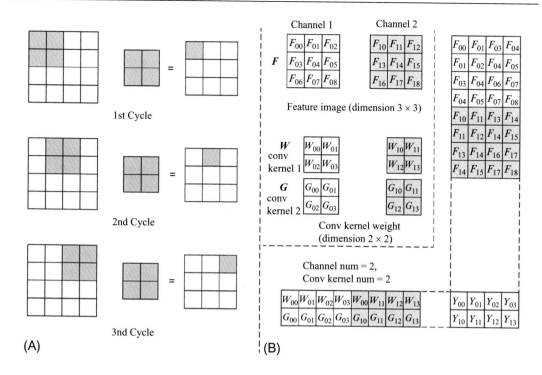

Fig. 2.2
Convolution operation transformed into matrix multiplication. (A) Direct convolution.
(B) Convolution based on matrix multiplication.

Similarly, for the input image F, the 2×2 block corresponding to the convolution kernel is expanded in row-major order. Consistent with the direct convolution order, the kernel slides one unit to the right and writes the block that is expanded later in the next column. Similar to the preprocessing of the convolution kernel, the two vectors of two different channels of the input image F can be concatenated into one vector and forms into the same column. Finally, a two-channel 3×3 input image is expanded in parallel into an 8×4 input feature matrix. After that, the input feature matrix is multiplied by the convolution kernel matrix, and the output obtained will be consistent with that of the traditional way of convolution.

It is worth noting that since the weights of the two channels of the same kernel have been arranged in the same row of the matrix, and the values of the two channels of the same input block are arranged in the same column, so the value of each unit of the 2×4 resulting matrix corresponds to the result of the accumulation of 2 channels. When the number of channels in the neural network is very large, the matrix will become so large that it might exceed the memory limit. In this way, the GPU cannot accommodate the expansion of all channels at a time. Based on the computing power of the GPU, each time an appropriate number of channels is selected and formed into an input matrix, and after some intermediate results are obtained, the outputs of multiple operations are accumulated to generate the final result.

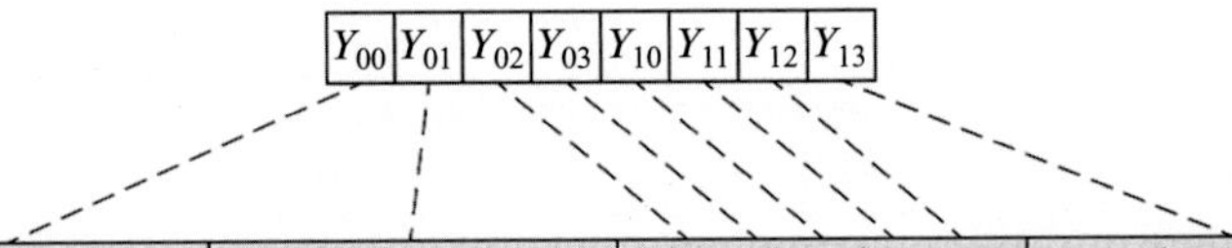

$$\boxed{Y_{00}}\boxed{Y_{01}}\boxed{Y_{02}}\boxed{Y_{03}}\boxed{Y_{10}}\boxed{Y_{11}}\boxed{Y_{12}}\boxed{Y_{13}}$$

Cycle	Thread1	Thread2	...	Thread8
1	$PS_1=W_{00}\cdot F_{00}+0$	$PS_2=W_{00}\cdot F_{01}+0$	...	$PS_8=G_{00}\cdot F_{04}+0$
2	$PS_1=W_{01}\cdot F_{01}+PS_1$	$PS_2=W_{01}\cdot F_{02}+PS_2$	...	$PS_8=G_{01}\cdot F_{05}+PS_8$
3	$PS_1=W_{02}\cdot F_{03}+PS_1$	$PS_2=W_{02}\cdot F_{04}+PS_2$	...	$PS_8=G_{02}\cdot F_{07}+PS_8$
4	$PS_1=W_{03}\cdot F_{04}+PS_1$	$PS_2=W_{03}\cdot F_{05}+PS_2$	...	$PS_8=G_{03}\cdot F_{08}+PS_8$
5	$PS_1=W_{10}\cdot F_{10}+PS_1$	$PS_2=W_{10}\cdot F_{11}+PS_2$	...	$PS_8=G_{10}\cdot F_{14}+PS_8$
6	$PS_1=W_{11}\cdot F_{11}+PS_1$	$PS_2=W_{11}\cdot F_{12}+PS_2$	...	$PS_8=G_{11}\cdot F_{15}+PS_8$
7	$PS_1=W_{12}\cdot F_{13}+PS_1$	$PS_2=W_{12}\cdot F_{14}+PS_2$	...	$PS_8=G_{12}\cdot F_{17}+PS_8$
8	$PS_1=W_{13}\cdot F_{14}+PS_1$	$PS_2=W_{13}\cdot F_{15}+PS_2$	...	$PS_8=G_{13}\cdot F_{18}+PS_8$

Fig. 2.3
Implementation of matrix multiplication on GPU.

For multiplication of the expanded matrix, the GPU uses single instruction multithreading (SIMT) manner. The GPU will assign a separate thread to compute one unit of the resulting matrix, corresponding to the result of the dot product of a row of the left matrix and a column of the right matrix. For this example, the GPU can use eight threads simultaneously to compute the matrix Y in parallel, where each thread executes the same instruction stream synchronously, but on different data.

As shown in Fig. 2.3, each thread of the GPU can perform a multiply-and-accumulate operation in each cycle, with multiple threads executing independently in parallel. In the figure, PS1, PS2,···, PS8, respectively, represent the partial sum in each thread, which corresponds to the intermediate results in the eight elements Y_{00}, Y_{01}, Y_{02}, Y_{03}, Y_{10}, Y_{11}, Y_{12}, and Y_{13}. In each clock cycle, a thread computes the multiplication of two input numbers and accumulates it to the partial sum. Ideally, after eight clock cycles, eight parallel threads will simultaneously output eight numbers in the resulting matrix.

2.2.1.2 Modern GPU architecture

With the development of the GPU industry, Nvidia's GPU architectures that support CUDA are also evolving from early-stage architectures like Fermi, Kepler, Maxwell, etc., which support the general floating-point computation, until the emergence of the latest architectures such as Volta and Turing that are optimized for deep learning and low-precision integer computation.

As shown in Fig. 2.4, the major functional modules of any generation of GPU architecture include stream processors, multilevel on-chip memory structures, and interconnection network

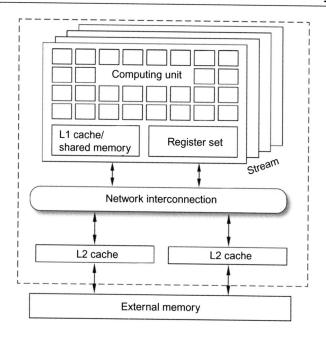

Fig. 2.4
Typical GPU architecture.

structures. A complete Turing-based TU102 processor contains 72 stream processors. The storage system consists of L1 cache, shared memory, register set, L2 cache, and off-chip storage. The L2 cache size of the TU102 GPU is 6 MB.

(1) **Turing Stream Processor**

In the Turing architecture [2], each stream processor contains 64 CUDA cores responsible for the computations of single-precision floating-point FP32. These CUDA cores are mainly used to support general-purpose computing programs. They can be programmed in the CUDA framework which maps to SIMT. Matrix multiplication or other types of computations can be implemented based on the methods described above.

Each stream processor in the Turing architecture also includes eight tensor cores, which is significantly different from previous generations of GPUs. The main purpose is to provide more powerful, more specialized, and more efficient computing power for deep neural network algorithms. The tensor core supports multiprecision computations such as FP16, INT8, and INT4, providing sufficient flexibility for different deep learning algorithms. With the newly defined programming interface (mainly through the use of WMMA instructions), the user can easily program the tensor core in the existing CUDA framework. The highest computational precision in the stream processor is provided by the two FP64 units, whose main target is scientific computing that have strict requirements for computational precision.

The stream processor provides space for data storage through a 256KB register set and a 96KB L1 cache. The large register set in the GPU is to meet the storage needs of the huge amounts of on-chip threads. Each thread running in the stream processor needs to be assigned a certain number of general-purpose registers (often used to store variables in the program). These are generally placed in the registers and directly cause an increase in the overall use of the register bank.

The GPU's architectural design can support the use of L1 cache as shared memory. The difference between the two is that the execution of the L1 cache is completely controlled by the hardware, invisible to the programmer, and operates on the data through a cache replacement strategy similar to the CPU; and the use and allocation of the shared memory can be directly controlled by the programmer, which is extremely useful for programs with significant patterns in data parallelism.

The Turing architecture applies a new way of partitioning to improve the utilization and overall performance of the stream processor. It divides the stream processor into four identical processing zones, except that the four zones share a 96KB L1 cache or shared memory, each of which includes a quarter of the computation and storage resources in the stream processor. Each zone is designated a separate L0 instruction cache, a warp scheduler, an instruction issue unit, and a branch jump processing unit. Compared to previous GPU architectures, the Turing architecture supports more threads, warps, and thread blocks running simultaneously. At the same time, the Turing architecture separately designed the independent FP32 and INT32 computing units, so that the pipeline can synchronize the address (INT32), and simultaneously load the data (FP32). This parallel operation increases the number of instructions transmitted per clock cycle and increases the computational speed.

The Turing architecture is designed to improve performance while balancing energy efficiency and ease of programming. It uses a specially designed multiprecision tensor core to meet the requirements of deep learning matrix operations. Compared to the older architecture, Turing's computational throughput of floating-point numbers and integers during training and inference is greatly improved. Under the usual computational load, the energy efficiency of the Turing architecture is 50% higher than that of the earlier GPU architectures.

(2) **Tensor core**

Tensor core is the most important feature of Turing architecture, which can greatly improve the computational efficiency of deep neural networks. It is a new type of matrix computing unit called multiprecision tensor core. The Turing GPUs have demonstrated excellent performance in the training and inference of large-scale neural networks with the introduction of tensor cores, further stabilizing the position of GPUs in the AI industry.

There are eight tensor cores in a stream processor, supporting INT4, INT8, and FP16 multiprecision calculations. The computation precision in the tensor core is relatively low but is sufficient for most neural networks while the energy consumption and the cost of the processor are greatly reduced. Each tensor core can perform 64 times of fused multiply and add (FMA) operations with the precision of FP16 in one clock cycle, so a stream processor can achieve 512 FMA operations per clock cycle, i.e., 1024 floating-point operations. If the INT8 precision is used in the same tensor core, it will be a double performance, achieving up to 2048 integer operations per clock cycle. Using INT4, then the performance can be doubled again.

The Turing architecture supports deep neural network training and inference on the tensor core by calling the WMMA instruction. The main function of the WMMA instruction is to achieve the multiplication of the large-scale input feature matrix and the convolution kernel weight matrix in the network connection layer. The tensor core is designed to increase computational throughput and energy efficiency. When a WMMA instruction enters the tensor core, it is broken down into a number of finer-grained HMMA instructions. The HMMA instruction controls the threads in the stream processor so that each thread can complete a four-point dot-products (FEDPs) in one clock cycle. Through careful circuit design, the tensor core ensures that each tensor core can achieve 16 FEDPs in one clock cycle, that is, each tensor core contains 16 threads. In other words, it can be guaranteed that each tensor core can complete the operation of multiplying two 4×4 matrices and accumulating a 4×4 matrix in one clock cycle. The formula (2.1) is as follows:

$$D = A \times B + C \tag{2.1}$$

In formula (2.1) A, B, C, and D, each represents a matrix of 4×4. The input matrices A and B are FP16 precision, and the accumulation matrices C and D can be either FP16 precision or FP32 precision. As shown in Fig. 2.5, $4 \times 4 \times 4 = 64$ multiplications and additions are needed to complete this process. The eight tensor cores in each stream processor can perform the computations above independently and in parallel.

When the tensor core is used to implement large matrix operations, the large matrix is first decomposed into small matrices and distributed in multiple tensor cores, respectively, and then the results are merged into a large result matrix. The Turing

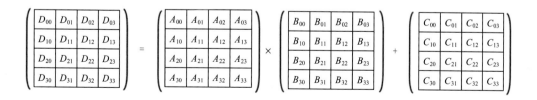

Fig. 2.5
Basic operations supported by tensor core.

tensor core can be manipulated as a thread block in the interface of CUDA C++ programming. This interface makes matrix and tensor operations in CUDA C++ programs more efficient.

Because of the strong capabilities in accelerating neural networks, high performance numerical computing, and graphics processing of the Turning GPUs, they have had a profound impact on scientific research and engineering. Turing currently exhibits outstanding computing power in the field of deep learning. The deep network model that used to take several weeks of training time often takes only a few hours to train with Turing GPUs, which greatly promotes the iteration and evolution of deep learning algorithms. In the meantime, people are also trying to apply the massive computing power of the tensor core to other application fields beyond artificial intelligence.

2.2.2 TPU acceleration theory

2.2.2.1 Systolic array for neural networks computing

The way in which the convolution is computed in the TPU is different from that of the GPU, which mainly relies on a hardware circuit structure called "systolic array." As shown in Fig. 2.6, the major part of the systolic array is a two-dimensional sliding array containing a number of systolic computing units. Each systolic computing unit can perform a multiply-add operation within one clock cycle. The number of rows and the number of columns in the systolic array may be equal or unequal, and the rightward or downward transfer of the data between the neighboring computing units is achieved through the horizontal or vertical data pathways.

The convolutional operation in Fig. 2.2 is used as an example to explain the process of computing in a systolic array. In this example, we use fixed convolution kernel weights, and the input feature values and partial sums are transferred laterally or longitudinally through the systolic array. According to Fig. 2.6, 2 two-channel W and G convolution kernel weights are first stored in the computational unit of the systolic array, wherein the two channels of the same convolution kernel are arranged in the same column. Then, the two channels of the input features F are arranged and expanded, and each row is staggered by one clock cycle and is prepared to be sequentially fed into the systolic array.

The state of the entire systolic array is shown in Fig. 2.7. When convolving with the two-channel input feature matrix F and the convolution kernels W and G, F is first re-arranged and loaded through the data loader into the leftmost column of the systolic array. The input data go from top to bottom, and each row entering the systolic array is delayed by one clock cycle from the previous row. In the first clock cycle, the input data F_{00} enters the W_{00} multiply-add unit and the multiply-add operation with W_{00} yields the unit result Y_{00}, which is the first partial sum of Y_{00}. In the second clock cycle, as shown in Fig. 2.8, the partial sum of the last W_{00} multiply-add unit Y_{00} is passed down to the W_{01} multiply-add unit, while the

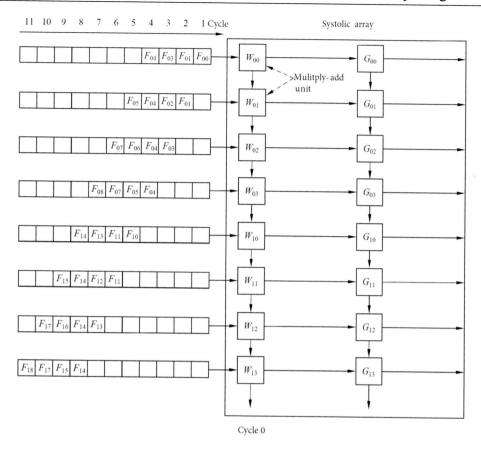

Fig. 2.6
Data arrangement for convolution acceleration in the systolic array.

second row of the input value F_{01} is multiplied by W_{01} and added to the second partial sum of the Y_{00}. On the other hand, F_{01} enters the W_{00} multiply-add unit and performs multiplication and addition to obtain the first partial sum of Y_{01}. At the same time, F_{00} slides to the right and enters the G_{00} multiply-add unit to obtain the first partial sum of the unit result Y_{10}.

Similarly, the data of the input feature matrix are continuously slid to the right along the horizontal direction of the systolic array to produce the partial sums of the different convolution kernels. In the meantime, the partial sums corresponding to each convolution kernel continuously slide down to the vertical direction of the column of the systolic array and accumulate with the result of the current multiply-add units, thereby obtaining the final convolution results for all channels of the convolution kernel in the lowermost computation unit of each column. As shown in Fig. 2.9, the first convolution result is obtained at the end of the eighth clock cycle. As shown in Fig. 2.10, after the ninth clock cycle, two results can be

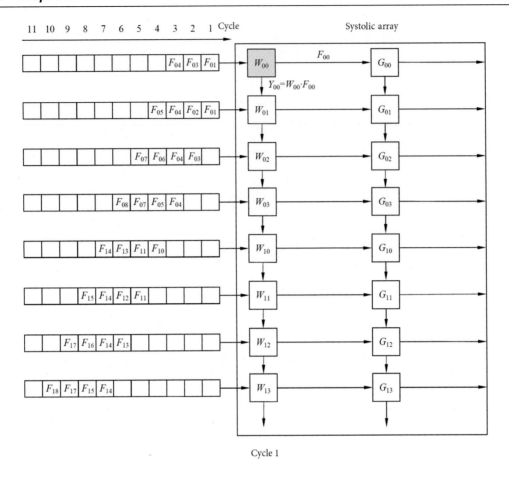

Fig. 2.7
State of the systolic array after the first cycle.

obtained each time. The convolution operation is not completed until all input data are convolved. The systolic array transfers data by simultaneous systolic in both directions, and the input data enters the array in a stepwise manner, and the final convolution results of each convolution kernel is sequentially generated.

The characteristics of the systolic array determine that the data must be fed sequentially, so each time to fill the entire systolic array, certain startup time is needed, and the startup time often causes a waste of hardware resources. The startup time can be estimated using {row number + column number − 1} where column number and row number are sizes of the systolic array. When the startup time is passed, the entire systolic array becomes fully loaded, and the maximum throughput can be obtained.

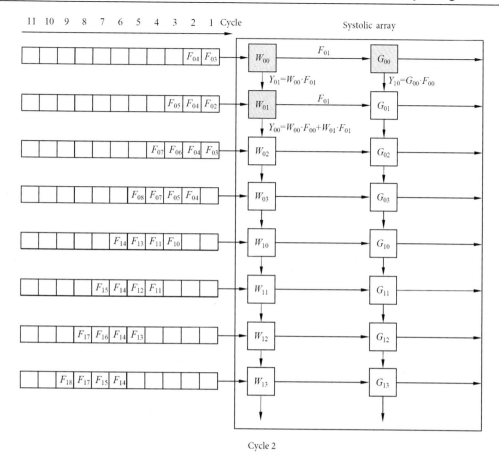

11 10 9 8 7 6 5 4 3 2 1 Cycle   Systolic array

$Y_{01}=W_{00} \cdot F_{01}$

$Y_{10}=G_{00} \cdot F_{00}$

$Y_{00}=W_{00} \cdot F_{00}+W_{01} \cdot F_{01}$

Cycle 2

Fig. 2.8
State of the systolic array after the second cycle.

The convolution results in the example of Figs. 2.6 are computed using fixed convolution kernel weights, with input data being fed through lateral systolic and partial sums being transferred through longitudinal systolic. Briefly speaking, we use fixed kernels and horizontally moving inputs and vertically moving partial sums. Actually, the same results can be obtained by fixing any one of the three and moving the other two. For example, we may fix the partial sums and horizontally move the inputs and vertically move the kernels. In practice, the selection of configurations will be determined based on the actual situation and application requirements.

It should be pointed out that when the convolution kernel is too large, there are too many channels, or if the weights of all channels are arranged in one column, it will inevitably cause the systolic array to be too large, which is not practical for the actual circuit design. To address

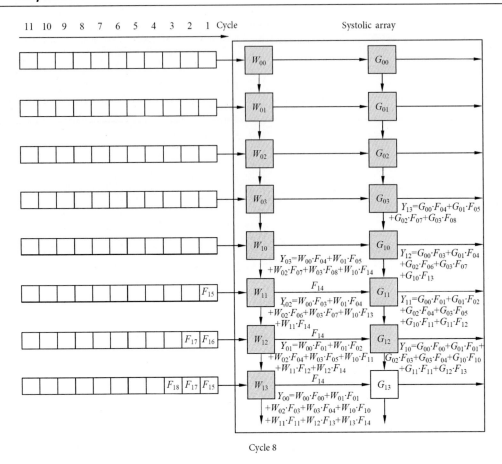

Cycle 8

Fig. 2.9
State of the systolic array after the eighth cycle.

this problem, split computation and accumulation are often used. The system divides the multichannel weight data into several blocks, each of which can fit the size of the systolic array. The weights of each block are then computed separately and sequentially, and the partial results of the computations are temporarily stored in a set of additive accumulators at the bottom of the systolic array. When the computation of a weights block finishes and the weight block is swapped with the next, the results are accumulated. After all the weight blocks are used, the accumulator accumulates all the results and outputs the final.

The systolic array in the TPU only performs the convolution operations, and the computation of the entire neural network requires the assistance of other computing units. As shown in Fig. 2.11, the vector computing unit receives the convolution results from the systolic array through the input data port and generates an activation value by a nonlinear function in the

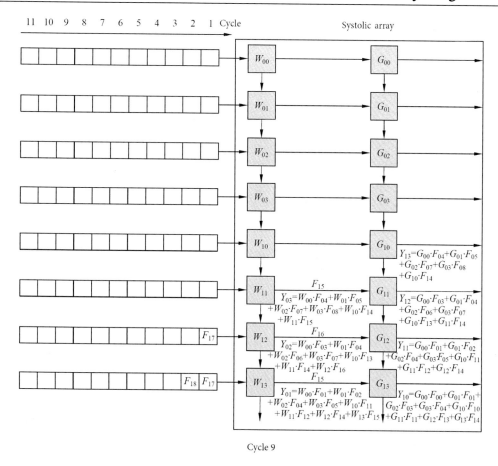

Cycle 9

Fig. 2.10
State of the systolic array after the ninth cycle.

activation unit, and the activation function can be customized based on requirements. In the vector computing unit, the activation value can also be normalized and then pooled. These operations are controlled by the queue module. For example, the queue module can specify an activation function, a normalization function, or a pooling function, and can also configure parameters such as step size through a parameter configuration port. After the processing of the vector computing unit, the activation values are sent to the unified buffer for temporary storage and as the input of the next layer. In this way, the TPU is able to perform the computation of the whole neural network layer by layer.

Although the systolic array is mainly targeted on the acceleration of neural networks, the architecture can handle much more than convolution operations. It is also efficient and powerful for the general matrix operations, so it can be used for a range of tasks other than convolution

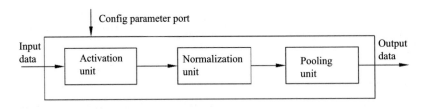

Fig. 2.11
Vector operation unit.

neural networks, such as fully connected neural networks, linear regression, logistic regression, clustering (such as K-means clustering), video en −/decoding, and image processing.

2.2.2.2 Google TPU architecture

Google's TPU processor, combined with its own TensorFlow software framework, can be used to accelerate the common algorithms for deep learning and has been successfully deployed to Google's cloud computing platform. The TPU is an application-specific processor for neural networks (please refer to https://cloud.google.com/blog/products/gcp/an-in-depth-look-at-googles-first-tensor-processing-unit-tpu for TPU architecture). Its main architecture modules include systolic array, vector computing unit, main interface module, queue module, unified buffer (UB), and direct memory access (DMA) control module.

The main interface is used to obtain parameters and configurations of the neural network, such as network-layer number, weights, and other initial parameters. After receiving the read command, the DMA control module will read the input features and weight data and store them in the on-chip UB. At the same time, the main interface sends an instruction to start execution of the queue module. After receiving the instruction, the queue module starts and controls the runtime mode of the whole neural network, such as loading the weight and feature data into the systolic array, splitting the data into blocks, and performing the computation by blocks. The main function of the unified buffer is to store the intermediate results of the input and output, or to send the intermediate result to the systolic array for the operation of the next layer. The queue module can send control signals to the unified buffer, the systolic array, and the vector computing unit, or directly communicate with the DMA control module and the memory.

In general, when applying TPU for the training or inference of neural networks, it operates on each layer of network sequentially. The system first obtains the input values from the off-chip memory and sends them to the systolic array to efficiently perform the convolution or other matrix operations. The vector unit utilizes special hardware for nonlinear activation and pooling. The output of each layer can be temporarily saved in the unified buffer to be used as input to the next layer. The overall process is a pipeline that is executed in an orderly manner under the control of instructions and hardware state machines.

The first generation of the TPU is equipped with 65,536 8-bit multiply-add units (MACs), which can support unsigned and signed integers, but does not support floating-point operations. A total of 4 MB of accumulator buffer is distributed around the systolic array and supports 32-bit accumulation. All intermediate results can be stored using a unified buffer of 24 MB. The TPU has an external 8 GB memory and can store a large number of images and convolution kernel data.

The instructions executed by the TPU are transmitted through the PCIe bus. The instructions belong to the CISC instruction set. The average number of clock cycles required to complete each instruction is approximately 10–20. Most of the instructions of the TPU belong to macros, which are essentially state machines controlled by hardware. This has the advantage of greatly reducing the overhead caused by instruction decoding and storage. The TPU has five main instructions for neural networks: data read instruction (Read_Host_Memory), weight read instruction (Read_Weight), matrix operation instruction (MatrixMultiply/Convolve, Activate), and data write back instruction (Write_Host_Memory). A complete instruction accounts for 12 bits in total, in which the unified buffer address accounts for 3 bits, the accumulator buffer address accounts for 2 bits, the operand length accounts for 4 bits, and the remaining 3 bits are the opcode and flag bits.

The basic instruction execution flow of the TPU is: first, the input feature data or image data are read from the system memory into the unified buffer by the Read_Host_Memory instruction; then the convolution kernel weight is extracted from the memory by the Read_Weight instruction and fed into the systolic array as part of the input of the systolic array; the function of the instruction MatrixMultiply/Convolve is to send the input data in the unified buffer to the systolic array based on certain rules and then load the results into the accumulator buffer for accumulation; then execute the Activate command to perform nonlinear activation functions, normalization and pooling by using the vector computing unit, and the results are stored in the unified buffer. Finally, the Write_Host_Memory instruction is used to write the final result of the completion in the unified buffer back into system memory.

2.3 Deep learning framework

With the popularity of deep learning, a variety of software frameworks has emerged. These frameworks are mostly open-source, and each of them has attracted many advocates in a short time. The main goal of these frameworks is to free deep learning researchers from tedious and detailed programming work, so their main focus can be on the tuning and improvement of AI algorithms. Since deep learning algorithms change rapidly and more and more hardware platforms begin supporting deep learning, the popularity of a framework often depends on how broad the ecosystem is and how well the framework can implement state-of-the-art algorithms while best exploiting the underlying hardware architectures.

2.3.1 MindSpore

MindSpore is a next-generation deep learning framework launched by Huawei originating from industry best practices [14]. It combines the computing power of the AI processor, supports flexible deployment of edge and cloud applications, and creates a new AI programming paradigm that simplifies the development of AI applications.

In the "Huawei CONNECT Conference" of 2018, ten challenges faced by artificial intelligence were put forward. Key among them was that algorithm training time was up to days or even months, that computing power was scarce and expensive, and that costs were prohibitive. Another issue was that AI still faced the challenge that there was no "intelligence" without considerable "manual" labor for practitioners with advanced skills to collect and label data. To date, the high technology threshold, high development cost, long deployment cycle, and other issues have hindered the development of industry-wide ecosystems. To help developers and industry more coherently address those systemic challenges, Huawei's next-generation artificial intelligence framework MindSpore focuses on simple programming with easy debugging, yet which yields high performance and flexible deployment options to effectively lower the development threshold. The details are as follows.

(1)   Programming in MindSpore is simple. As shown in Code 2.1, MindSpore introduces a new paradigm for AI programming. It incorporates an innovative functional differential programming architecture that allows data scientists to focus on the mathematical representation of model algorithms. The operator-level automatic differentiation technology makes it unnecessary to manually implement and test the inverse operator when developing a new network, reducing the effort required to deliver cutting-edge scientific research.

(2)   MindSpore is easy to debug. MindSpore provides a GUI which enables an easier debugging experience. It also provides both dynamic and static development and debugging modes where lines of code or a statement allows developers to switch the debugging mode. As shown in Code 2.2, when high-frequency debugging is required, the dynamic graph mode is selected, and the single operator/subgraph is executed to facilitate

---

CODE 2.1 MindSpore automatic differential code example.

```
import ms
from ms ops import focal_loss
def focalloss_ad logits labels out gamma
  loss = focal_loss logits labels gamma
  #Automatic differential derivation
  dout = ms autodiff loss logits out
  return dout
```

CODE 2.2 **Code example for MindSpore's debugging mode switching.**

```
def ssd_forward_run data gt_boxes gt_classes
  net = ssd_resnet34_224 batch_size=8
  # Switch to graph execution mode
  context switch_to_graph_mode
  loss = net data gt_boxes gt_classes
  # Switch to eager execution mode
  context switch_to_eager_mode
  loss = net data gt_boxes gt_classes
```

---

development and debugging. When it is required to run efficiently, it can be switched to the static graph mode which is compiled and executed using advanced optimization.

(3) MindSpore offers excellent performance. MindSpore executes models through AI Native which maximizes computing power across device, edge, and cloud platforms. Utilizing Huawei's AI processor for local execution, efficient data format processing, deep graph optimization, and other characteristics helps to achieve maximum performance, in turn helping developers to reduce training time and improve inference performance. As the datasets and models of modern deep neural networks get bigger and bigger, the memory and computing power of the single machine cannot meet the demands placed on it leading to a need for model parallelism. Manually partitioning tasks is slow and challenging to debug. As shown in Code 2.3, MindSpore automates model segmentation and tuning through flexible policy definition and cost models leading to optimal efficiency and performance.

(4) MindSpore has flexible deployment options. MindSpore provides consistent development across all platforms, facilitates on-demand collaboration between platforms and enables flexible deployment letting developers quickly deploy mobile, edge-to-cloud AI applications in all scenarios that achieve higher efficiency and unmatched privacy protection. MindSpore is open-source and scalable, which improves the prosperity of artificial intelligence and enables developers to flexibly extend third-party frameworks and third-party hardware for their needs. MindSpore provides sufficient tutorials and guides on the portal and open-source communities.

CODE 2.3 **Code example of MindSpore's automatic parallelism.**

```
def ssd_forward_compile_auto_parallel data gt_boxes gt_classes
  net = ssd_resnet34_224 batch_size=8
  #Automatic parallel between 8 devices
  compile_graph net data gt_boxes gt_classes auto_parallel=True
device_num=8
```

2.3.2 Caffe

In early neural network research, researchers needed to develop programs for heterogeneous architectures such as CPUs and GPUs in order to carry out and accelerate large-scale neural network operations. This required programmers to have advanced programming skills and a deep understanding of programming environments such as CUDA. Such requirements have severely impeded the development and promotion of deep learning. In 2012, AlexNet made waves in deep learning research with large-scale training and $10 \times$ performance improvement by using GPUs [15]. This prompted the development of many deep learning frameworks, often developed by global technology giants, including the most representative of them: the open-source framework, Caffe [16].

Caffe (Convolutional Architecture for Fast Feature Embedding) was created by Jia Yangqing during his PhD at the University of California at Berkeley based on C++/Cuda, and subsequently adapted to Python with PyCaffe. Caffe performs computations on either CPU or GPU with developers only defining the structure and parameter configuration of neural networks. Command-line options control either efficient training or inference of networks. In addition, Caffe also supports the development of customized network layers. Developers only need to implement layer parsing, feed-forward, and back-propagation functions of a layer to support new functionality. Debugging of programs and porting between different systems very easy since Caffe is based on C++. Lastly, Caffe provides a number of pretrained models that enable researchers to perform rapid iterative studies on neural networks by modifying parameters or fine-tuning the network based on pretrained models. For these reasons, Caffe stood out in the early days of the deep learning.

In the Caffe framework, structure and parameters of a neural network are defined by a prototxt file. Prototxt is the Google Protocol Buffer library (protobuf) for storing text. It is a lightweight and efficient structured data storage format that can be used for structured data serialization. It is very suitable for data storage or RPC data exchange, like JSON or XML but more efficient. The three most important concepts in protobuf are the proto file, the prototxt file, and the protoc compiler.

The proto file is used to define the organization of the data and is mainly composed of a package name (PackageName) and a message definition (MessageDefinition). Code 2.4 shows a definition of a proto file, where syntax specifies the protobuf version, package specifies the namespace, message defines a message type that contains multiple field definitions, and the field can be Required, Optional, and Repeatable, and the type of the field can be a common Int32, Double, String, or an enumerated type. Caffe source code defines caffe.proto itself to define various message types used internally. The most important ones are LayerParameter for defining layer parameters, SolverParameter for defining solver parameters and NetParameter for defining network structure.

CODE 2.4 Illustration of proto file contents.

```
syntax = "proto3"; // specify the protobuf version
package university; // claim the namespace
message Person // define the message type
{
  required int32 id = 1;  // define the required key
  required string name = 2;
  repeated string email = 3;  // define the repeatable key
  repeated string phone = 4;
  optional string birthday = 5; // define the optional key
  enum Type {      // define the enumerate key
   TEACHER = 0;
   STUDENT = 1;
  }
  required Type type = 6 [default = STUDENT]
}
```

The prototxt file is a text file that is serialized according to the format defined in the proto file. There is also a corresponding binary file, but the text file is easier to read and modify. Caffe's prototxt file contains two types of information: one is to define the neural network structure and the other is to define the training network parameters. The data structure in the prototxt file defining the neural network structure is defined by NetParameter, where "layer" represents each layer in the neural network, the structure of which is defined by the LayerParameter. As shown in Code 2.5, a prototxt representing a neural network structure can have multiple layers, depending on which parameters are used to determine the type of layer, parameters, and connections between them. Caffe builds the structure of the neural network by parsing the prototxt file. In addition, network training parameters used by Caffe optimizers such as learning rate are defined in the prototxt files. After parsing this information, Caffe is able to train the network.

During Caffe compilation, the protoc compiler compiles caffe.proto to get caffe.pb.cc and caffe.pb.h, which contain the serialization and deserialization interfaces for all defined

---

CODE 2.5 Prototxt structure.

```
name: "test"
layer {
  ...
}
layer {
  ...
}
```

CODE 2.6 An example of the max pooling layer.

```
layer {
name: "pool1"
type: "Pooling"
bottom: "conv1"
top: "pool1"
pooling_param {
 pool: MAX
 kernel_size: 2
 stride: 2
 }
 }
```

message types. Caffe can use these interfaces to generate or parse all message types defined by caffe.proto. For example, through the LayerParameter definition, each layer in the prototxt file can be parsed into a LayerParameter class, which is further passed according to the parsed type field. Subclasses of the corresponding LayerParameter class, such as ConvolutionParameter, parse specific layer parameters. Code 2.6 shows an example of a concrete maximum pooling layer whose format follows the LayerParameter definition, where the pooling_param field format follows the PoolingParameter definition.

In the Caffe framework, the intermediate feature map data is usually arranged in a four-dimensional array, called a Blob, and its specific format is defined in caffe.proto. Input image data needs to be stored in either lmdb or leveldb database format. The corresponding path of dataset and information are stored in prototxt through DataParameter. Currently, caffe also supports direct reading of image data through OpenCV [17] although this requires the OpenCV library and a separate ImageDataParameter.

After compiling Caffe, you can control the corresponding inference and training process merely through the command line, and the corresponding commands are as follows. As shown in Code 2.7, Caffe is a compiled executable program that requires only the solver file for training. The inference requires the prototxt file of the neural network and the corresponding weight file.

CODE 2.7 How to use Caffe for training and inference.

```
caffe train -solver=lenet_solver.prototxt
caffe test -model lenet_train_test.prototxt -weights lenet_i-
ter_10000.caffemodel
```

Since Caffe is written in C++, the structure of the library is clear: each layer has a special C++ implementation as well as a Cuda implementation for GPUs. This allows users to easily develop their own models in Caffe and is a large part of why Caffe is still widely used by major companies and universities for algorithm research and application deployment. Developing a customized layer in Caffe generally requires the following steps:

(1) add information defining the parameters of the customized layer, LayerParameter in caffe.proto;
(2) inherit Caffe built-in classes, build customized layer classes, provide methods for parameter parsing, memory allocation, shape calculation, layer registration, etc. This step provides providing the most important feed-forward and back-propagation implementations on CPU and GPU;
(3) write a test file, recompile Caffe, and the customized layer is added successfully if no error is reported;
(4) modify the prototxt file for training and inference.

The original Caffe is no longer updated and has been gradually replaced by Caffe2 since the original framework supports only single-GPU computing, and does not support distributed training among other drawbacks such as model level parallelism. In spite of this, Caffe provides an efficient and convenient learning platform for many beginners in the development of deep learning and is often their first step into deep learning.

2.3.3 TensorFlow

TensorFlow is Google's second-generation open-source deep learning framework [18]. It is based on DistBelief which was originally developed by GoogleBrain team for Google research and development. Released under the Apache 2.0 open-source license on November 9, 2015, it supports running on CPU, GPU, and Google's own TPU. TensorFlow is currently the most widespread and widely used open-source framework in the deep learning community.

After AlphaGo defeated Lee Sedol, the top professional chess player, Google used the opportunity to launch TensorFlow, gaining support from many developers. This is in large part due to Google sparing no effort in developing and promoting TensorFlow by maintaining a quick update schedule, complete documentation, wide platform support, and a rich interface, particularly for Python. TensorFlow also supports a wide range of neural networks so that developers can quickly build cutting-edge applications without reinventing the wheel is also appreciated by many users.

TensorFlow's name comes from its own operating principle. Tensor refers to the storage and transfer format of data between nodes in TensorFlow which are similar to arrays in NumPy library but different in many ways. Flow refers to the flow of tensor data. Input data flows as tensors through layers eventually flowing to the output node like a water stream after which the output data is obtained. TensorFlow abstracts network into simple data-flow diagrams that allow users to build models flexibly, without having to care about the underlying hardware scheduling or computational implementation details. By defining the computational graph in this manner, TensorFlow can further optimize the computational graph including operations such as memory allocation, data rearrangement, and so on. TensorFlow also supports distributed computing which may involve communication between different devices, unlike Caffe.

Although TensorFlow is a Python library, the computational graph formalism brings a completely different programming style. Typical Python libraries often provide a set of variables, functions, and classes. Using these libraries feels similar to writing normal Python code. However, when using TensorFlow, users find that the code used to define the computational graph in TensorFlow cannot be debugged or printed, and they even cannot use Python's If-else and While statements.

This is because TensorFlow is essentially a new domain-specific language (DSL) based on Declarative programming. Users need first define the computational graph need run by TensorFlow. The computational graph has inputs, outputs, and the mapping between them, which is equivalent to defining a new program. This programming concept is called Metaprogramming which sounds very complex and difficult to understand. However, this concept will be elaborated upon later in this book to teach readers how to use it. For now, to develop a neural network program using TensorFlow, just follow these steps:

(1)   define the computational graph using the interfaces provided by TensorFlow;
(2)   read data using normal Python code;
(3)   provide data to the computational graph, run the computational graph, and get the output.

Taking the computation graph in Fig. 2.12 as an example, both A and B are arrays of shape {10}. After the Element-Wise Product, an array C of shape {10} is obtained, and then after adding another scalar, an array D of the same shape {10} is obtained. The corresponding TensorFlow code for this example is shown in Code 2.8.

The first concept of TensorFlow programming is the computational graph. Each TensorFlow program will build a computational graph by default, so the declaration of the graph is not

Fig. 2.12
An example of TensorFlow computation graph.

> **CODE 2.8** **TensorFlow code.**
>
> ```
> import numpy as np
> import tensorflow as tf
> # define the computing graph
> A = tf.placeholder(tf.int32, 10, 'A')
> B = tf.placeholder(tf.int32, 10, 'B')
> C = tf.multiply(A, B, 'Mult')
> D = tf.add(C, tf.constant(1, tf.int32), 'Add')
> # run the computing graph
> with tf.Session() as sess:
>   print(sess.run(D, feed_dict={A: np.ones(10), B: np.ones(10)}))
> ```

explicitly displayed in the code. TensorFlow can define multiple computational graphs by tf.Graph, but there will only be one default computational graph at any time.

The second concept of TensorFlow programming is Nodes. Nodes may be compute nodes or data nodes. Compute nodes define a specific computation. In Code 2.8, tf.add defines tensor addition, and tf.multiply defines tensor multiplication. In addition, more high-level compute nodes like convolution, fully connected computation, and so on are equivalent to the layers defined in Caffe. The other type of node is data nodes. In Code 2.8, tf.placeholder in the above code defines a placeholder node which acts as an input to the computational graph. Other types of data nodes, like (1)tf.constant: defines constant nodes (2) tf.Variable: defines variables. Trainable parameters, such as weights, offsets, and so on are represented in the form of data nodes.

The third concept of TensorFlow programming is Tensor, which represents actual data in TensorFlow. It is reflected in the computational graph as the connection between nodes. In Code 2.8, A, B, C, and D are all tensor objects. There are two types of tensors: one is the tensor corresponding to placeholder output and is used to provide input data at runtime. The other is the tensor passed between compute nodes. When the user runs the computational graph TensorFlow computes the minimum dependency graph between inputs and outputs and uses this reduced graph to compute the output value(s).

The fourth concept of TensorFlow programming is the Session. It provides context for the computation of the entire computational graph, including configuration information for the GPU, etc.

2.3.4 PyTorch

PyTorch is a deep learning framework launched by Facebook in October 2016 [19]. It is an open-source Python machine learning library based on Torch. The official version was launched on December 7, 2018. It is very popular as Google's TenosrFlow.

PyTorch is a second-generation deep learning framework like TensorFlow, but has some distinctive features. Although PyTorch is also based on a computational graph mechanism it feels very similar to ordinary Python code. This is because PyTorch uses Imperative Programming to dynamically generate graphs.

Each time a line of code is executed, the system constructs a corresponding computational graph and data is calculated in real-time. Such a computational graph is called a dynamic graph. In contrast, TensorFlow can only obtain data by running an existing computational graph. Such a computational graph is called a static graph. There is an animation on PyTorch's GitHub official website that explains how it works. Interested readers can check it out.

Why does PyTorch, which introduces dynamic graphs, not count as a new generation of deep learning frameworks compared to TensorFlow? This is because the introduction of "dynamic graphs" in essence is only a change of user interface and interaction. Such flexibility is partly at the expense of runtime performance, and it cannot be regarded as true technological innovation. In fact, static graph based frameworks like TensorFlow are also introducing dynamic graphing mechanisms such as TensorFlow Eager and MxNet Gluon.

But in any case, imperative programming and dynamic graphing mechanisms make it easier for users to carry out deep learning development and programming. For example, recursive neural network and word2vec, which are challenging in TensorFlow, can be implemented easily with PyTorch.

Implementing the computations in Code 2.8, using PyTorch in Code 2.9 is much simpler and more similar to the typical Python code.

2.4 Deep learning compilation framework—TVM

With the introduction of many new deep learning frameworks and the emergence of an increasing number of hardware products, researchers in the field of deep learning have found that it is not easy to handle end-to-end software deployment and execution perfectly and efficiently. Although frameworks such as TensorFlow can support a variety of hardware such as CPU, GPU, and TPU, the migration of algorithm models among different deep learning

---

CODE 2.9 PyTorch code.

```
import torch
A = torch.ones(10)
B = torch.ones(10)
C = A * B
D = C + 1
```

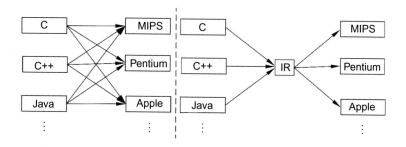

Fig. 2.13
Intermediate representation of LLVM.

frameworks (such as PyTorch, TensorFlow, and Caffe) is difficult. As shown in the left half of Fig. 2.13, different software programming methods and frameworks have different implementations on different hardware architectures, such as mobile phones, embedded devices, or servers in data centers. These factors increase the user's costs.

The compiler-level intermediate representation framework LLVM [20] solves this problem by setting up an intermediate instruction representation (IR), as shown in the right half of Fig. 2.14. All software frameworks are not directly mapped to specific hardware but are first compiled into an intermediate format of instruction representation by a front-end compiler. For specific hardware, the vendor can provide a back-end compiler that bridges the intermediate instructions and the specific hardware instructions, and implements the IR with the specific hardware instructions.

Motivated by this idea, a number of intermediate representations, compilers, and actuators dedicated to deep learning have emerged over the past few years. These are collectively referred to as a Compiler Stack. For example, nGraph proposed by Microsoft and SystemML published by IBM, and the TVM (Tensor Virtual Machine) framework proposed by Tianqi Chen's team of University of Washington [21].

More details about TVM will be introduced in the following chapters but here is a brief introduction to the overall structure and major components. Similar to the LLVM framework, TVM is also divided into front-end, middle, and back-end. However, TVM introduces many additional features in the middle. As shown in Fig. 2.14, TVM provides the following functionalities:

(1) converts computational graph representations of different frameworks into a unified NNVM intermedia representation (IR), and then perform graph-level optimizations upon the intermediate representations, such as operator fusion;
(2) provides tensor-level intermediate representation (or TVM primitives), which separates the computing from the scheduling. It allows the implementation of different scheduling methods for the same operator on different hardware architectures; and

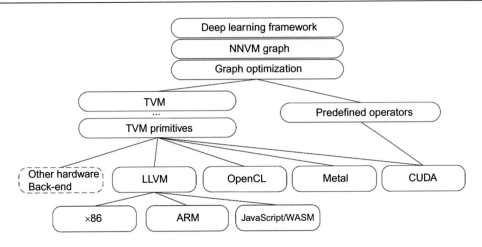

Fig. 2.14
TVM/NNVM architecture.

(3) provides a learning-based optimization method that finds optimal scheduling methods
within search space then quickly and automatically generates kernels whose performance
can exceed those produced by manual optimization.

TVM's contribution is not only to provide a set of compiler stacks that translate from the deep
learning framework to the underlying hardware but more importantly to propose the
abstractions from graph-level to operator-level by dividing the graph into primitive operations,
combining the operators when needed and providing specific scheduling for each architecture.
This enables users to use TVM to automatically or semiautomatically generate code or kernels
that exceeds the performance of handwritten code. It greatly improves the efficiency of the
development of high-performance deep learning applications.

References

[1] Volta (Microarchitecture), Wikipedia. https://en.wikipedia.org/wiki/Volta_(microarchitecture) (Accessed
2020).
[2] Turing (Microarchitecture), WikiPedia. https://en.wikipedia.org/wiki/Turing_(microarchitecture) (Accessed
2020).
[3] What are Field-Programmable Gate Arrays (FPGA) and How to Deploy, Microsoft. https://docs.microsoft.
com/en-us/azure/machine-learning/how-to-deploy-fpga-web-service (Accessed 2020).
[4] Tensor Processing Unit, Wikipedia. https://en.wikipedia.org/wiki/Tensor_processing_unit (Accessed 2020).
[5] Ascend AI Processor, Huawei. http://www.hisilicon.com/en/Products/ProductList/Ascend (Accessed 2020).
[6] Comparison of Deep Learning Software, Wikipedia. https://en.wikipedia.org/wiki/Comparison_of_deep-
learning_software (Accessed 2020).
[7] Moore's Law, Wikipedia. https://en.wikipedia.org/wiki/Moore%27s_law (Accessed 2020).
[8] What's the Difference Between a CPU and a GPU, Nvidia. https://blogs.nvidia.com/blog/2009/12/16/whats-
the-difference-between-a-cpu-and-a-gpu/ (Accessed 2020).

[9] CUDA, Wikipedia. https://en.wikipedia.org/wiki/CUDA (Accessed 2020).

[10] RTX-2080, Nvidia. https://www.nvidia.com/en-us/geforce/graphics-cards/rtx-2080/ (Accessed 2020).

[11] Application Specific Integrated Circuit, Wikepedia. https://en.wikipedia.org/wiki/Application-specific_integrated_circuit (Accessed 2020).

[12] Field Programmable Gate Array, Wikipedia. https://en.wikipedia.org/wiki/Field-programmable_gate_array (Accessed 2020).

[13] Versal, Xilinx. https://www.xilinx.com/products/silicon-devices/acap/versal.html (Accessed 2020).

[14] MindSpore, Huawei. https://e.huawei.com/ca/products/cloud-computing-dc/atlas/mindspore (Accessed 2020).

[15] A. Krizhevsky, I. Sutskever, G.E. Hinton, Imagenet classification with deep convolutional neural networks, NIPS, 2012.

[16] Caffe, Wikipedia. https://en.wikipedia.org/wiki/Caffe_(software) (Accessed 2020).

[17] OpenCV, Wikipedia. https://en.wikipedia.org/wiki/OpenCV (Accessed 2020).

[18] Tensorflow, Google. https://www.tensorflow.org/ (Accessed 2020).

[19] Pytorch, Facebook. https://pytorch.org/ (Accessed 2020).

[20] LLVM, https://llvm.org/ (Accessed 2020).

[21] TVM, https://tvm.apache.org/ (Accessed 2020).

## CHAPTER 3

Hardware architecture

In order to meet the increasing demands on the computing power of deep neural networks, Huawei launched the Ascend AI processor series in 2018 [1]. The Ascend AI processor provides powerful and highly efficient computing power for integer- and floating-point multiplication and addition operations. The Ascend AI processors not only have a large computational capacity, but also implement many special optimizations at the level of hardware architecture, which achieves high efficiency in performing forward computation of current mainstream deep neural networks. Therefore, it has great potential for various smart device applications.

3.1 Hardware architecture overview

The Ascend AI processor is a System on Chip (SoC) [2], as shown in Fig. 3.1. It can be used in many applications such as image, video, voice, and language processing. Its main architectural components include special computing units, large-capacity storage units, and the corresponding control units. The processor can be roughly divided into Control CPU, AI Computing Engine (including AI Core and AI CPU), multilevel on-chip system cache (Cache) or buffer (Buffer), Digital Vision Preprocessing module (DVPP), and etc. The processor adopts high-speed LPDDR4 [3] as the main memory controller interface which is more cost-effective than other alternatives. At present, the main memory of most SoC chips is generally composed of DDR (Double Data Rate) or HBM (High Bandwidth Memory) [4] to store large data. HBM has a higher storage bandwidth than DDR does, and it is the trend in the storage industry. Other common peripheral interface modules include USB, disk, network card, GPIO [5], I2C [6], power management interfaces, and so on.

When Ascend AI processors are used to accelerate servers, a PCIe interface [7] is used for data exchange between the processors and other hardware units. All of the above units are connected by an on-chip ring bus based on the CHI protocol, which defines the data exchange mechanism among modules and ensures data sharing and consistency.

The Ascend AI processor integrates multiple ARM CPU cores, each of them has its own L1 and L2 caches with all CPUs sharing an on-chip L3 cache. The integrated CPUs can be divided into the main CPU that controls the overall system and AI CPUs for nonmatrix complex

Ascend AI Processor Architecture and Programming. https://doi.org/10.1016/B978-0-12-823488-4.00003-5
© 2020 Tsinghua University Press Limited. Published by Elsevier Inc.

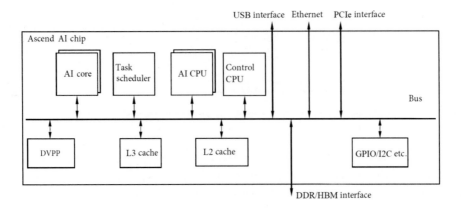

Fig. 3.1
Ascend AI processor hardware architecture.

calculations. The number of cores of CPUs can be allocated dynamically through software based on the immediate requirements.

Besides CPUs, the main computing power of Ascend AI processors is achieved by AI Core, which uses the DaVinci hardware architecture. These AI Cores, through specially designed hardware architectures and circuits, can achieve high throughput, high computational power, and low power consumption. They are especially suitable for matrix multiplications, the essential computation for neural networks in deep learning. At present, the processor can provide powerful multiplication and addition computations for integer-type (INT8 and INT4) or floating-point numbers (FP16). Taking advantage of modular design allows further increases to computational power by incorporating various modules.

In order to store and process large amounts of parameters needed by deep networks and intermediate temporary results, the processor also equips the AI computing engine with an 8 MB on-processor buffer to provide high bandwidth, low latency, and high-efficiency data exchange. The ability to quickly access needed data is critical to improving the overall running performance of the neural network. Buffering a large amount of intermediate data to be accessed later is also significant for reducing overall system power consumption. In order to achieve efficient allocation and scheduling of computing tasks on the AI Core, a dedicated CPU is used as a Task Scheduler (TS). This CPU is dedicated to scheduling tasks between AI Core and AI CPUs only.

The DVPP module is mainly in charge of the image/video encoding and decoding tasks. It supports 4 K[a] resolution video processing and image compressions such as JPEG and PNG.

---

[a]   4 K means 4096 × 2160 pixel resolution, which represents ultrahigh-definition video.

The video and image data, either from host memory or network, need to be converted to meet processing requirements (input formats, resolutions, etc.) before entering the computing engine of the Ascend AI processor. The DVPP module is called to convert format and precision accordingly. The main functionality of Digital Vision Preprocessing Module includes video decoding (Video Decoder, VDEC), video encoding (Video Encoder, VENC), JPEG encoding and decoding (JPEG Decoder/Encoder, JPEGD/E), PNG decoding (PNGD) and vision preprocessing (Vision Preprocessing Core, VPC), etc. Image preprocessing can perform various tasks such as up/downsampling, cropping, and color conversion. The DVPP module uses dedicated circuits to achieve highly efficient image processing functions, and for each function, a corresponding hardware circuit module is designed to implement it. When the DVPP module receives an image/video processing task, it reads the image/video data and distributes it to the corresponding processing module for processing. After the processing completes, the data is written back to memory for the subsequent processing steps.

3.2 DaVinci architecture

Unlike traditional CPUs and GPUs that support general-purpose computing, or ASIC processors dedicated to a particular algorithm, the DaVinci architecture is designed to adapt to common applications and algorithms within a particular field, commonly referred to as "domain-specific architecture (DSA)" processors.

AI Core is the main computing core in Ascend AI processor, which is responsible for executing scalar, vector, and tensor-related computation-intensive operations. AI Core adopts the DaVinci architecture, whose basic structure is shown in Fig. 3.2. It can be seen as a relatively simplified basic architecture of modern microprocessors from the control point of view. It includes three basic computing resources: Cube Unit, Vector Unit, and Scalar Unit. These three computing units correspond to three common computing modes: tensor, vector, and scalar. In the process of computation, each unit performs its own duties, forming three independent execution pipelines, which cooperate with each other under the unified scheduling of system software to achieve optimal computing efficiency. In addition, different calculation modes are designed with different precision requirements in Cube and Vector units. Cube Unit in AI Core can support the calculation of INT8, INT4, and FP16; and Vector Unit can support the calculation of FP16 and FP32 at the moment.

In order to coordinate the data transmission of AI Core, a series of on-chip buffers are distributed around three kinds of computing units. These on-chip buffers, e.g., Input Buffer (IB) and Output Buffer (OB), are used to store the entire image features, model parameters intermediate results, and so on. These buffers also provide high-speed register units that can be used to store temporary variables in the computing units. Although the design architectures and organization of these storage resources are different, they serve the same goal, i.e., to better meet the different input formats requirements, accuracy, and data layout for different

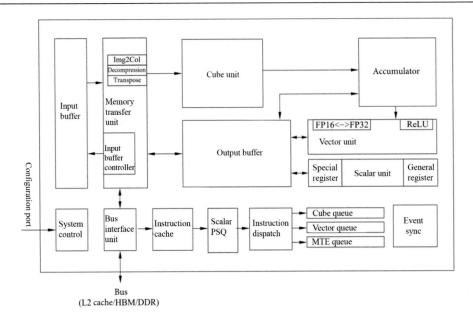

Fig. 3.2
AI core architecture framework.

computing modes. These storage resources are either directly connected to the associated computing hardware resources or to the bus interface unit (BIU) to obtain data on the external bus.

In AI Core, a memory transfer unit (MTE) is set up after the IB, which is one of the unique features of DaVinci architecture, the main purpose is to achieve data format conversion efficiently. For example, as mentioned earlier, GPU needs to apply convolution by matrix computation. It first needs to arrange the input network and feature data in a certain format through Img2Col. This step in GPU is implemented in software, which is inefficient. DaVinci architecture uses a dedicated memory conversion unit to process this step, which is a monolithic hardware circuit and so can complete the entire conversion process quickly. The customized circuit modules for transpose operation, one of the frequent operations in a typical deep neural network, can improve the execution efficiency of AI Core and achieve uninterrupted convolution operations.

The control unit in AI Core mainly includes System Control, Scalar PSQ, Instruction Dispatch, Matrix Queue, Vector Queue, Memory Transfer Queue, and Event Sync. The system control is responsible for commanding and coordinating the overall operation of AI Core, configuring parameters, and doing power control. Scalar PSQ mainly implements the decoding of control instructions. When instructions are decoded and sent out sequentially through Instruction

Dispatch, they are sent to Matrix Queue, Vector Queue, and Memory Transfer Queue according to the types of instructions. The instructions in the three queues are independently given to the Cube Unit, the Vector Unit, and the MTE according to a first-in-first-out (FIFO) mechanism. Since different instruction arrays and computing resources construct independent pipelines, they can be executed in parallel to improve instruction execution efficiency. If there are dependencies or mandatory time sequence requirements during instruction execution, the order of instruction execution can be adjusted and maintained by Event Sync. Event Sync is entirely controlled by software. In the process of coding, the execution sequence of each pipeline can be specified synchronizer symbols, to adjust the execution sequence of instructions.

In AI Core, the Memory Unit provides transposed data which satisfies the input format requirements for each computing unit, the computing unit returns the result of the operation to the Memory Unit, and the control unit provides instruction control for the various computing units and the Memory Unit. The three units coordinate together to complete the computation task.

3.2.1 Computing unit

Computing Unit is the core unit of AI Core, which provides powerful computing power, it is the main force of AI Core. AI Core computing units mainly include the Cube Unit, Vector Unit, Scalar Unit, and accumulator, as shown in Fig. 3.3. Cube Unit and accumulator mainly complete matrix-related operations, Vector Unit is responsible for vector operations, and Scalar Unit is mainly responsible for all types of scalar data operations and program control flow.

3.2.1.1 Cube unit

(1) Matrix multiplication

Due to the extensive use of matrix computing in the common deep neural network, the DaVinci architecture specifically optimizes matrix computing in-depth and customizes Cube Units to support high-throughput matrix operations. Fig. 3.4 shows the multiplication operation $C = A \times B$ between matrix A and B, where M represents the number of rows of matrix A, K represents the number of columns of matrix A and the number of rows of matrix B, and N represents the number of columns of matrix B.

The matrix multiplication computation in a traditional CPU is shown in Code 3.1. This program needs three loops to perform a complete matrix multiplication calculation. If it is executed on a single instruction dispatch CPU, it needs at least $M \times K \times N$ clock cycles to complete the operation. When the matrix is very large, the execution process is extremely time consuming.

In the computation process using CPU, matrix A is scanned row-by-row and matrix B is scanned column-by-column. Considering how a matrix is typically stored in the memory,

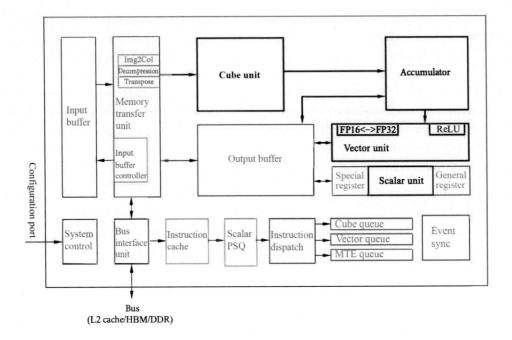

Fig. 3.3
Computing unit.

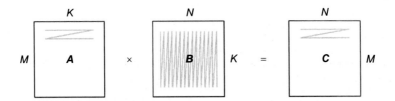

Fig. 3.4
Matrix multiplication illustration.

CODE 3.1 CPU matrix multiplication calculation.

```
for (int m=0; m<M, m++)
    for (int n=0; n<N, n++)
        for (int k=0; k<K, k++)
            C[m][n] += A[m][k]*B[k][n];
```

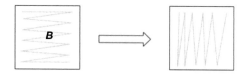

Fig. 3.5
Matrix B storage mode.

both matrix **A** and matrix **B** are stored row-by-row, so-called row-major mode. Memory accessing often has strong patterns. For example, when reading a number in a matrix into memory, it puts a whole line in memory and reads all the numbers of the same line together. This method of memory reading is very efficient for matrix **A**, but very inefficient for matrix **B** because matrix **B** in the code needs to be read column by column. In this case, it is beneficial to convert the storage mode of matrix **B** into column-by-column storage, so-called Column-Major (Fig. 3.5) mode, so as to conform to the efficient memory reading. The efficiency of matrix computing is often improved by changing the storage mode of a relevant matrix.

Generally speaking, when the matrix is large, due to the limitations of computing and memory on the processor, it is often necessary to split the matrix (Tiling), as shown in Fig. 3.6. Due to the capacity of on-chip cache, when it is difficult to load the whole matrix **B** at one time, matrix **B** can be divided into several submatrices such as B_0, B_1, B_2, and B_3. Each submatrix can be stored in a cache on the processor to calculate with matrix **A** to get the result submatrix. The purpose of this method is to fully utilize the data locality principle, reuse the submatrix data in the cache as much as possible to get all relevant submatrix results, then read the new submatrix for the next cycle. In this way, all the submatrices can be moved to the cache one by one, and the whole process of matrix calculation can be completed efficiently. Finally, the resulting matrix **C** can be obtained. As one of the common optimization methods for matrix computation, the advantage of partitioning is that it makes full use of caching capacity and maximizes the use of data locality in the process of computation. This allows it to achieve high efficiency especially for large-scale matrix multiplication computations.

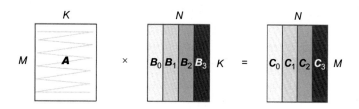

Fig. 3.6
Matrix operation using tiling.

(2) Computing method of cube unit

To implement the convolution process in deep neural networks, the key step is to convert the convolution operation into matrix operation. Large matrix computation in CPUs often becomes a performance bottleneck, however, such computations are crucial for deep learning. In order to solve this dilemma, GPUs use General Matrix Multiplication (GEMM) to implement matrix multiplications. For example, to multiply a 16×16 matrix with another 16×16 matrix, 256 parallel threads are used, and each thread can calculate one output point in the resulting matrix independently. Assuming that each thread can complete a multiplication and addition operation in one clock cycle, the GPU needs 16 clock cycles to complete the whole matrix calculation. This delay is an inevitable bottleneck for GPU. The Ascend AI processor has made further optimizations to avoid this bottleneck. The high efficiency of AI Core for matrix multiplication guarantees high performance for the Ascend AI processor when used as an accelerator for deep neural networks.

In AI Core, DaVinci architecture specially designed a Cube Unit as the core computing module of Ascend AI processor, aiming at removing the bottleneck of matrix computations. Cube Unit (CU) provides powerful parallel multiplication and addition computations, enabling AI Core to finish matrix computations rapidly. Through the elaborate design of customized circuits and aggressive back-end optimizations, the Cube Unit can complete the multiplication operation of two 16×16 matrices with one instruction (referred to as 16^3, also the name origin of Cube). This corresponds to $16^3 = 4096$ multiplication and addition operations with FP16 precision in a single instruction. As shown in Fig. 3.7, to compute matrix operation of $A \times B = C$, the Cube Unit stores matrix A and B in the IB, and after computation, the result matrix C is stored in the OB. In matrix multiplication (Fig. 3.7), the first element of matrix C is obtained through 16 multiplications and 15 additions (using Cube Unit subcircuits) on 16 elements in the first row of A and 16 elements in the first column of B. There are 256 matrix computing subcircuits in the Cube Unit, which can calculate 256 elements of matrix C in parallel using only one instruction.

In matrix computations, it is very common to accumulate the result of one matrix multiplication with itself such as $C = A \times B + C$. The design of the Cube Unit also takes this situation into account. A group of accumulator units is added after the Cube Unit, which can accumulate the last intermediate results with the current results. The total number of accumulations can be controlled by software, and the final results can be written to the output after the accumulation is completed. For convolution operations, the accumulator can be used to complete the addition of the bias term.

Cube Unit can quickly accomplish matrix multiplication of 16×16. However, when a matrix is larger than 16×16, it needs to be stored in a specific format in advance and read in a specific block-splitting way during the step of the computation. As shown in Fig. 3.8, the partitioning and sorting method shown as A is called "big Z and small Z." It is intuitive

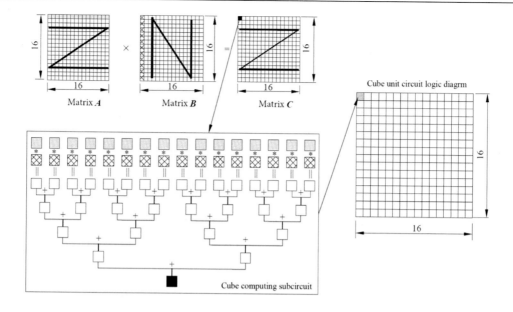

Fig. 3.7
Cube unit calculation illustration.

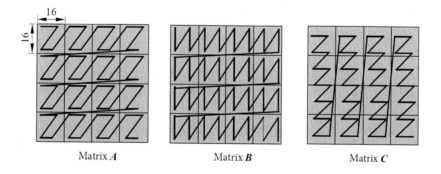

Matrix *A*   Matrix *B*   Matrix *C*

Fig. 3.8
Data storage format requirement.

to see that each block of *A* is sorted according to the index order of rows, and it is called "big Z." The data of each internal block is also arranged row-by-row, which is called as "small Z." Each block of matrix B is sorted by rows, while the inner part of each block is sorted by columns, which is called the "big Z small N" partitioning method. According to the general rule of matrix calculation, the resulting matrix *C* obtained by multiplying the *A* and *B* matrices, which is arranged as each block matrix being partitioned by columns, and the data inside each block being partitioned by row, so-called "big N and small Z" arrangement.

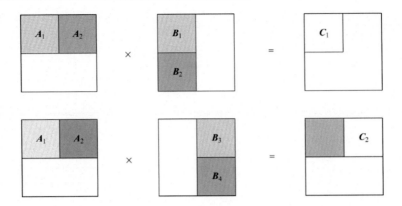

Fig. 3.9
Matrix computation using partitions.

When using the Cube Unit to compute large-scale matrices, due to the memory limitation, it is impossible to store the entire matrix at once. Therefore, it is necessary to partition the matrix and perform the calculation step-by-step. Fig. 3.9 shows the matrix A and matrix B are equally divided into blocks of the same size, as 16×16 submatrixes. During partitioning, the missing row/columns are padded with zeros. At first, obtain the resulting submatrix C_1, which needs to be calculated in two steps: the first step moves A_1 and B_1 to the Cube Unit and calculates the intermediate result of $A_1 \times B_1$. At the second step, moves A_2 and B_2 to the Cube Unit and calculate $A_2 \times B_2$. After that, accumulate these two results to get the final submatrix C_1, then C_1 is written into the output buffer. Since the output buffer capacity is also limited, it is necessary to write the C_1 submatrix into the memory as soon as possible, in order to leave spaces for the next result, e.g., submatrix C_2. By repeating the same mechanisms, the computation of the entire large-scale matrix multiplication can be achieved efficiently.

In addition to FP16-type operations, the Cube Unit can also support lower precision types such as INT8. For INT8, the Cube Unit can perform a matrix multiplication operation of 16×32 or 32×16 at once. By adjusting the precision of the Cube Unit accordingly to the computation requirement of deep neural networks, it is possible to achieve better performance.

Along with FP16 and INT8 operations, the Cube Unit also supports UINT8, INT4, and U2 data types. In terms of U2 data type, only the two-bit weight (U2 Weight) calculation is supported. Due to the popularity of the lightweight neural network using two-bit weights, U2 weight data will be converted into FP16 or INT8 for computations.

3.2.1.2 Vector unit

The Vector Unit in AI Core is mainly responsible for performing vector-related operations. It supports computations for one vector, computations between one vector and scalar, and

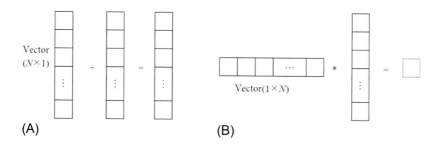

Fig. 3.10

Vector unit calculation illustration. (A) Vector addition. (B) Vector dot product.

computations between two vectors. All the computations support various data types, such as FP32, FP16, INT32, and INT8.

Fig. 3.10 shows the Vector Unit can quickly complete two FP16 type vector computations. Note that both the input and output data of the Vector Unit are usually stored in the OB (Fig. 3.2). For Vector Units, the input data can be stored in discontinuous memory space, depending on the addressing mode of the input data. The addressing mode supported by Vector Unit includes continuous addressing mode and fixed interval addressing mode. In special cases where vectors having irregular addresses, the Vector Unit also provides vector address registers to be used for addressing those vectors.

As shown in Fig. 3.2, the Vector Unit could serve as a data bridge between the Cube Unit and the output buffer. In the process of transferring the result of matrix computation to the output buffer, the Vector Unit can conveniently complete some common computations of deep neural networks, especially in convolutional neural networks, such as the activation functions (ReLU [8]) and various pooling functions, etc. The Vector Unit can also perform data format conversion before the data are written back to the OB or Cube Unit for the next operation. All these operations can be implemented by software with corresponding Vector Unit instructions. Vector Unit provides abundant basic computations together with many special vector computations to complement the matrix computations of the Cube Unit and provides AI Core with comprehensive computation for nonmatrix data.

3.2.1.3 Scalar unit

Scalar Unit is responsible for scalar-related computations in AI Core. It also behaves like a mini-CPU that controls the entire AI Core. Scalar Unit can control the iterations in programs and recognize conditional statements. It can also control how other modules are executed in the AI Core pipeline by inserting synchronizer in the Event Sync module. In addition, it calculates the address of data and related parameters to support the Cube Unit or Vector Unit.

Furthermore, it provides many basic arithmetic operations. Note that other highly complex scalar operations are fulfilled by the AI CPU with customized operators.

There are several general purpose registers (GPR) and special purpose registers (SPR) around the Scalar Unit. GPRs can be used to store variables or addresses, providing input data for arithmetic logic operations and storing intermediate computation results. SPRs are designed to support the special functionality of specific instructions in the instruction set. Generally, they cannot be accessed directly, only part of SPR can be read and written by special instructions.

The SPRs in AI Core include CoreID (used to identify different AI Core), VA (vector address register), and STATUS (AI Core run state register), and so on. Programmers can control and change the running state and mode of AI Core by monitoring these special registers.

3.2.2 Memory system

The Ascend AI processor memory system includes two parts: (1) on-chip memory unit, (2) the corresponding data transfer bus. It is well known that almost all deep learning algorithms are data intensive. Therefore, a well-designed data memory and transfer structure are crucial to the performance of Ascend AI processors. The suboptimal design generally creates performance bottlenecks, which could waste other resources in the processor. Through optimization and coordination among various types of distributed buffers, AI Core provides very fast data transfer for the deep neural network. It eliminates the bottleneck of data transmission to improve overall computing performance and to support efficient extraction and transfer of large-scale, concurrent data required in deep learning neural networks.

3.2.2.1 Memory unit

To achieve optimal computing power in the processor, it is essential to ensure that the input data can be fed into the computing unit rapidly and without corruption. The DaVinci architecture ensures accurate and efficient data transfer among computing resources through well-designed memory units which are the logistics system in AI Core. The memory units in AI Core is composed of Memory Control Units, Buffers, and Registers (bold in Fig. 3.11). Memory Control Unit can directly access lower-level caches outside AI Core through the data bus interface and can also access memory directly through DDR or HBM. The MTE is also set up in the memory control unit, which aims at converting the input data into data formats compatible with various types of computing units in AI Core. Buffers include IBs that temporarily store the input image feature maps and OBs which are placed in the center of the processor can temporarily store various forms of intermediate and final outputs. The various registers in AI Core are mainly used by Scalar Unit.

Read and write operations of all buffers and registers can be explicitly controlled by the underlying software. Experienced programmers can use advanced programming techniques to

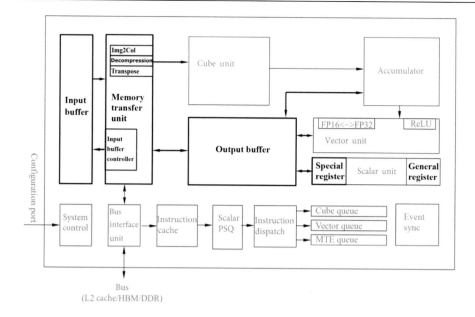

Fig. 3.11
Memory unit architecture.

avoid read and write conflicts that affect the performance of the pipeline. For regular neural network computations such as convolution or matrix operations, the corresponding programs can realize the whole process without blocking the execution of the pipeline.

The Bus Interface Unit in Fig. 3.11, as the "gate" of AI Core, is a bridge that connects the system bus and the external world. AI Core reads/writes data from/to the external L2 buffer, DDR, or HBM through the bus interface. In this process, the Bus Interface Unit can convert the read and write requests from AI Core to the external read and write requests that meet the bus requirements and complete the transaction and conversion using the predefined protocol.

The input data is read from the bus interface and processed by the MTE. As the data transmission controller of AI Core, the MTE is responsible for managing the internal data read and write operations among different buffers inside the AI Core. It includes tasks such as format conversion operations, zero-filling, Img2Col, transpose, and decompression, etc. The MTE can also configure the IB in AI Core to achieve local data caching.

For a deep neural network, the input image feature normally has a large number of channels and the input data volume is huge as well. The IB is often used to temporarily store the data that requires frequent reuse, in order to reduce power consumption and improve overall performance. When temporarily stored in the IB, the frequently used data does not need to be fed into the AI Core through the bus interface every time. It reduces data access frequency and the risk of congestion on the bus. This is important when data format conversion operation is carried out by the MTE. The DaVinci architecture stores the source data in the IB first, then it is possible to process data conversion. The entire data flow is controlled by the IB Controller. Storing in the IB makes it more efficient to move a large amount of data into AI Core at one time. This allows the data format to be converted rapidly using customized hardware eliminating performance bottlenecks that would otherwise be caused.

In the neural network, intermediate results of each layer can be placed in the OB, so that the data is easily obtained when processing the following layer. Using the OB greatly improves the computational efficiency when compared to reading data through the system bus which has low bandwidth and high latency.

The Cube Unit also contains a Supply Register which directly stores two input matrices of a 16×16 matrix multiplication. After the result is calculated, the accumulator caches the result matrix using a Result Register. With the help of the accumulator, the results of previous matrix calculation can be accumulated continuously, which is very common in running convolutional neural networks. The results in the Result Register can be transferred to the OB only once when all required cumulative operations complete, which can be controlled using software API.

Since the Memory System in AI Core provides continuous data flow, it fully supports the computing units to achieve high computing power. Therefore, it improves the overall computing performance of AI Core. This is similar to the Unified Buffer (UB) concept in Google's TPU design, and AI Core uses a large-capacity on-chip buffer design to increase the on-chip cache volume, which further reduces the frequency of data transmission between off-chip storage and AI Core. This also helps reduce power consumption effectively to control the overall energy consumption of the entire system.

DaVinci Architecture uses customized circuits in the MTE to implement format conversion operations such as Img2Col, etc. These not only reduce power consumption but also save the instruction cost of data conversion. Such instructions, which can do data format conversion while transmitting, are called accompanying instructions. The hardware support of accompanying instructions is beneficial since it doesn't need to schedule the conversion and transmission processes.

3.2.2.2 Data flow

Data flow refers to the data flowing path in AI Core when AI Core executes a computational task. The data flow path was briefly introduced in the previous section using matrix multiplication as an example. Fig. 3.12 shows the complete data flow within an AI Core in the DaVinci architecture. This includes DDR or HBM, as well as L2 caches, which belong to data storage systems outside the AI Core. All other types of data buffers in the diagram belong to the core memory system.

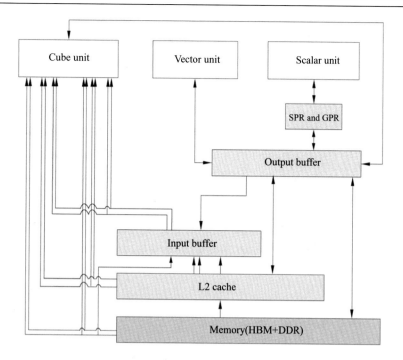

Fig. 3.12
Basic data flow illustration.

Data in the off-chip storage system can be directly transferred to the Cube Unit using LOAD instructions, and the output results will be stored in the OB. In addition to being transferred directly to the Cube Unit, data can also be transmitted to the IB first through LOAD then to the Cube Unit later by other instructions. The advantage of the latter approach is that the available large IB of temporary data can be reused many times by Cube Units.

Cube Units and OB can transfer data to each other. Because of limited storage in the Cube Unit, some matrix operation output is written into the OB in order to provide enough space for subsequent computations. When the time comes, data in the OB can also be moved back to the Cube Unit as input for subsequent calculations. Moreover, there are separate bidirectional data transmission buses between the OB and the Vector Unit as well as the Scalar Unit and the off-chip storage system, respectively. For example, data in the OB can be written into the Scalar Unit through a dedicated register or a general register.

It is worth to note that all data in AI Core must pass through the OB before being written back to the external storage. For example, if image feature data in the IB output to system memory, it is processed by the Cube Unit first with the output stored in the OB and finally is sent to off-chip storage from the OB. There is no data transmission bus directly from the IB to the OB in AI Core. Therefore, by serving arbiter of AI Core data outflow, the OB controls and coordinates the output of all core data accordingly.

The data transmission bus in the DaVinci architecture is characterized as multiple-input and single-output (MISO). Data can be fed into AI Core directly from outside to any of the Cube Unit, IB, and OB through multiple data buses. The data sinking path is flexible because data can be fed into the AI Core using different data pipelines separately controlled by software. On the other hand, output data must pass through the OB before it can be transferred to the off-chip storage.

The design is based on the characteristics of deep neural network computations, where input data has a great variety such as weights, bias terms of convolution layers, or eigenvalues of multiple channels. In AI Core, data can be stored accordingly in different memory units based on their type and can be processed in parallel. This greatly improves the data inflow efficiency in order to satisfy the needs of intensive mathematical computations. The advantage of multiple input data buses in AI Core is that they facilitate continuous data transmission of the source data into AI Core with few restrictions. On the contrary, outputs of deep neural networks are relatively simple, often only feature maps stored as matrices. According to this characteristic of neural network output, a single output data path is designed. As a result, the output data is centrally managed, thus reducing the hardware control units for output data.

To summarize, the data buses among storage units and the MISO data transmission mechanism in DaVinci architecture are designed based on the thorough study of most mainstream convolutional deep learning networks. The design principle is to reduce processor cost, improve data mobility, increase computing performance, and decrease control complexity.

3.2.3 Control units

In the DaVinci architecture, the Control Unit provides instructions for the entire computation process and is considered to be the heart of AI Core. It is responsible for the overall processing of the entire AI Core and so plays a vital role. The main components of the Control Unit are System Control, Instruction Cache, Scalar PSQ, Instruction Dispatch, Cube Queue, Vector Queue, MTE Queue, and Event Sync, shown as bolded in Fig. 3.13.

In the process of instruction execution, the instructions can be prefetched in advance, and multiple instructions can be read into the cache at the same time to improve the efficiency. Multiple instructions enter the instruction cache of AI Core from system memory through the bus interface where they wait to be decoded and executed quickly and automatically by the hardware. After the instruction is decoded, it will be imported into the Scalar PSQ for address decoding and execution control. These instructions include matrix computing instructions, vector computing instructions, and memory transfer instructions. Before entering the

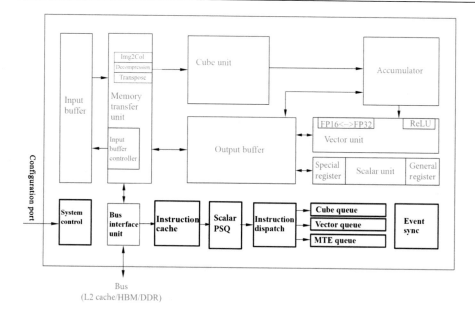

Fig. 3.13
Control unit logic diagram.

Instruction Dispatch module, all instructions are processed sequentially as conventional scalar instructions. After the address and parameters of these instructions are decoded by Scalar PSQ, the Instruction Dispatch sends them to the corresponding execution queue according to their types, only scalar instructions reside in Scalar PSQ for subsequent execution, as shown in Fig. 3.13.

Instruction execution queues consist of Matrix Queue, Vector Queue, and Memory Transfer Queue. Matrix computing instructions enter the Matrix Queue, vector computing instructions enter the Vector Queue, and memory transfer instructions enter the Memory Transfer Queue, respectively. The instructions in the same instruction execution queue are executed in the order they are entered. Different instruction execution queues can be executed in parallel and through multiple instruction execution queues. Parallel execution improves overall instruction execution efficiency.

When the instruction in the instruction execution queue arrives at the head of the queue, it begins the execution process and is distributed to the corresponding execution unit. For example, the matrix computing instructions will be sent to the Cube Unit, and the memory transfer instructions will be sent to the MTE. Different execution units can calculate or process data in parallel according to the corresponding instructions. The instruction execution process in the instruction queue is defined as the instruction pipeline.

When there is data dependence between different instruction pipelines, DaVinci architecture uses Event Sync to coordinate the process of each pipeline to maintain the correct execution order. Event Sync monitors the execution status of each pipeline at all times and analyzes the dependencies between different pipelines in order to solve the problem of data dependence and synchronization. For example, if the current instruction in the Matrix Queue depends on the result of the Vector Unit, the Event Sync will suspend the execution process of Matrix Queue, requiring it to wait for the result of the Vector Unit. When the Vector Unit completes the computation and outputs the results, the Event Sync notifies the Matrix Queue that the data is ready and can continue to execute the remaining instructions. The Matrix Queue executes the current instruction only after receives notification from Event Sync. In the DaVinci architecture, both internal synchronization and interpipeline synchronization can be achieved through Event Sync using software control.

As shown in Fig. 3.14, the execution flow of four pipelines is illustrated. Scalar PSQ first executes scalar instructions S_0, S_1, and S_2. Both the instruction V_0 in Vector Queue and the instruction MT_0 in Memory Transfer Queue have a dependency on S_2. Therefore, they need to wait until S_2 is completed before start execution. Because of these dependencies, the instructions have to be executed in sequential order. For the same reason, the matrix operation instructions M_0 and scalar instructions S_3 can only be executed at time 4. From time 4, the four instructions pipeline can be executed in parallel since all previous dependencies are resolved. The parallelization stops after scalar instruction S_7 is executed in the Scalar PSQ. At this point, the Event Sync controls the matrix instruction pipeline, the vector instruction pipeline, and the memory transfer instruction pipeline in order to wait until the matrix operation instruction M_0, the vector operation instruction V_1, and the memory transfer instruction MT_1 are all executed. After that, the scalar pipeline is allowed to continue executing scalar instruction S_8.

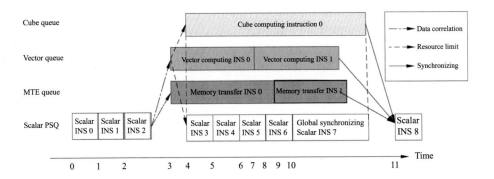

Fig. 3.14
Process and control of instructions.

There is also a System Control Module in the control units. Before AI Core runs, an external task scheduler is required to configure and initialize various interfaces of the AI Core, such as instruction configuration, parameter configuration, and task block configuration. One task block is defined as the smallest computational task that represents the task granularity in the AI Core. After the configuration is completed, the System Control Module will control the execution process of the task block. At the same time, after one task is completed, the System Control Module will process interrupts and report the status. If there is an error in the execution process, the System Control Module will report the execution error status to the task scheduler, which is merged into the current AI Core status information and finally exported to the Ascend AI processor top-level control system.

3.2.4 Instruction set design

When a program executes a computing task in the processor chip, it needs to be converted into a language that can be understood and processed by the hardware following a certain specification. Such language is referred to as the Instruction Set Architecture (ISA) or Instruction Set for short. The Instruction Set contains data types, basic operations, registers, addressing modes, data reading and writing modes, interruption, exception handling, and external I/O, etc. Each instruction describes a specific operation of the processor. An instruction set is a collection of all of the processor's operations that can be invoked by a computer program. It is an abstract model of a processor's functionality and an interface between computer software and hardware.

The instruction set can be classified into one of the Reduced Instruction Set Computer (RISC) and the Complex Instruction Set Computer (CISC). The advantages of simplified instruction sets include simple command functions, fast execution, and high compilation efficiency. However, simplified instruction sets cannot access the memory directly without using corresponding instructions. Common simplified instruction sets include ARM, MIPS, OpenRISC, and RISC-V, etc. [9]. On the other hand, in complex instruction sets, a single instruction is more powerful and supports more complex functionalities. And they support direct access to memory. However, it requires a longer command execution period. A common complex instruction set is x86.

There is a customized instruction set for the Ascend AI processor. The complexity of the instruction set in the Ascend AI processor is somewhere in between the simplified and complex instruction set. The instruction set includes scalar instructions, vector instructions, matrix instructions, and control instructions. A scalar instruction is similar to a simplified instruction set, while the matrix, vector, and data transfer instructions are similar to a complex instruction set. The Ascend AI processor instruction set combines the advantages of the simplified instruction set and complex instruction set, i.e., simple function, fast execution, and flexible memory access capability. Therefore, it is simple and efficient to transfer a large block of data.

Table 3.1 Common scalar instructions.

Type	Example instruction
Operation instruction	ADD.s64 Xd, Xn, Xm
	SUB.s64 Xd, Xn, Xm
	MAX.s64 Xd, Xn, Xm
	MIN.s64 Xd, Xn, Xm
Comparison and selection instruction	CMP.OP.type Xn, Xm
	SEL.b64 Xd, Xn, Xm
Logic instruction	AND.b64 Xd, Xn, Xm
	OR.b64 Xd, Xn, Xm
	XOR.b64 Xd, Xn, Xm
Data transfer instruction	MOV Xd, Xn
	LD.type Xd, [Xn], {Xm, imm12}
	ST.type Xd, [Xn], {Xm, imm12}
Flow control instruction	JUMP {#imm16, Xn}
	LOOP {#uimm16, LPCNT}

3.2.4.1 Scalar instruction set

A scalar instruction is executed by a Scalar Unit and is mainly used to configure address and control registers for vector instructions and matrix instructions. It also controls the execution process of a program. Furthermore, the scalar instruction is responsible for saving and loading data in the OB and performing some simple data operations. Table 3.1 lists the common scalar instructions in the Ascend AI processor.

3.2.4.2 Vector instruction set

A vector instruction is executed by a Vector Unit, which is similar to a conventional Single Instruction Multiple Data (SIMD) instruction. Each vector instruction can perform the same type of operations on multiple samples. And the instruction can directly be run on the data in the OB without loading the data into the vector register with a data loading instruction. The data types supported are FP16, FP32, and INT32. The vector instruction supports recursive execution and the direct operation of vectors that are not stored in continuous memory space. Table 3.2 describes common vector instructions.

3.2.4.3 Matrix instruction set

The matrix instruction is executed by the Matrix Calculation Unit to achieve efficient matrix multiplication and accumulation operations{$C = A \times B + C$}. In the neural network computation process, a matrix A generally represents an input feature map, a matrix B generally represents a weight matrix, and a matrix C is an output feature map. The matrix instruction supports input data of INT8 and FP16 data types and supports computation for INT32, FP16, and FP32 data types. Currently, the most commonly used matrix instruction is the matrix multiplication and accumulation instruction MMAD:

Table 3.2 Common vector instructions.

Type	Example instruction
Vector operation instruction	VADD.type [Xd], [Xn], [Xm], Xt, MASK
	VSUB.type [Xd], [Xn], [Xm], Xt, MASK
	VMAX.type [Xd], [Xn], [Xm], Xt, MASK
	VMIN.type [Xd], [Xn], [Xm], Xt, MASK
Vector comparison and selection instruction	VCMP.OP.type CMPMASK, [Xn], [Xm], Xt, MASK
	VSEL.type [Xd], [Xn], [Xm], Xt, MASK
Vector logic instruction	VAND.type [Xd], [Xn], [Xm], Xt, MASK
	VOR.type [Xd], [Xn], [Xm], Xt, MASK
Vector data transfer instruction	VMOV [VAd], [VAn], Xt, MASK
	MOVEV.type [Xd], Xn, Xt, MASK
Customized instruction	VBS16.type [Xd], [Xn], Xt
	VMS4.type [Xd], [Xn], Xt

```
MMAD.type [Xd], [Xn], [Xm], Xt
```

[Xn] and [Xm] are the start addresses of input matrix A and B, and [Xd] is the start address of output matrix C. Xt is a configuration register which consists of three parameters: M, K, and N, indicating the sizes of matrix A, B, and C, respectively. In matrix computation, the matrix multiplication and accumulation operation is performed using the MMAD instruction repeatedly, to accelerate the convolution computation of the neural network.

3.3 Convolution acceleration principle

In a deep neural network, convolution computation plays an important role. In a multilayer convolutional neural network, the convolution computation is often the most important factor that affects the performance of the system. The Ascend AI processor, as an artificial intelligence accelerator, puts more focus on convolution operations and optimizes the convolution calculation in both hardware and software architectures.

3.3.1 Convolution acceleration

Fig. 3.15 shows a typical computation process of a convolution layer, where X is an input feature map, and W is a weight matrix; b is the bias values. Y_o is the intermediate output. Y is the output feature map, and GEMM refers to the General Matrix Multiplication. Matrices X and W are first processed by Img2Col to obtain the reconstructed matrices X_{I2C} and W_{I2C}, respectively. A matrix multiplication operation is performed on the matrices X_{I2C} and W_{I2C} to obtain an intermediate output matrix Y_o. Then the bias term b is accumulated to obtain the final output feature map Y, which completes the convolution operation in a convolutional neural network.

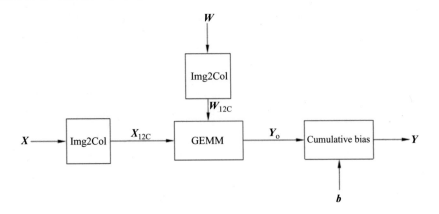

Fig. 3.15
Process of convolution operation.

The AI Core uses the following processes to accelerate the convolution operation. First, the convolutional program is compiled to generate low-level instructions which are stored into external L2 buffer or memory. Then these instructions are fed into the instruction cache through the bus interface. After that, the instructions are prefetched and wait for the Scalar PSQ to perform decoding. If no instruction is being executed, the Scalar PSQ reads the instruction in the cache immediately, configures the address and parameters, and then sends it to the corresponding queue according to the instruction type. In the convolution operation, the first instruction to fire is data transfer, which is sent to the memory transfer queue and then finally forwarded to the MTE.

As shown in Fig. 3.16, all data is stored in the DDR or HBM. After receiving the data read instruction, the MTE first reads the matrix X and W from the external memory to the IB by using the bus interface ①. After that, through data path ③, X and W are transferred to the MTE, which performs zero-padding on X and W and obtains two reconstructed matrices (X_{I2C} and W_{I2C}) through Img2Col operation. This completes the format conversion process which converts the convolution computation to the matrix calculation. To improve the efficiency, during the format conversion process, the Memory Transfer Queue can send the next instruction to the MTE to request sending X_{I2C} and W_{I2C} through the data path ⑤ to the Cube Unit, waiting for calculation after the format conversion ends. According to the general rule of data locality, if the weight W_{I2C} needs to be repeatedly used in the convolution process, the weight may be frozen in the IB by using the data path ⑰, and then transmitted to the Cube Unit through the data path ⑱ whenever the weight W_{I2C} needs to be used. Furthermore, during the format conversion process, the MTE reads the bias data from the external storage to the OB through the data path ④. And after the MTE reassembles the bias data from the original vector format into the matrix format through the data path ⑥, the data is transferred to the OB the data path ⑦. After that, the

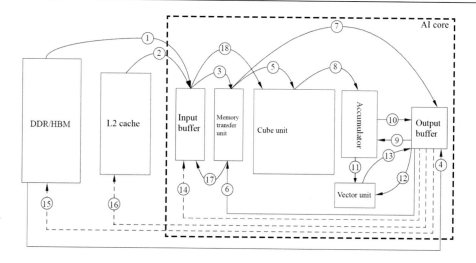

Fig. 3.16

Typical data flow in convolution operation.

data is stored in the registers of the accumulator through path ⑨, for the convenience of accumulating the bias values later using the accumulator.

When both the left and right matrix data are ready, the Matrix Queue sends the matrix multiplication instruction to the Cube Unit through the data path ⑤. The X_{I2C} and W_{I2C} matrices are grouped into a 16×16 matrix, and the Cube Unit performs multiplication operations. If the input matrix is large, the aforementioned steps may be repeated multiple times and accumulated to obtain the Y_o as the intermediate result, which is stored in the Cube Unit. After the matrix multiplication is complete, the accumulator will receive the bias term accumulation instruction if the bias values need to be added. The accumulator then reads the bias values from the OB through data channel ⑨, reads the intermediate result Y_o in the Cube Unit through data channel ⑧, and accumulates all values to obtain the final output feature matrix Y, which is transferred to the OB through the data path ⑩ and waits for subsequent instructions to be processed.

After the AI Core finishes the convolution operation through matrix multiplications, the Vector Unit will receive the pooling and activation instructions. The output feature matrix Y then enters the Vector Unit through the data path ⑫ to perform pooling and activation operations. The result Y is stored in the OB through the data channel ⑬. It is very convenient that the Vector Unit can perform some special operations, such as activation functions and can also efficiently implement dimensionality reduction, especially for pooling operations. When conducting the computation of a multilayer neural network, the previous layer output Y is transferred from the OB to the IB through the data channel ⑭, to be used as the input to the computation of the next layer of the neural network.

By considering the unique characteristic of computation and data flow in the convolution operation, the DaVinci architecture design considers many optimizations combining the transferring, computing, and control units more effectively. The overall optimization is achieved without compromising the functionality of each module. The AI Core combines the Cube Unit and data buffer efficiently, shortens the data transmission path from transferring to computing, and greatly reduces the system delay.

In addition, the AI Core integrates a large-capacity input and output buffers on the processor, which allows the AI Core to read and buffer sufficient data at one time, reduce the access to the external storage and significantly improve the data transfer efficiency. At the same time, each on-chip buffer has a much higher speed to access than external storage does, the use of a large amount of on-chip buffers greatly improves the data bandwidth in many computations.

Furthermore, based on the structural diversity of the deep neural network, the AI Core adopts a flexible data path, so that data can be quickly moved back and forth among the on-chip buffer, the off-chip storage system, the MTEs, and the computing units. This flexibility aligns well with the computing requirements of the deep neural network with different structures, which empowers the AI Core to have great adaptability for various types of computations.

3.3.2 Architecture comparison

In this section, we will compare the implementation of convolution on the DaVinci architecture of the Ascend AI processor to that on GPUs and TPUs described earlier. Referring to the convolution example in Fig. 2.2, GPUs use GEMM to convert the convolution calculation into a matrix calculation and obtain the output feature maps through parallel processing in multiple clock cycles using massive threads. With SIMD of the stream processor, GPUs execute multiple threads at the same time, and these threads complete an operation step, such as matrix multiplication, activation, or pooling, in a certain period. After threads in the GPU complete a step, data needs to be written back to the memory because the on-chip memory capacity is small. When the threads execute the next calculation, the data in the memory is read in again. Aimed at the general purpose of computations, GPUs process in similar schemes for convolution, pooling, and activation operations.

Although GPUs achieve flexible task allocation and scheduling control through centralized register management, multithread parallel execution, and CPU-like structure, the overall power consumption is increased. The advantage of centralization is that it facilitates the development of programs. However, in order to meet the general purpose requirement, each computation process needs to comply with the common rules. For example, one rule is that each computation needs to read data from a register and save the result back to the register. In this way, the power consumption of data transfer increases, and GPUs are always considered to be power hungry.

On the other hand, Google's TPU adopts the systolic array, which directly accelerates the convolution operation. The TPU has a large-capacity buffer on the processor. It can read almost all the data required for convolution operation to the on-chip buffer at once. After that, the data flow control unit transfers the data in the buffer to the computing array for the convolution computation. When all the computing units of the systolic array are fully occupied, the saturation is reached. At each clock cycle, TPU outputs the convolution results of one line. After the convolution operation on the systolic array is finished, the TPU uses a customized vector operation unit to perform activation or pooling.

During the calculation of the convolution neural network, the TPU reads a large amount of data into the buffer at a time by using simplified instructions and uses a fixed data flowing mode to fed the data into the systolic array, which greatly reduces the number of times data must be moved and reduces the overall power consumption of the system. However, this highly customized design limits the scope of the applications supported by the processor. In addition, because the buffer occupies too large a portion on the processor, other valid resources are inevitably compressed, thereby limiting the overall capability of TPU.

The Ascend AI processor accelerates convolution operation through matrix multiplication. First, the input feature map and the weight matrix are reconstructed to perform convolution using matrix multiplication. This is similar to GPU which also uses matrix multiplication to implement convolution calculation. However, due to different hardware architecture and design, the Ascend AI processor differs significantly from the GPU in matrix processing operations. First of all, the Cube Unit in the Ascend AI processor can perform calculations on matrices with size 16×16 at a time. Therefore, the throughput rate of the matrix calculation is greatly improved compared with that of the GPU. In addition, due to the careful design of the Vector and Scalar Unit, multiple computations such as convolution, pooling, and activation can be concurrently processed, which further improves the computation parallelism of the deep neural network.

The high computational efficiency in matrix or convolution operations of Ascend AI processor is due primarily to the advanced hardware design used by the DaVinci architecture, which significantly accelerates 16×16 matrix multiplications. In addition, DaVinci architecture uses a large number of distributed caches to cooperate with computing units, which effectively reduces data transmission to various computation units. As a result, it improves computing power and reduces the power consumption of data transmission simultaneously. Therefore, Ascend AI processors have huge advantages in the applications of deep convolution neural networks, especially in large-scale convolution calculations. However, because the DaVinci architecture adopts a fixed 16×16 Cube Unit when processing a small neural network, the computing power of Ascend AI processors cannot be fully utilized due to the low usage of hardware resources.

In conclusion, every architecture has its own pros and cons. It is meaningless to judge whether a hardware architecture is better or worse without specifying certain applications. Even for the same applications, data size and distribution, type of computation and precision requirements, structure, and layout of the neural network, all these affect whether or not a hardware architecture can fully achieve its advantages. Unfortunately, every case needs to be analyzed separately.

Domain-specific processors are becoming more and more important in the near future for computer industries. Unlike traditional ASICs that need to only consider hardware design, its overall performance strongly depends on efficient software operating on the processor as well. In the following chapters, we will introduce methods of software optimization using examples that will help readers to embrace the concepts of software and hardware collaborative programming and to adapt to the computer industry's new trend in this post-Moore era.

References

[1] Ascend AI Processor, Huawei. http://www.hisilicon.com/en/Products/ProductList/Ascend. (Accessed 2020).
[2] System on Chip, Wikipedia, https://en.wikipedia.org/wiki/System_on_a_chip. (Accessed 2020).
[3] LPDDR, Wikipedia, https://en.wikipedia.org/wiki/LPDDR. (Accessed 2020).
[4] High Bandwidth Memory, Wikipedia, https://en.wikipedia.org/wiki/High_Bandwidth_Memory. (Accessed 2020).
[5] General-Purpose Input/Output, Wikipedia, https://en.wikipedia.org/wiki/General-purpose_input/output. (Accessed 2020).
[6] I2C, Wikipedia, https://en.wikipedia.org/wiki/I%C2%B2C. (Accessed 2020).
[7] PCI express, Wikipedia, https://en.wikipedia.org/wiki/PCI_Express. (Accessed 2020).
[8] Rectifier (Neural Networks), Wikipedia, https://en.wikipedia.org/wiki/Rectifier_(neural_networks). (Accessed 2020).
[9] Reduced Instruction Set Computer, Wikipedia, https://en.wikipedia.org/wiki/Reduced_instruction_set_computer. (Accessed 2020).

## CHAPTER 4

Software architecture

The DaVinci architecture of the Ascend AI processor uses the customized computing resources in hardware design. The function execution is highly adapted to hardware which provides a powerful basis for improving the computing performance of the convolutional neural network. For a neural network algorithm, during the process from various open-source frameworks to the implementation of the model, and to the running on the actual processor, a multilayer software structure is required to manage the network model, computing flow, and data flow. The neural network software flow provides powerful support for the implementation of the neural network on the Ascend AI processor. In addition, the development tool chain is convenient for the application development of the neural network based on the Ascend AI processor. The software flow and development tool chain construct the foundation of the software stack of the Ascend AI processor, hence support from top to bottom of the execution process of the entire chipset.

4.1 Ascend AI software stack overview

To make the Ascend AI processor provide excellent performance, it is very important to design a complete software stack containing computing resources, a performance tuning framework, and various corresponding toolkits. The software stack of the Ascend AI processor can be divided into the neural network software flow, tool chain, and other software modules.

The neural network software flow mainly includes the process orchestration (Matrix), the framework manager (Framework), the execution manager (Runtime), the Digital Vision Pre-Processing (DVPP) module, the Tensor Boost Engine (TBE), and the Task Scheduler (TS). Neural network software flow is mainly used to complete the generation, loading, and execution of a neural network model. The tool chain mainly provides the auxiliary convenience for the realization process of the neural network.

As shown in Fig. 4.1, the functions of the main components in the software stack depend on each other to carry data flow, computing flows, and control flows. The software stack of the Ascend AI processor consists of four layers and an auxiliary tool chain. The four layers are the L3 application enabling layer, L2 execution framework layer, L1 processor enabling layer, and L0 computing resource layer. The tool chain provides auxiliary capabilities such as

Ascend AI Processor Architecture and Programming. https://doi.org/10.1016/B978-0-12-823488-4.00004-7

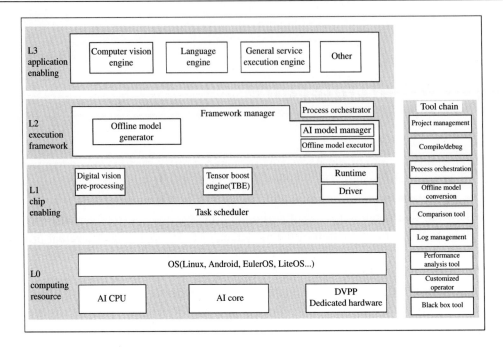

Fig. 4.1

Ascend AI software stack logical architecture.

program development, compilation and commissioning, application process orchestration, log management, and performance analysis.

4.1.1 L3 application enabling layer

The L3 application enabling layer is application-level encapsulation. It provides different processing algorithms for specific domains, including the general service execution engine, computer vision engine, and language text engine. The general service execution engine provides a general neural network inference capability. The computer vision engine provides some algorithm encapsulation for video or image processing in the field of computer vision. In the speech and other fields, the language engine provides basic processing algorithms for data such as speech and text and provides language processing functions based on specific application scenarios.

In general service requirements, the corresponding computation process is defined based on the process orchestrator (Matrix), and then the general service execution engine implements specific functions. The L3 application enabling layer provides computing and processing capabilities for various domains, can directly use the framework scheduling capability provided by the next L2 execution framework layer and generates a corresponding neural network through a general framework to implement specific engine functions.

4.1.2 L2 execution framework layer

The L2 execution framework layer encapsulates the framework utilization capability and offline model generation capability. After developing and encapsulating the algorithm of a specific domain into an engine at the L3 application enabling layer, the L2 layer invokes the appropriate deep learning framework according to the characteristics of related algorithms. For example, it invokes the Caffe [1] or TensorFlow [2] framework to obtain the corresponding neural network and then generates an offline model through the framework manager. The L2 execution framework layer contains the framework manager and process orchestrator.

The online and offline framework is used in the L2 execution framework layer. The online framework uses mainstream deep learning open-source frameworks (such as Caffe and TensorFlow) to convert and load offline models so that they can perform acceleration operations on Ascend AI processors. For the network model, the online framework provides training and inference capabilities for network models and supports training and inference acceleration in different deployment scenarios, such as a single card, single machine, and multimachine. In addition to the common deep learning open-source framework, the L2 execution framework layer also provides the Huawei-developed MindSpore [3] deep learning framework, which functions similarly to TensorFlow. However, the neural network model generated by the MindSpore framework can directly run on the Ascend AI processor without hardware adaptation and conversion.

For the Ascend AI processor, the neural network supports online generation and execution. In addition, the offline framework provides the offline generation and execution capabilities of the neural network, that is, the Offline Model (OM) can have the same capability (mainly for the inference) under the deep learning framework. The framework manager includes the Offline Model Generator (OMG), Offline Model Executor (OME), and offline model inference interface. The framework manager supports model generation, loading, unloading, and inference calculation execution.

The Offline Model Generator converts the generated model and weight files in the Caffe or TensorFlow framework into offline model files and executes the files independently on the Ascend AI processor. The Offline Model Executor loads and unloads the offline model, converts the loaded model file into an instruction sequence that can be executed on the processor, and compiles the program before the execution. The load and execution of these offline models need to be coordinated by the process orchestrator (Matrix). It provides developers with a development platform for deep learning including computing resources, running frameworks, and related tools. In this way, developers can easily and efficiently compile AI applications running on specific hardware devices and schedule the generation, loading, and operation of the models. After transforming the original model of the neural network into an offline model that can be executed on the Ascend AI processor at the L2 layer, the Offline Model Executor transfers the offline model to the L1 processor enabling layer for task allocation.

4.1.3 L1 processor enabling layer

The L1 processor enabling layer is the bridge between the offline model and the Ascend AI processor. After receiving the offline model generated by the L2 execution framework layer, the L1 enabling layer provides the acceleration function for the offline model by using the acceleration library (Library) for different computing tasks. The L1 processor enabling layer is the layer closest to the underlying computing resources and is responsible for outputting the tasks of the operator level to the hardware. The L1 processor enabling layer mainly includes the DVPP module, TBE, Runtime, driver, and TS.

In the L1 processor enabling layer, the TBE is used as the core, and the acceleration calculation of the online and offline models is supported. The TBE contains the standard operator acceleration library. These operators have a good performance after being optimized. During the execution, the operator interacts with the Runtime at the upper layer of the operator acceleration library, and the Runtime communicates with the L2 execution framework layer to provide the standard operator acceleration library interface for the L2 to execute the framework layer. So a network model can find the optimized, executable, and accelerative operators to achieve the optimal implementation. If the standard operator acceleration library of the L1 processor does not contain the operators required by the L2 to execute the framework layer, you can use the TBE to write a new custom operator to support it, therefore, the TBE provides an operator with functional completeness for the L2 execution framework layer by providing both a standard operator library and a customized operator capability.

Under the TBE, the TS generates a specific computation kernel function according to the corresponding operator. The TS processes and distributes the corresponding computing kernel function to the AI CPU or AI Core according to the specific task type and activates the hardware using the driver. The TS itself runs on a dedicated CPU core.

The DVPP module is a multifunctional package oriented to the field of image and video processing. In a scenario where the common image or video preprocessing needs to be performed, the module provides various data preprocessing capabilities for the upper layer using dedicated hardware in the bottom layer.

4.1.4 L0 computing resource layer

The L0 computing resource layer is the hardware foundation of the Ascend AI processor. After the L1 enabling layer distributes the tasks corresponding to the operators, the execution of specific computing tasks starts from the L0 computing resource layer. It consists of the operating system, AI CPU, AI Core, and DVPP dedicated hardware modules.

AI Core is the computing core of the Ascend AI processor, which is for matrix computation of the neural network. And AI CPU completes the general computation of the control operator, scalar, and vector. If the input data needs to be preprocessed, the DVPP dedicated hardware module is activated and is used to preprocess image and video data. In specific scenarios, the AI Core provides the data format that meets the calculation requirements. The AI Core is responsible for computing intensive tasks. The AI CPU is responsible for complex computing and execution control functions. The DVPP hardware completes the data preprocessing function. The operating system is used to closely assist the three components to form a complete hardware system to provide execution assurance for the calculation on the Ascend AI processor.

4.1.5 Tool chain

The tool chain is a tool platform that supports Ascend AI processors and can be used for development by programmers. It provides support for customized operator development, debugging, network migration, optimization, and analysis. In addition, the programming interface provides a visual AI engine with a drag-and-drop programming interface, which greatly reduces the development effort of the applications related to the deep neural network.

The tool chain includes project management, compilation debugging, process orchestration, offline model conversion, comparison tool, log management, performance analysis tool, customized operator, and black box tool. Therefore, the tool chain provides multilevel and multifunction services convenient for application development and execution on this platform.

4.2 Neural network software flow

To implement and execute a neural network application, the Ascend AI software stack is a bridge between the deep learning framework and the processor. It is a software flow that supports the high-performance computing for the neural network. It provides a quick conversion shortcut for the neural network from the original model, to the IR graph, and then to the independent execution of the offline model. It focuses on the generation, loading, and execution of offline models and aggregates functional blocks such as process orchestrator, DVPP module, TBE, framework manager, Runtime, and the TS to form a complete functional cluster, as shown in Fig. 4.2.

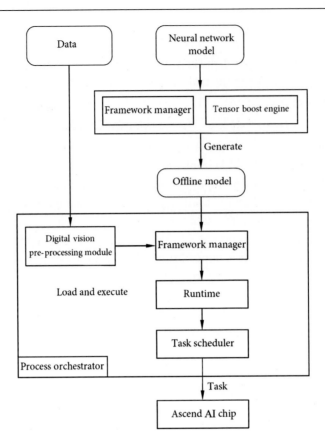

Fig. 4.2
Neural network software flow.

Each of these functional blocks has its specialty: the process orchestrator is responsible for implementing the neural network on the Ascend AI processor, coordinating the effective process of the entire neural network, and controlling the loading and execution of the offline model. The DVPP module performs data processing and modification to meet the format requirement. As a neural network operator, TBE provides a powerful computing operator for the neural network model. The framework manager uses the original neural network model to create the form supported by the Ascend AI processor and integrates the model with the Ascend AI processor to guide the running of the neural network and further improve the performance. The Runtime provides various resource management channels for the task delivery and allocation of the neural network. As a task driver for hardware execution, the TS provides specific target tasks for the Ascend AI processor. The Runtime and TS interact together to form a system of neural network tasks flowing to the hardware resources and monitor and distribute effectively different types of execution tasks in real time. In short, the entire neural network software flow provides a software and hardware combination and complete implementation process for the Ascend AI processor, contributing to the development of the relevant application ecosystem.

4.2.1 Process orchestrator (matrix)

4.2.1.1 Functions

The Ascend AI processor divides the network execution layers into basic execution units to obtain the granular computing engine (Engine). Each engine performs specific operations on data during process orchestration, such as classifying images, preprocessing input data, and outputting image data. In short, the computing engine is customized by developers to perform the required functions.

Generally, through the unified invoking of the process orchestrator, the entire deep neural network application includes four engines: data engine, preprocessing engine, model inference engine, and postprocessing engine. The data engine prepares the dataset (for example, MNIST dataset [4]) required by the neural network and processes the corresponding data (such as image filtering) as the data source of the subsequent computing engines. Generally, input media data needs to be preprocessed to meet the computing requirements of the Ascend AI processor. The preprocessing engine preprocesses the media data, performs operations such as image and video encoding and decoding, and format conversion. In addition, all functional modules of the DVPP need to be called by the process orchestrator.
The model inference engine needs to be used when data flows are based on neural network inference. The model inference engine mainly uses the loaded model and the input data flow to complete the feed-forward calculation of the neural network. After the model inference engine outputs the result, the postprocessing engine performs subsequent processing on the output of the model inference engine, for example, adding a frame and adding a label to the image recognition. The four engines can be used to construct multiple types of neural network applications and implement service functions based on the neural network in a combination of computing engines. The computing engine integrates functions similar to operators, abstracts the functional structure of the neural network from a higher level, and brings concise basic functional modules for the specific application development of the neural network, accelerating the development process of the neural network application.

In addition to engine encapsulation of the execution layer, the Ascend AI processor performs offline model conversion on the neural network model, so that it can be executed on the Ascend AI processor in the form of an offline model. The neural network model can be converted to an offline model by using the Offline Model Generator. The offline model includes the dependency of operators on the network and the training weight information. These dependencies and weight information constitute a neural network calculation diagram in essence. The offline model can run independently on the hardware, so that the processor can completely separate from the basic neural network open-source framework when completing the specific inference task, thereby saving a lot of resource overhead. The offline model can also reduce the size of the model, save storage space, and adapt to lightweight applications by means of quantization and compression. In addition, the offline model is closely related to the hardware and is highly optimized based on the hardware of the Ascend AI processor. In this way, performance and efficiency are greatly improved.

In fact, the process of implementing a neural network offline model is achieved through the orchestration and design of the computing engine process. After the orchestration is complete, the computing engine flowchart is generated. Fig. 4.3 shows a typical example. In the computing engine flowchart, each data processing node is a computing engine. Data flows are processed and calculated based on the orchestrated paths, and the results are output. The final output of the entire flow chart is the result generated by the corresponding neural network. Two adjacent computing engine nodes establish a connection based on the configuration file in the flowchart of the computing engine. The actual data between nodes flow according to the node connection defined by a specific network model. After node attributes are configured, data is imported to the start node of the computing engine flowchart to start the running process of the entire computing engine.

As the process orchestrator of the entire neural network, which is between the L1 processor enabling layer and the L3 application enabling layer, it provides unified standard intermediate interfaces for multiple operating systems (such as Linux and Android), in addition, it is responsible for establishing, destroying, and reclaiming computing resources.

During the process of creating a computing engine flowchart, the process orchestrator completes the computing engine flowchart creation based on the configuration file of the computing engine. Before execution, the process orchestrator provides input data. If the form of video input data does not meet the processing requirement, the DVPP module may be invoked by using a corresponding programming interface to perform data preprocessing. If the data meets the processing requirements, the Offline Model Executor is invoked to perform inference calculation. During the execution, the process orchestration apparatus has multiple node scheduling and multiprocess management functions. It is responsible for computing

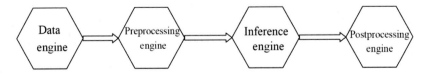

Fig. 4.3
Computing engine flowchart.

the running of the process on the device, guarding the computing process, and collecting and summarizing related execution information. After the model is executed, it provides the application on the active node with the functionality of obtaining the output result.

The Ascend AI processor uses the computing engine and process orchestrator to orchestrate and execute the computing engine diagram. The process orchestrator provides four common computing engines, which effectively enables multiple neural network offline models to be object oriented and process based. In addition, the data flow control is enhanced, so that the execution of different models has a general process template for development and design. The concept of computing engine also allows data flows and computing flows to be centrally managed in the flowchart.

4.2.1.2 Application scenarios

The Ascend AI processor can set up a hardware platform with different dedicated hardware for different services. Therefore, based on the collaboration between the device and host, there are two common application scenarios: Accelerator and Atlas DK. The applications of the process orchestrator in these two typical scenarios are different.

Acceleration card form

In an acceleration card application scenario, as shown in Fig. 4.4, a PCIe [5] card based on an Ascend AI processor is mainly oriented to a data center or an edge server scenario. It is a dedicated acceleration card for accelerating neural network computing. The PCIe accelerator card supports multiple types of data precision. Compared with other similar acceleration cards, the PCIe accelerator card provides more powerful computing power for the calculation of the neural network. In the accelerator scenario, a host needs to be connected to the accelerator card, and the host is a server or a personal computer that supports the PCIe card. The host invokes the neural network computing capability of the acceleration card to perform corresponding processing.

Fig. 4.4
PCIe acceleration card based on Ascend AI processor set.

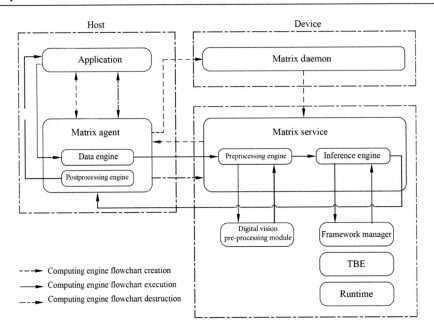

Fig. 4.5
Computing process for acceleration card.

As shown in Fig. 4.5, the process orchestrator function in the acceleration card scenario is implemented by three subprocesses: process orchestration agent subprocess (Matrix Agent), process orchestration daemon (Matrix Daemon), and process orchestration service subprocess (Matrix Service). The process orchestration agent subprocess runs on the host, controls and manages the data engine and postprocessing engine, processes data interaction with the host application, controls the application and communicates with the processing on the device. The process orchestration daemon and service subprocesses run on the device. The process orchestration daemon process creates processes on devices based on the configuration file, starts the process orchestration process on the device, and manages the process orchestration process. After the calculation is complete, the process orchestration process is released and resources are reclaimed. The process orchestration service subprocess starts and controls the preprocessing engine and model inference engine on the device. It controls the preprocessing engine to call the programming interface of the DVPP module to implement the video and image data preprocessing function. The process orchestration service subprocess can also call the AI model manager programming interface in the Offline Model Executor to load and inference offline models.

Fig. 4.5 shows the process of calculating the offline model of the neural network through the process orchestrator. The process consists of three steps: creating a computing engine flowchart, executing a computing engine flowchart, and destroying a computing engine. The process of creating a computing engine is to use the computing engine of different functions to orchestrate the execution process of the neural network. The computing engine flowchart is used to calculate and implement the neural network function based on the defined flowchart. The process of destroying the computing engine is used to release the system resources occupied by the computing engine after all computing is complete.

The process of executing an application in the system is as follows: first, the application program invokes a subprocess of the host's process orchestration agent to orchestrate the computing engine flowchart according to a precompiled configuration file of the corresponding neural network, creates an execution process of it and defines a task of each computing engine. Then, the computing engine orchestration unit uploads the offline model file and the configuration file of the neural network to the process orchestration daemon process on the device, and then the process orchestration service subprocess of the device initializes the engine. The process orchestration service subprocess controls the model inference engine to invoke the initialization interface of the AI model manager to load the offline model of the neural network.

After the offline model is loaded, the process orchestration agent subprocess on the host is notified of the application data input. The application directly sends the data to the data engine for processing. If the input is media data and does not meet the calculation requirements of the Ascend AI processor, the preprocessing engine starts immediately and calls the interface of the DVPP module to preprocess media data, such as encoding, decoding, and scaling. After the preprocessing is complete, the preprocessing engine sends the data to the model inference engine. In addition, the model inference engine invokes the processing interface of the AI model manager to combine the data with the loaded offline model to complete inference calculation. After the output result is obtained, the model inference engine invokes the data sending interface of the process orchestration unit to return the inference result to the postprocessing engine, which completes the postprocessing operation of the data, and finally returns it to the application program by using the process orchestration unit, then completes the flowchart of executing the computing engine.

After all engine data is processed and returned, the application notifies the process orchestration agent subprocess to release the hardware resources of the data engine and postprocessing engine. The process orchestration agent subprocess instructs the service subprocess to release resources of the preprocessing engine and the model inference engine. After all, resources are released, the computing engine flowchart is destroyed. The process orchestration agent subprocess instructs the application program to perform the next neural network execution.

The three software units implement the computing engine process in an orderly manner and work together to implement the function application of a neural network offline model on the Ascend AI processor.

Developer board form

In the developer board scenario, Huawei launches the Atlas developer suite (Atlas200 Developer Kit, Atlas 200DK), as shown in Fig. 4.6, including the hardware of a developer board that uses the Ascend AI processor as the core. The developer board provides the kernel functions of the Ascend AI processor through the peripheral interfaces on the board. This facilitates the control and development of the processor from the external. It can easily and intuitively display the neural network processing capability of the Ascend AI processor. Therefore, the developer board based on the Ascend AI processor can be widely used in different AI fields and is also the main hardware on edge devices in the future.

In the developer board environment, the control function of the host is integrated into the developer board. Therefore, the process orchestrator has only one software unit to run the process, which includes the subprocess functions of the host process orchestration agent, device process orchestration service, and process orchestration daemon process in the acceleration card scenario, as shown in Fig. 4.7.

In this case, as the functional interface of the Ascend AI processor, the process orchestrator function implements data interaction and commands between the computing engine flowchart and applications. The process orchestrator creates a computing engine flowchart based on the configuration file of the computing engine process to orchestrate, control, and manage processes. After the calculation is complete, the process orchestrator releases the computing engine flowchart and reclaims resources. During preprocessing, the process orchestrator invokes the interface of the preprocessing engine to perform media preprocessing. During the inference process, the process orchestrator can also invoke the programming interface of

Fig. 4.6
Developer board—Atlas 200DK.

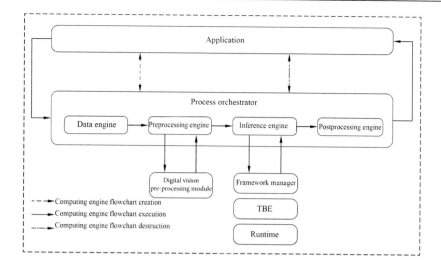

Fig. 4.7
Computing flowchart for the developer board.

the AI model manager to load and inference offline models. In the developer board application scenario, the process orchestrator orchestrates the implementation process of the entire computing engine flowchart and does not need to interact with other devices.

Similarly, in the developer board scenario, the offline model of the neural network uses the process orchestrator to perform inference calculation. The process is also divided into three main steps: creating, executing, and destroying a computing engine flowchart, as shown in Fig. 4.7.

Specifically, the application invokes the process orchestrator, creates a flowchart of the computing engine according to the network model, and initializes the computing engine. During initialization, the model inference engine loads the model through the initialization interface of the AI model manager to complete the creation of the computing engine flowchart. Then, the data is imported to the data engine. If the media data format does not meet the requirements, the preprocessing engine performs preprocessing. Then, the model inference engine invokes the AI model manager in the Offline Model Executor to perform inference calculation. After the calculation is complete, the model inference engine invokes the data output interface provided by the process orchestrator to return the inference result to the postprocessing engine, which returns the reasoning result to the application program through the callback function to complete the execution of the calculation engine flowchart. Finally, after the program calculation is complete, the process orchestrator destroys the computing engine flowchart and releases resources, then completes implementation of the neural network function in the developer board scenario.

4.2.2 Digital vision pre-processing module

As the encoding, decoding, and image conversion module in the whole software flow execution process, the DVPP module plays the assistant role for the neural network. Before the video or image data from the system memory and network enters the computing resources of the Ascend AI processor, the DaVinci architecture has a fixed format requirement for the input data. If the data does not meet the input format and resolution requirements specified in the architecture, the digital vision processing module needs to be invoked to convert the format so that the subsequent neural network calculation steps can be performed.

4.2.2.1 Functional architecture

The DVPP module provides six modules: video decoding (VDEC) module, video encoding (VENC) module, JPEG decoding (JPEGD) module, JPEG encoding (JPEGE) module, PNG decoding (PNGD) module, and visual preprocessing (VPC) module. The video decoding module provides the video decoding function of the H.264/H.265, which decodes the input video streams and outputs images for scenarios such as video recognition. For the counterparts, the video encoding module provides the encoding function of the output video. For the output data of the vision preprocessing module or the raw input YUV [6] format data, the video encoding module encodes and outputs the H.264/H.265 video, so as to directly play and display the video. This function is commonly used in high-speed data transmission scenarios such as cloud games and simulated mobile phone service. For pictures in JPEG format, the corresponding encoding and decoding module is also available. The JPEG decoding module decodes the JPEG picture, converts the original JPEG picture into YUV data, and preprocesses input data of the neural network. After the image processing is complete, the JPEG encoding module needs to be used to restore the processed data in JPEG format for training of the neural network and postprocessing of the inference output data. When the input picture is in PNG format, the flow orchestrator needs to invoke the PNGD decoding module to decode the picture and output the PNG picture in RGB format to the Ascend AI processor for training or inference calculation. In addition to the encoding and decoding modules for video and image formats, the DVPP module also provides other functions such as format conversion (for example, conversion from YUV/RGB format to YUV420 format), resizing, and cropping.

The execution process of the digital visual processing module is shown in Fig. 4.8 and needs to be completed by a process orchestrator, a digital vision processing module, a DVPP driver, and a DVPP hardware module. The top layer of the framework is the process orchestrator, which is responsible for scheduling the functional modules in the DVPP for processing and managing data flows. The digital vision processing module is located at the upper layer of the functional architecture and provides a programming interface for the process orchestrator to invoke the video or image processing module. Through these interfaces, parameters related to the encoding/decoding or vision preprocessing module can be configured. The DVPP driver

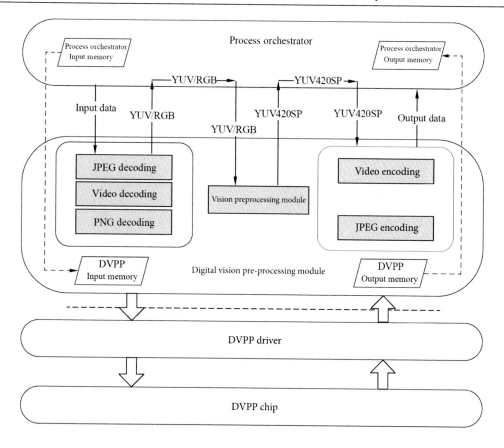

Fig. 4.8
DVPP function architecture.

is located in the middle and lower layers of the functional architecture and is closest to the hardware module of the DVPP. It is responsible for device management, engine management, and engine module driver. The driver allocates the corresponding DVPP hardware engine according to the tasks delivered by the digital vision processing module and reads and writes the registers in the hardware module to complete other hardware initialization. The bottom layer is the real hardware computing resource DVPP module group. It is a dedicated accelerator independent of other modules in the Ascend AI processor. It is responsible for executing the encoding, decoding, and preprocessing tasks corresponding to images and videos.

4.2.2.2 Preprocessing mechanisms

When the input data enters the data engine, if the engine detects that the data format does not meet the processing requirements of the subsequent AI Core, the DVPP module can be enabled to perform data preprocessing. The data flow shown in Fig. 4.8 is taken as an example. First, the process orchestrator moves the data from the memory to the buffer of the DVPP module for caching. According to the format of the specific data, the preprocessing engine completes parameter configuration and data transmission through the programming interface provided by the digital vision processing module. After the programming interface is started, the digital vision processing module transfers the configuration parameters and the original data to the driver. The DVPP driver invokes the PNG or JPEG decoding module for initialization and task delivery. In this case, the PNG or JPEG decoding module starts the actual operation to decode the picture and obtain the YUV or RGB data to meet the subsequent processing requirements.

After the decoding is complete, the process orchestrator uses the same mechanism to continue to invoke the DVPP module to convert the image into the YUV420SP format, because the YUV420SP data storage efficiency is high and the occupied bandwidth is small. Therefore, more data can be transmitted under the same bandwidth to meet the powerful computing throughput requirement of the AI Core. In addition, the DVPP module can also crop and resize images.

A typical image crop and zero-padding operation are shown in Fig. 4.9. The vision preprocessing module extracts the part of the to-be-processed image from the original image, and then performs zero padding, so as to retain the edge feature information during the calculation of the convolutional neural network. The zero-padding operation requires four padding sizes namely, upper, lower, left, and right. The image edge is expanded in the zero areas, and finally, a zero-padded image that can be directly calculated is obtained.

After a series of preprocessing, the image data that meets the format requirements will enter the AI Core for the required neural network calculation under the control of the AI CPU. After that, the output image data is encoded by the JPEG encoding module. After encoding, the data is stored in the buffer of the DVPP module. The process orchestrator obtains the data for subsequent operations, releases DVPP of computing resources, and reclaims the cache.

During the preprocessing, the process orchestrator implements functions of different modules. As a customized data supply module, the DVPP module uses a heterogeneous and

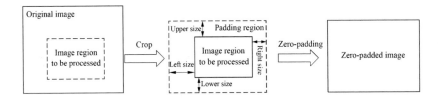

Fig. 4.9
Change image size.

dedicated processing method to quickly transform image data and provides sufficient data sources for AI Core, thereby satisfying a requirement of a large amount of data and a large bandwidth in a neural network calculation.

4.2.3 Tensor boost engine

Generally, in a neural network structure, an operator is used to form a network structure of different application functions. The TBE, being the arsenal of operators, provides the operator development capability for the neural network based on the Ascend AI processor, and constructs various neural network models by using the TBE operator written in the TBE language. In addition, the TBE provides encapsulation and invoking capabilities for operators. In the TBE, there is a neural network TBE standard operator library optimized by dedicated personnel. Developers can directly use the operators in the standard operator library to implement high-performance neural network calculations. In addition, the TBE also provides the fusion capability of the TBE operator, which opens a unique path for the optimization of the neural network.

4.2.3.1 Functional framework

The TBE provides the capability of developing customized operator based on TVM [7]. Through the TBE language and custom operator programming interface, the corresponding neural network operators can be developed. The structure of the TBE is shown in Fig. 4.10, which includes a domain-specific language (DSL) module, a scheduling (Schedule) module, an intermediate representation (IR) module, a compiler transfer (Pass) module, and a Code Generation (CodeGen) module.

TBE operator development is divided into computing logic writing and scheduling development. The domain-specific language module provides the programming interface of the operator calculation logic and writes the calculation and scheduling process of the operator directly based on the domain-specific language. The operator calculation process describes the calculation methods and steps of the operator, and the scheduling process describes the planning of the data block and data flow direction. Each calculation is processed according to a fixed data dimension. Therefore, data dimension splitting needs to be performed on the operators executed on different computing units in the Ascend AI processor in advance. For example, the Cube Unit, the Vector Unit, and the operator executed on the AI CPU have different requirements for the input data dimension.

After defining the basic implementation process of the operator, you need to start the tiling (Tiling) submodule in the scheduling module, divide the data among the operator according to the scheduling description, and specify the data transfer process to ensure that the execution on the hardware is optimal. In addition to data dimension segmentation, the operator

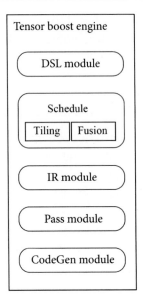

Fig. 4.10
Tensor boost engine module components.

fusion and optimization capabilities of the TBE are also provided by the fusion (Fusion) submodule in the scheduling module.

After the operator is written, an IR needs to be generated for further optimization, and the IR module generates an IR by using an IR format similar to TVM. After the generation, the module needs to compile and optimize the modules for various application scenarios. The optimization modes include double-buffer (Double Buffer), pipeline (Pipeline) synchronization, memory allocation management, instruction mapping, and block adaptation Cube Unit.

After the operator is processed by the Pass module, the code generation module generates a temporary file of the C-like code. The temporary code file may generate an implementation file of the operator by using the compiler and may be directly loaded and executed by the Offline Model Executor.

To sum up, a complete customized operator uses the submodule of the TBE to complete the entire development process and provides the primitive operator calculation logic and scheduling description from the domain-specific language module. After the operator prototype is formed, the scheduling module performs data segmentation and operator fusion and enters the IR module to generate the IR of the operator. The Pass module performs compilation optimization such as memory allocation by means of the IR. Finally, the code generation module generates a C-like code for compiler. In the definition process of the operator, the TBE not only completes the operator writing but also completes the related optimization, which improves the execution performance of the operator.

4.2.3.2 Application scenarios

Fig. 4.11 shows the three application scenarios of the TBE. Generally, a neural network model implemented by using a standard operator in the deep learning framework has been trained by using a GPU or another type of neural network processor. If the neural network model continues to run on the Ascend AI processor, it is naturally expected to benefit the portability of the model and perform optimally without changing the original code. Therefore, the TBE provides a complete TBE operator acceleration library. The operator function in the library has a one-to-one mapping to common standard operators in the neural network. Meanwhile, the software stack provides a programming interface for the operator to use. Thus, it provides acceleration for various frameworks or applications in the upper-layer deep learning, and avoids the development of adaptation code for the bottom-layer adaptation of the Ascend AI processor.

If a new operator appears in the neural network model construction, the standard operator library provided by the TBE may not meet the development requirements. In this case, you need to develop a customized operator in the TBE language. This development mode is similar to that of the CUDA C++ on the GPU. In this way, more multifunctional operators can be implemented, and various network models can be flexibly compiled. The implemented operator is delivered to the compiler, and finally executes on the processor, revealing the acceleration capability of the AI Core or AI CPU.

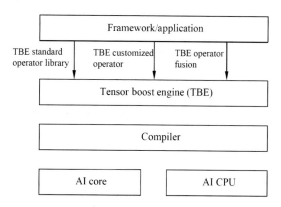

Fig. 4.11
TBE operator application scenarios.

In an appropriate scenario, the operator fusion capability provided by the TBE improves operator performance, and the neural network operator can perform multilevel cache fusion based on different levels of buffers so that the Ascend AI processor improves the on-chip resource utilization when the integrated operator is executed.

To sum up, because the TBE provides the operator development capability, the capability of standard operator invoking and operator fusion optimization, the Ascend AI processor can meet various function requirements in the actual neural network application, the network construction method is more convenient and flexible, and the fusion and optimization capabilities will also improve the running performance.

4.2.4 Runtime

Being the gateway of neural network software task flowing to the system hardware resources, the Runtime provides the resource management channel for the task allocation of the neural network. The Ascend AI processor runs in the application process space through the Runtime. It provides the following functions: memory (Memory) management, device (Device) management, stream (Stream) management, event (Event) management, and kernel (Kernel) execution.

As shown in Fig. 4.12, the TBE standard operator library and Offline Model Executor provided by the upper layer of the Runtime for the TBE are shown in Fig. 4.12. The TBE standard operator library is the operator used by the Ascend AI processor to provide the neural network. The Offline Model Executor is used to load and execute the offline model.

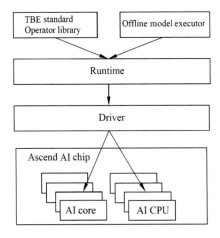

Fig. 4.12
Runtime context.

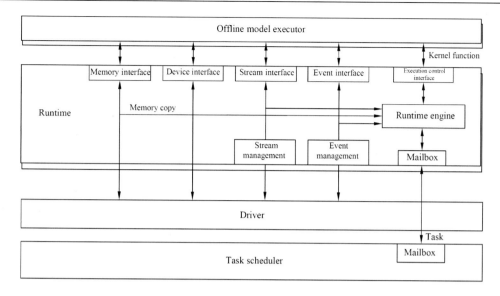

Fig. 4.13
Runtime functional module and external interfaces.

The lower layer of the Runtime is a driver and interacts with the Ascend AI processor at the bottom layer.

As shown in Fig. 4.13, the Runtime provides various invoking interfaces, such as memory interfaces, device interfaces, stream interfaces, event interfaces, and execution control interfaces. Different interfaces are controlled by the Runtime engine. The memory interface is used to apply for, release, and copy the HBM or DDR memory on the device, including data copy from the device to the host, from the host to the device, and from the device to the device. There are two types of memory copy: synchronous and asynchronous. Synchronous copy indicates that the next operation can be performed only after the memory copy is complete. Asynchronous copy indicates that other operations can be performed at the same time.

The device interface provides the function of querying the number and attributes of underlying devices and selecting and resetting the devices. After the offline model invokes the device interface and selects a specific device, all tasks in the model will be executed on the selected device. If a task needs to be dispatched to another device during the execution, the device interface needs to be invoked to select the device again.

The stream interface provides stream creation, release, priority definition, callback function setting, and event dependency definition and synchronization. These functions are related to task execution in the stream, and tasks in a single stream must be executed in sequence.

If multiple streams need to be synchronized, the event interface needs to be invoked to create, release, record, and define synchronization events to ensure that multiple streams are synchronized and output the final model result. The event interface is used to allocate the dependency between tasks or execution flows. It can also be used to mark the time during the program running and record the execution time sequence. During execution, the execution control interface is also used. The management engine executes the control interface and mailbox (Mailbox) to load the kernel functions and store asynchronous copies.

4.2.5 Task scheduler

The TS and the Runtime form a channeling system between software and hardware. During execution, the TS drives and supplies hardware tasks, provides specific target tasks for the Ascend AI processor, completes the task scheduling process with the Runtime, and returns the output data to the Runtime, which serves as a channel for task delivery and data backhaul.

4.2.5.1 Functions

The TS runs on the task scheduling CPU on the device side to distribute specific tasks assigned by the Runtime to the AI CPU. It can also allocate tasks to the AI Core through the hardware task Block Scheduler (BS) and return the execution result to the Runtime after the execution is complete. Generally, the TS processes the following transactions: AI Core tasks, AI CPU tasks, memory copy tasks, event recording tasks, event waiting tasks, cleanup and maintenance (Maintenance) tasks, and performance analysis (Profiling) tasks.

Memory copy is mainly performed in asynchronous mode. The event recording task records the event information. If a task is waiting for the current event, it can continue execution after the event record being completed, so that the stream is not blocked due to the event record itself. The event-waiting task could refer to: (1) if the waiting event has occurred, then the task is accomplished directly, or (2) if the waiting event has not yet occurred, then waiting task is put into the to-be-processed list, and all subsequent tasks of the waiting task in the same execution stream are paused, then resumes to process when it occurs.

After the task execution is complete, the maintenance task performs cleaning based on the respective parameters of each task and reclaims the computing resources. During the execution, you may need to record and analyze the computing performance. In this case, you need to use the performance analysis task to control the start and pause of the performance analysis operation.

Fig. 4.14 shows the functional framework of the TS. The TS is usually located at the device end and has the task scheduling CPU. The task scheduling CPU consists of the scheduling interface (Interface), scheduling engine (Engine), scheduling logic processing module, AI CPU

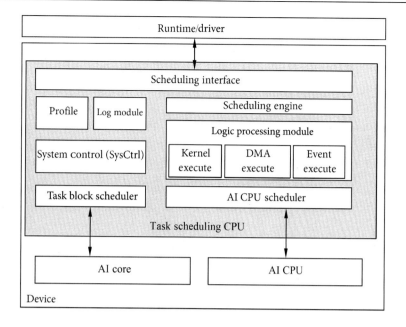

Fig. 4.14
Task Scheduler function framework.

scheduler, task block scheduler, system control (SysCtrl) module, performance analysis (Profile), and log (Log) module.

The task scheduling CPU implements communication and interaction with the Runtime and the driver through the scheduling interface. The task scheduling engine sends the task execution result to the task scheduling engine. The task scheduling engine is responsible for task organization, task dependency, and task scheduling control. The task scheduling engine manages the execution process of the task scheduling CPU. Based on the task type, the task scheduling engine divides tasks into three types: computing, storage, and control. The task scheduling engine distributes the tasks to different scheduling logic processing modules and starts specific kernel function tasks, storage tasks, and interflow event dependency management and scheduling.

The logic processing module is divided into a kernel execute module (Kernel Execute), a direct memory access module (DMA Execute), and an event execute module (Event Execute). The kernel executes module schedules and processes the computing task, implements the task scheduling logic on the AI CPU and AI Core, and schedules the specific kernel function. The direct memory access executes module implements the scheduling logic of the storage task, and schedules and processes the memory copy. The event execute module implements the scheduling logic of synchronization control tasks and implements the logic processing of interflow event dependency. After the scheduling logic of different types of tasks is processed, the corresponding control units start to perform hardware execution.

For the AI CPU task execution, the AI CPU scheduler in the task scheduling CPU uses software to manage the status of the AI CPU and schedule tasks. For the task execution of the AI Core, the task scheduling CPU distributes the processed task to the AI Core by using a separate task block scheduler hardware, and the AI Core performs the specific calculation, and the result of the calculation is returned by the task block scheduler to the task scheduling CPU.

During task scheduling, the system controls the system configuration and processor function initialization. The performance analysis and log modules monitor the entire execution process and record key execution parameters and detailed execution details. When the execution ends or an error occurs, performance analysis or error locating can be performed to provide a basis for detailed efficiency evaluation and correctness analysis of the execution process.

4.2.5.2 Scheduling process

During the execution of the offline model of the neural network, the TS receives specific execution tasks from the Offline Model Executor. The tasks depend on each other. Therefore, the TS needs to release the dependency relationship, perform task scheduling, distribute the tasks to the AI Core or AI CPU based on the specific task type and completes the calculation or execution of specific hardware. During task scheduling, a task is composed of multiple execution instructions (CMD). The TS interacts with the Runtime to schedule the entire task instruction. The Runtime executes on the CPU of the host, the instruction queue is located in the memory of the device, and the TS delivers the specific task instruction.

Fig. 4.15 shows the scheduling process. First, the Runtime invokes the dvCommandOcuppy interface of the driver to enter the instruction queue, queries the available storage space in the instruction queue according to the tail information of the instruction, and returns the available instruction storage space address to the Runtime. After receiving the address, the Runtime fills the currently prepared task instruction into the storage space of the instruction queue and invokes the dvCommandSend interface of the driver to update the current tail information and the credit (Credit) information of the instruction queue. After receiving the new task instruction, the queue generates a doorbell interrupt and instructs the TS to add a task instruction in the instruction queue in the device memory. After receiving the notification, the TS enters the device memory, moves the task instruction to the buffer of the scheduler, and updates the header information of the instruction queue in the DDR memory of the device. Finally, the TS sends the instruction in the cache to the AI CPU or the AI Core for execution according to the condition.

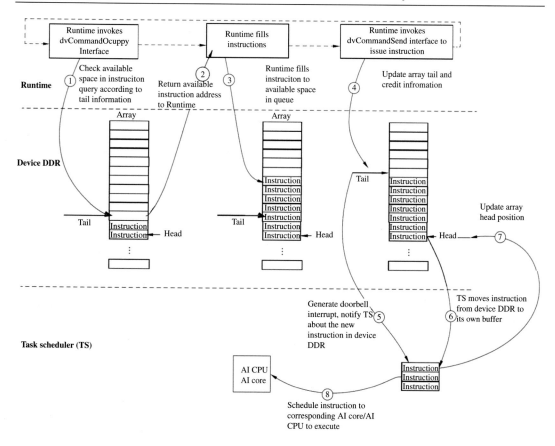

Fig. 4.15
Runtime and task scheduler collaboration flowchart.

The structure of the software stack is basically the same as that of most accelerators. The Runtime, driver, and TS in the Ascend AI processor works closely together to distribute tasks to corresponding hardware resources and executes the tasks in an orderly manner. This scheduling process carries out tasks closely and orderly in the process of deep neural network calculation, which ensures the continuity and efficiency of task execution.

4.2.6 Framework manager

As the modeler and execution participant of the neural network in the implementation of the Ascend AI processor, the framework manager generates an executable offline model for the neural network in the neural network software flow. Before the neural network is executed, the framework manager and the Ascend AI processor combine to generate a high-performance offline model with hardware matching and streamline the process orchestrator and Runtime to deeply integrate the offline model and Ascend AI processor. When the neural network is executed, the framework manager together with the process orchestrator, Runtime, TS, and underlying hardware resources, combines the offline model, data, and the DaVinci architecture, and optimizes the execution process to obtain the application output of the neural network.

4.2.6.1 Functional framework

The framework manager consists of three parts: Offline Model Generator (OMG), Offline Model Executor (OME), and AI Model Manager, as shown in Fig. 4.16. Developers use the Offline Model Generator to generate an offline model and save the file with the suffix of om. Then, the process orchestrator in the software stack invokes the AI model manager in the framework manager to start the Offline Model Executor, load the offline model to the Ascend AI processor, and complete the offline model execution through the entire software stack. From the birth of the offline model to the loading and entering to the Ascend AI processor hardware until the last function operation, the offline framework manager always plays a management role.

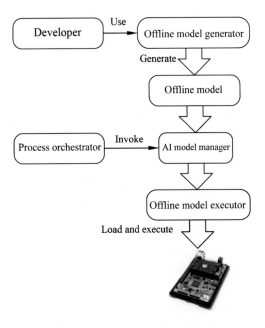

Fig. 4.16
Offline model function framework.

4.2.6.2 *Offline model generation*

Taking the convolutional neural network as an example, the network model is first constructed under the deep learning framework and trained on the original data. And then the Offline Model Generator converts the original model and generates the optimized offline model, by performing operator scheduling optimization, weight data rearrangement and compression, and memory optimization. The Offline Model Generator is used to generate an offline model that can be efficiently executed on the Ascend AI processor.

Fig. 4.17 shows the principle of the Offline Model Generator. After receiving the original model, the Offline Model Generator performs model parsing, quantization, compilation, and serialization on the convolutional neural network model. The steps are described as follows:

Parsing

During the parsing process, the Offline Model Generator supports the parsing of original network models in different frameworks, abstracts the network structure and weight parameters of the original model, and redefines the network structure by using the unified intermediate graph (IR Graph). The intermediate graph consists of a compute node and a data node. Compute node consists of TBE operators with different functions. The data node receives different tensor data and provides various input data for the entire network. This intermediate graph is composed of computing graphs and weights, covering all the original model information. The intermediate graph sets up a bridge between the deep learning framework and the Ascend AI software stack. In this way, the neural network model constructed by the external framework can be easily converted into the offline model supported by the Ascend AI processor.

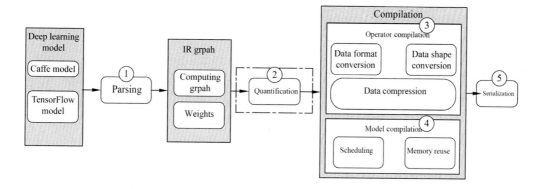

Fig. 4.17
Offline model generation flowchart.

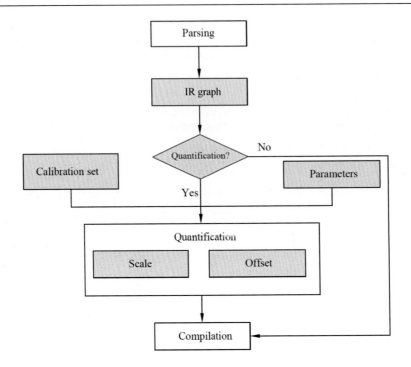

Fig. 4.18
Quantization process during offline model generation.

Quantification

As shown in Fig. 4.18, an intermediate graph is generated after the parsing is complete. If the model needs to perform quantization processing, it may be performed by using an automatic quantization tool based on the structure and weight of the intermediate graph. In the operator, the weight and the offset can be quantized. During the offline model generation, the quantized weight and offset are stored in the offline model. During inference calculation, the quantized weight and offset can be used to calculate the input data, and the calibration set is used to train the quantization parameter in the quantization process, so as to ensure the quantization precision. If no quantization is required, the offline model is directly compiled to generate an offline model.

The quantization mode is divided into data offset quantization and nonoffset quantization. The quantization scale (Scale) and the quantization offset (Offset) parameters need to be output. In the data quantization process, when no offset is specified, the quantization scale of the quantized data is calculated by using the nonoffset mode. If the specified data offset is quantized, the data uses the offset mode. In this case, the quantization scale and offset of the output data are calculated. In the weight quantization process, because the weight has a high requirement on the quantization precision, the nonoffset mode is always used. For example, INT8-type quantization is performed on the weight file according to the quantization algorithm, so that the INT8 weight and the quantization degree may be output. In the process of offset quantization, the FP32-type offset data can be quantized into INT32-type data output according to the quantization degree of weight and the quantization degree of the data.

You can perform quantization operations when there are higher requirements for the size and performance of the model. In the offline model generation process, the high-precision data is quantized to the low-bit data, so that the final offline model is lighter, thereby saving the network storage space, reducing the transmission delay, and improving the operation efficiency. In the quantization process, because the model storage size is greatly influenced by parameters, the Offline Model Generator focuses on the quantization of the convolution operator, full connection operator, and depth separable convolution (ConvolutionDepthwise).

Compilation

After the model is quantified, you need to compile the model. The compilation consists of two parts: operator compilation and model compilation. The operator compilation provides the specific implementation of the operator. The model compilation associates the operator model with the aggregation connection to generate the offline model structure.

Operator compilation

Operator compilation is used to generate operator-specific offline structures. Operator generation consists of three processes: input tensor description, weight data conversion, and output tensor description. The input tensor description calculates the input dimension and memory size of each operator and defines the form of operator input data in the Offline Model Generator. In the weight data conversion, the weight parameters used by the operator are processed such as data format (for example, conversion from FP32 to FP16), shape conversion (such as fractal rearrangement) and data compression. The output tensor description calculates the output dimension and memory size of the operator.

Fig. 4.19 shows the operator generation process. During operator generation, the interface of the TBE operator acceleration library is used to analyze and determine the shape of the output data. The TBE operator acceleration library interface can also convert the data format. The Offline Model Generator receives the intermediate graph generated by the neural network and describes each node in the intermediate graph, and parses the input and output of each operator one by one. The Offline Model Generator analyzes the input data source of the current operator, obtains the operator type directly connected to the current operator in the previous layer, accesses the operator library through the interface of the TBE operator acceleration library, searches for the output data description of the source operator, and returns the output data information of the source operator to the Offline

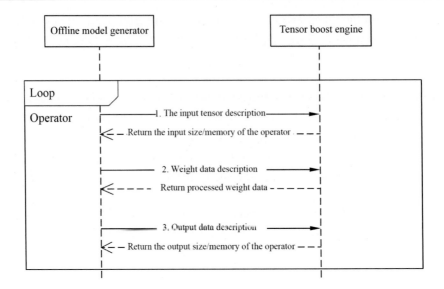

Fig. 4.19
Operator generation process.

Model Generator as the description of the input tensor of the current operator. Therefore, the output information of the source operator can be used to obtain the description of the input data of the current operator.

If the node in the intermediate graph is not an operator but a data node, the input tensor description is not required. If the operator has weight data, such as the convolution operator and full connection operator, the weight data needs to be described and processed. If the input weight data type is FP32, the Offline Model Generator needs to invoke the type conversion (ccTransTensor) interface to convert the weight to the FP16 data type to meet the data-type requirements of the AI Core. After the type conversion is complete, the Offline Model Generator invokes the shape setting (ccTransFilter) interface to perform fractal rearrangement of the weight data, so that the input shape of the weight can meet the format requirement of the AI Core. After obtaining the weight of a fixed format, the Offline Model Generator invokes the compression optimization (ccCompressWeight) interface provided by the TBE to compress and optimize the weight, reduce the weight storage space, and make the model more lightweight. After the weight data is converted, the weight data that meets the calculation requirement is returned to the Offline Model Generator.

After the weight data is converted, the Offline Model Generator also needs to describe the output data information of the operator and determine the output tensor form. For high-level complex operators, such as convolution operators and pooling operators, the Offline Model Generator can directly use the computing interface provided by the TBE operator acceleration library. For example, the convolution operator corresponds to the ccGetConvolution2dForwardOutputDim interface, and the pool operator corresponds to the ccGetPooling2dForwardOutputDim interface, and the output tensor information of the operator is obtained by combining the input tensor information and weight information of the operator. If a low-level simple operator, such as an addition operator, is directly used to determine the output tensor form by using the input tensor information of the operator, then it is finally sent into the Offline Model Generator. According to the foregoing running process, the Offline Model Generator traverses all operators in the intermediate network diagram, cyclically executes the operator generation steps, describes input and output tensor and weight data of all operators, completes the offline structure representation of the operator, and provides an operator model for the next model generation.

Model compilation

After the operator is generated during compilation, the Offline Model Generator also needs to generate a model to obtain the offline structure of the model. The Offline Model Generator obtains an intermediate graph, performs parallel scheduling analysis on the operator, splits multiple intermediate graph nodes, and obtains multiple streams formed by an operator and data input, where the stream may be regarded as an execution sequence of the operator. Nodes that do not depend on each other are directly allocated to different execution flows. If nodes in different execution flow depend on each other, the rtEvent synchronization interface is used to perform interflow synchronization. When the AI Core computing resources are sufficient, multiexecution flow splitting can provide multistream scheduling for AI Core, thereby improving the computing performance of the network model. However, if a large number of parallel tasks are processed by the AI Core, resource preemption is aggravated and performance is deteriorated. Generally, a single stream is used to process the network by default, which prevents congestion caused by concurrent execution of multiple tasks.

In addition, based on specific relationships of execution sequences of multiple operators, the Offline Model Generator may perform operator fusion optimization independent of hardware and memory reuse optimization operations. Based on the input and output memory information of the operator, the memory is reused, and the related multiplexing information is written into the model and operator description to generate an efficient offline model. These optimization operations can redistribute computing resources that are executed by multiple operators to minimize memory usage during running and avoid frequent memory allocation and release during running. In this way, the minimum memory usage and data migration frequency can be used to implement multiple operators, improving performance, in addition, the requirements for hardware resources are reduced.

Serialization

The offline model generated after compilation is stored in the memory and needs to be serialized. In the serialization process, the signature and encryption functions are provided for the model file to further encapsulate and protect the offline model. After serialization, the offline model can be exported from the memory to external files for the remote Ascend AI processor to invoke and execute.

4.2.6.3 Loading offline model

After the Offline Model Generator in the framework manager completes the offline model generation, the Offline Model Executor loads the model to the Runtime and integrates with the Ascend AI processor to perform inference calculation. In this process, the Offline Model Executor plays the main model execution function. Fig. 4.20 shows the process of loading an offline model. First, the process orchestrator, as the entry for interaction between applications and software stacks, provides the management capability for the execution process of inference tasks, divides the process that needs to be completed in the entire offline model into the engine of each execution phase and invokes the loading interface of the AI model manager to initialize the process of the device and load the offline model. Then, the Offline Model Executor is started to load the offline model, deserialize the offline model file, decode the executable file, invoke the storage interface of the execution environment to apply for memory, and copy the weight of the operator in the model to the memory. In addition, resources such as the model execution handle, execution flow, and event of the Runtime are applied for, and resources such as execution flows are bound to the

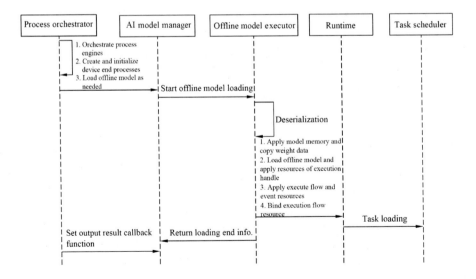

Fig. 4.20
Offline model loading process.

corresponding models one by one. An execution handle executes a neural network computing graph. An execution handle can have multiple execution flows. Different execution flows contain AI Core or AI CPU computing tasks. A task is performed by a kernel function on AI CPU or AI Core, and events refer to the synchronization operations between different execution flows.

After a model is calculated, all operators in the offline model need to be traversed and the task information is updated. The Offline Model Executor invokes the running manager interface to deliver the task to the TS. Then, the Offline Model Executor returns the loading end information to the AI model manager, then, the process orchestrator sets the output result callback function to obtain the execution result. So far, the offline executor completes the loading process of the offline model, and the next step can directly perform inference calculation. This loading process is equivalent to adapting the model to the Ascend AI processor. The hardware resource and the operator in the offline model are planned in a coordinated manner. In this way, the offline model is executed in an orderly manner in subsequent execution, and the prespeed capability is provided for inference calculation.

4.2.6.4 Offline model inference

After the offline model is loaded, the inference function of the model can be implemented. Because the offline model is essentially a neural network model, corresponding functions, such as image recognition, are performed in the inference process. During the generation and loading of the offline model, no specific data to be processed is used. Only the software stack is used to construct, orchestrate, optimize, encapsulate, and perform hardware adaptation for the operator and calculation process in the model. In the specific inference execution process, the specific input data is read to drive the execution and output the result.

Fig. 4.21 shows the offline model inference process. When an application needs to process data, it prepares data to be processed. The process orchestrator invokes the processing interface of the AI model manager to inject data into the Offline Model Executor. Then, the Offline Model Executor invokes the execution flow (rtModelExecute) interface of the Runtime to deliver multiple inference tasks in the execution flow to the TS. The TS splits the task into task blocks and delivers them to the AI Core or AI CPU for execution. After the tasks are completed, the TS returns the result. The task scheduler traverses the tasks in the execution flow, cyclically transmits the task blocks, and returns the execution result. After all the tasks are complete, the TS returns the result to the memory of the Runtime. When the task of multiple executions flows is calculated, the operator synchronization between multiple streams needs to be performed through the event record and event waiting interface in the Runtime, and the operator calculation is completed in an orderly manner. After all operators in a stream are invoked, the Offline Model Executor synchronizes the execution completion of all execution flows through the execution flow synchronization (rtStreamSychronize) interface of the Runtime. After all related execution flow tasks are completed, the final results of all result generation models are integrated. In this case, the Offline Model Executor notifies the

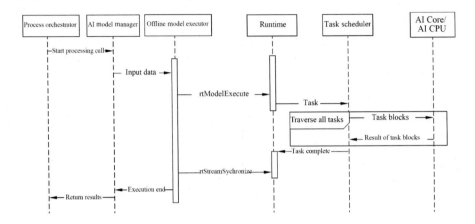

Fig. 4.21
Offline model inference process.

AI model manager that the stream has been executed. Finally, the AI model manager invokes the preset output callback function to return the result of the offline model reasoning execution to the process orchestrator, which then sends the result to the application.

4.2.7 Application of neural network software flow

The overall process of application of the neural network software flow includes defining a neural network structure under the deep learning network framework, generating a neural network model, and transferring the neural network software flow to the Ascend AI processor for function implementation. Now the Inceptionv3 classification network is used as an example to show the practical application of the neural network software flow.

The Inceptionv3 [8] classification network is a convolutional neural network designed for image classification. Users can define the network structure and complete training in the Caffe deep learning framework provided by the neural network software flow. The network structure is saved through the prototxt format and the weight is saved in the caffemodel file. The structure of the Inceptionv3 classification network consists of the convolution layer, pooling layer, and fully connected layer. The input data is processed layer by layer and fed forward.

After the original Inceptionv3 network model is created, the offline model conversion is required. The Offline Model Generator and TBE in the neural network software flow are used to generate the original model in offline mode. You can invoke the running program of the Offline Model Generator through the command line, and then the Offline Model Generator completes the model parsing, model compilation, and serialization in sequence to generate the final offline model. If the network needs to be quantified, the Offline Model Generator can also quantify the model parameters.

After the offline model conversion is complete, the offline model can be obtained, and the execution sequence of operators in the model and related data dependency can be presented in a directed loop-free diagram. As shown in Fig. 4.22, the offline model structure of the InceptionV3 network is shown in Fig. 4.22. When the Caffe model is converted to an offline model, operator integration is performed, and the input data changes. In the original Caffe model, the default values are used for parameters such as step and convolution kernel. However, in the converted offline model, a constant (Const) node is used to represent input, and these constant nodes can receive parameters such as a convolution stride and convolution kernels, and pass the parameters into the model. In this way, a variable network parameter may be input according to a specific requirement, and the implemented function may be relatively flexible.

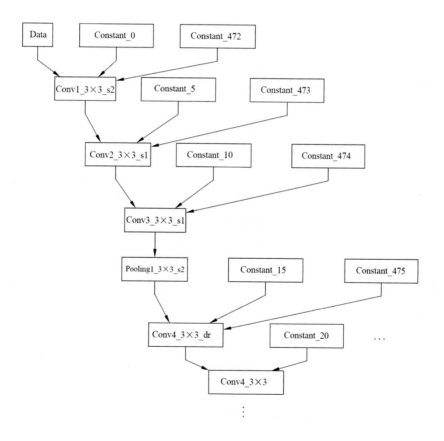

Fig. 4.22
InceptionV3 offline model partial visualization.

After the Inceptionv3 network offline model is generated, to enable the classification function of the Inceptionv3 network on the Ascend AI processor, the process orchestrator needs to create a computing engine flowchart and implement the Inceptionv3 network offline model by executing the flowchart of the computing engine. Therefore, you need to define the following four computing engines: the data engine, preprocessing engine, model inference engine, and postprocessing engine. Besides, it is needed as well to define the connection between four computing engines and the configuration file of node attributes.

Assuming that the network function is implemented on the developer board, the process orchestrator generates a flowchart of the computing engine based on the configuration of the computing engine and then invokes the initialization interface of the AI model manager to load the offline model of the Inceptionv3 network.

During offline model loading, the application program starts loading through the AI model manager through the process orchestrator, and then the Offline Model Executor deserializes the Inceptionv3 network offline model. After deserialization, the Offline Model Executor invokes the runtime interface to copy the weight to the memory, applies for hardware resources for the execution handle, execution flow, and event, and binds the hardware resources. After the resource configuration is complete, the operator in the model is mapped to the stream. Each stream completes the calculation submap of the corresponding operator and allocates events to the synchronization management of multiple streams. In addition, the Offline Model Executor invokes the runtime interface to map the tasks in the execution flow to the kernel functions on the AI Core or AI CPU and updates the execution information in the task. Each kernel function completes a specific task during the offline model execution. Finally, the Offline Model Executor calls the task interface in the Runtime to distribute the tasks in the model to the execution hardware. By now, the InceptionV3 network function has been split into tasks and matched with hardware resources. The InceptionV3 network offline model has been loaded, and the calculation engine flowchart has been created.

After the computing engine flowchart is created, execute the flowchart of the computing engine. The data engine receives images to be classified by the InceptionV3 network, and then the process orchestrator starts the preprocessing engine. The engine invokes the DVPP module through the DVPP interface to preprocess image data, including encoding, decoding, and scaling. The processed image data enters the model inference engine through the process orchestrator and starts inference calculation.

During inference calculation, the model inference engine invokes the interface of the AI model manager to start the inference calculation process. The preprocessed image data is transferred from the AI model manager to the Offline Model Executor. Then the Offline Model Executor invokes the interface in the Runtime to inject data configured during the loading process to the TS. After receiving the task, the TS schedules the hardware AI Core or AI CPU, and the task is executed by the hardware. All tasks in the execution flow are executed in sequence. Under the control of event synchronization, the output results of different streams are integrated and the final result is generated. In this case, the AI model manager returns the result of the classified image to the process orchestrator. Finally, the process orchestrator sends the result to the postprocessing engine, which then displays the classification result through the callback function.

After the classification result is output, the process orchestrator needs to be used to destroy the computing engine flowchart of the InceptionV3 network to release computing resources. To this end, the whole function implementation of the InceptionV3 network on the Ascend AI processor is completed.

This section uses the InceptionV3 classification network as an example. This section describes how to generate an offline model from the original network model, create a flowchart of the computing engine, and execute the flowchart of the computing engine. The execution process also experiences the loading and inference calculation of the offline model of the network, and finally the destruction of the flowchart of the computing engine. All of these are implemented based on the software modules provided by the Ascend AI software stack. The neural network software stream provides a perfect world for software to support the functions of various neural networks on the Ascend AI processor.

4.3 Development tool chain

If a worker wants to do something good, he must first sharpen his tools. The design of the Ascend AI software stack was deeply practiced, and various functional tools were developed to form a versatile tool chain. From the construction of neural networks, to offline model generation, to hardware-related execution, each link has some tools to assist.

In the process of building network execution, if there is no corresponding development tool, it requires a lot of manpower and energy in the development process, and each development requires human intervention, which increases the difficulty and cycle of development. The tool chain of the Ascend AI software stack will be processed by tools so that developers can focus on the performance mining of neural networks and promote the efficient application of the AI processor from the speed of process development.

4.3.1 Introduction to functions

All toolchains are integrated on the Mind Studio development platform. Mind Studio is a Huawei-based AI processor development toolchain platform that provides processor-based operator development, debugging, tuning, and third-party operator development capabilities, as well as network migration, optimization, and analysis capabilities. It brings great convenience for users to develop applications. Mind Studio provides developers with a variety of functions such as operator development, network model development, computation engine development, and application development through web pages:

(1) For operator development, Mind Studio provides a full set of operator development and tuning capabilities to support the operation of analog operators in real-world processor runtime environments. The toolchain provided by Mind Studio can also be used for third-party operator development, which reduces the threshold for operator development, improves the efficiency of operator development and debugging, and effectively enhances product competitiveness.

(2) For the development of the network model, Mind Studio integrates offline model conversion tools, model quantification tools, model precision comparison tools, model operation performance analysis tools, and log analysis tools to improve the efficiency of network model migration, analysis, and optimization.

(3) For computing engine development, Mind Studio provides a visual drag-and-drop programming technology for the computational engine and a large number of automatic code generation techniques to reduce the technical effort of the developer and preset a rich algorithmic engine such as ResNet-18 [9], etc., adding the developer's preparation of the AI algorithm engine and porting efficiency.

(4) For application development, Mind Studio integrates various tools such as Profiler and Compiler to provide developers with a graphically integrated development environment, which can be used for project management and compilation through Mind Studio. Full process development such as debugging, simulation, performance analysis, etc., can greatly improve development efficiency.

4.3.2 Functional framework

The function framework of Mind Studio is shown in Fig. 4.23. The toolchain currently includes project management tools, compiler commissioning tools, process orchestration tools, offline model tools, comparison tools, log management tools, customized operator tools, performance analysis tools, black box tools (BlackBox), device management tools, Device Development Kit (DDK), and many other tools.

Mind Studio can be installed on a regular PC or workstation and supports running on Ubuntu Linux. Currently, it supports browser access. If you just do ordinary project management, writing code, compiling, model conversion, or running debugging in the simulation environment, you can do it on the machine with Mind Studio installed. If you need to run the development project on the real Ascend AI processor, you need to connect Mind Studio to the host and cooperate with the tool background service module on the host to complete the running, debugging, logging, and performance analysis of the developed project.

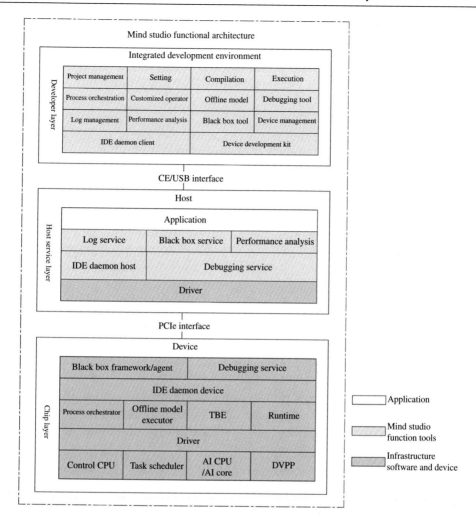

Fig. 4.23
Toolchain functional architecture.

4.3.3 Tool functions

The tools provided in the Mind Studio toolchain are powerful. The following are the main features of the toolchain:

(1) Project management tools: provide developers with functions such as project creation, project opening, project closure, project deletion, project export, project file directory addition, and property settings.

(2) Compilation tools: provide development and compilation of operators, computation engines and applications to meet the development and compilation requirements of different scenarios of developers.

(3) Operation tool: the operator and computation engine supporting development are run in the real processor environment, and the operation related information can be viewed in the interface uniformly.

(4) Process orchestration tools: for business process developers, the process orchestration tool provides a drag-and-drop programming method based on business nodes. By dragging and dropping business nodes on Mind Studio and connecting them, the business can be arranged with "zero" coding. One-stop services such as compiling, running, and displaying results make the process development more intelligent. The whole process requires no programming. It is completely done by drag and drop and configuration. It is very simple. It allows developers to get started quickly, so that they can focus more on application performance improvement. And the tool itself does not bring any additional learning costs.

(5) Customized operator tool: provides the industry's first integrated development environment for operator programming development and debugging based on TBE, which makes the operator transplantation under different platforms more rapid, and adapts to the Ascend AI processor fast.

(6) Offline model tool: the trained third-party network model can be directly imported and converted into an offline model through the offline model tool, and the model interface can be automatically generated in one click, which is convenient for developers to program based on the model interface, and also provides visualization of offline models.

(7) Log management tool: Mind Studio provides the system-wide log collection and log analysis solution for the Ascend AI processor to improve the efficiency of identifying runtime algorithm problems. The unified system-wide log format provides cross-platform log visualization analysis capabilities and runtime diagnostic capabilities in a web-based format, improving the ease of use of the log analysis system.

(8) Performance analysis tools: Mind Studio provides two-node, multimodule heterogeneous systems for efficient and easy-to-use, flexible, and scalable system performance analysis based on graphical interface and command-line user interface presentation. It also enables the synchronous analysis of performance and power consumption for the AI processor device, which meets the needs of algorithm optimization for system performance analysis.

(9) Black box tool: the device saves the necessary key information of the system before the software reset and hardware reset and provides the interface visual viewing mode. Referred to as the black box, it is mainly used for the positioning of subsequent problems.

(10) Device Management: Mind Studio provides device management tools to implement management functions for the developer board connected to the host.

(11) Comparison tool: it can be used to compare the result of the customized operator by the TBE with the result of the Caffe standard operator, so as to confirm the cause of the neural network operation error. Mind Studio provides three comparison methods: Lower Bound, Vector, and User-define. The Lower Bound alignment is a TBE customized operator alignment. The Vector comparison contains an operator comparison of cosine similarity, maximum absolute error, cumulative relative error, and Euclidean relative distance. The user-define comparison refers to user-defined operator comparison.

(12) Device Development Kit: provides developers with a related algorithm development kit based on the Ascend AI processor, designed to help developers develop fast and efficient artificial intelligence algorithms. Developers can install device development kits on Mind Studio, use Mind Studio development tools for rapid algorithm development, or use separate device development kits for algorithm development. The device development kit includes header files and library files, compiler toolchains, debugging and tuning tools, and other tools that are dependent on the development of the AI processor algorithm.

References

[1] Caffe, Wikipedia. https://en.wikipedia.org/wiki/Caffe_(software) (Accessed 2020).
[2] Tensorflow, Google. https://www.tensorflow.org/ (Accessed 2020).
[3] MindSpore, Huawei. https://e.huawei.com/ca/products/cloud-computing-dc/atlas/mindspore (Accessed 2020).
[4] Y. LeCun, C. Cortes, C.J.C. Burges, The MNIST Database, http://yann.lecun.com/exdb/mnist/ (Accessed 2020).
[5] PCI Express, Wikipedia. https://en.wikipedia.org/wiki/PCI_Express (Accessed 2020).
[6] YUV, Wikipedia. https://en.wikipedia.org/wiki/YUV (Accessed 2020).
[7] TVM, https://tvm.apache.org/ (Accessed 2020).
[8] C. Szegedy, V. Vanhoucke, S. Ioffe, J. Shlens, Z. Wojna, Rethinking the inception architecture for computer vision, in: Proceedings of the IEEE Conference on Computer Vision and Pattern Recognition, 2016, pp. 2818–2826.
[9] K. He, X. Zhang, S. Ren, J. Sun, Deep residual learning for image recognition, in: Proceedings of the IEEE Conference on Computer Vision and Pattern Recognition, 2016, pp. 770–778.

## CHAPTER 5

Programming methods

With the development of deep learning, various deep learning frameworks have been proposed, from Caffe and Torch in academia to Google's TensorFlow and Facebook's Pytorch and Caffe2 in industry. The emerging deep learning framework provides developers a complete, efficient, and convenient platform for developing, training, managing, and deploying models. Meanwhile, the requirement of high-performance inference in the deep learning field also promotes the emergence of Inference Engines such as TensorFlow XLA [1], TVM, and TensorRT [2]. These Inference Engines introduce multiple optimization methods, which greatly improve the inference performance of the deep learning models much more than the training performance using the deep learning frameworks, and are more suitable for specific application deployment.

In this context, Huawei has built a complete software stack for its Ascend AI processor computing architecture. It is designed to be compatible with various deep learning frameworks and to efficiently run on Ascend AI processors, enabling developers to quickly develop inference applications, and providing convenient solutions for developers.

This chapter focuses on Ascend AI processor programming. However, before introducing specific programming processes and practices for Ascend AI, it is necessary to introduce the general programming ideas of deep learning applications and the principles of the deep learning Inference Engine. After understanding these concepts, the software stack of the Ascend AI processor will no longer be a black box that cannot be opened, and readers can have a better understanding on how to develop a program.

5.1 Basics of deep learning development

5.1.1 Deep learning programming theory

Developing programs using deep learning models is very different from the traditional Python programming. It involves programming concepts such as declarative programming, metaprogramming, and domain-specific language. In addition, for the Ascend AI software stack, the inputs are usually the model files defined by the mainstream deep learning frameworks. It is important to understand how these model files are generated and saved for programming on Ascend AI processors.

Ascend AI Processor Architecture and Programming. https://doi.org/10.1016/B978-0-12-823488-4.00005-9

5.1.1.1 Declarative programming and imperative programming

Declarative programming, also known as symbolic programming, is often compared with imperative programming. The former only needs to define the operations, and when the program is running, it is explicitly or implicitly compiled and converted into the actual low-level kernel function calls. In this way, the definition steps of the computing graph can be separated from the actual compilation and running steps. In contrast, the latter will start the computation immediately as soon as each line of code is executed.

The Python code shown in Code 5.1 uses the imperative programming style. It implements vector multiplication and addition using the NumPy[a] library. When a program is executed to any line, the corresponding operation is performed immediately. Taking $c=a*b$ as an example, when the program executes to this line, the computer immediately executes the corresponding vector multiplication operation and returns the result c. In this case, if the print function is used, the result can be printed.

The TensorFlow code in Code 5.2 shows an implementation of the same vector multiplication and vector addition operations in a declarative programming style. When the application

---

CODE 5.1 Imperative programming style Python code (NumPy API).

```python
import numpy as np
# Start computing
a = np.ones(10)
b = np.ones(10)
c = a * b
d = c + 1
print(d)
```

CODE 5.2 Declarative programming style Python code (TensorFlow API).

```python
import numpy as np
import tensorflow as tf
# Define the computing graph
A = tf.placeholder(tf.int32, 10, 'A')
B = tf.placeholder(tf.int32, 10, 'B')
C = tf.multiply(A, B, 'Mult')
D = tf.add(C, tf.constant(1, tf.int32), 'Add')
# Run the computing graph
with tf.Session() as sess:
    print(sess.run(D, feed_dict={A: np.ones(10), B: np.ones(10)}))
```

---

[a] The use of Numpy can be referred to https://www.numpy.org/.

executes the line of C=tf.multiply (A, B, 'Mult'), the computer does not perform the calculation right away but constructs the corresponding graph structure in the memory. In this case, if calling the print function, only the data object information will be returned instead of the actual calculation result. This is because the calculation is not performed until the last line of code sess.run() is executed. Then, the corresponding output is returned.

In short, declarative programming tells the computer what to do (What) and lets the computer decide how to do (How). And imperative programming tells the computer in detail how to do (How), and what kind of task to accomplish (What).

Why are declarative programming and imperative programming the most important concepts in the deep learning framework? Because different programming styles bring different programming flexibility and development efficiency to developers. In general, declarative programming provides better running efficiency, and imperative programming offers better flexibility.

For example, in the TensorFlow code of Code 5.2, as the computing graph is defined first, all information about the graph is known when the program is running. Here, the computing graph is referred to as a static graph. The framework can then optimize the computing graph, including operator fusion, memory reuse, and computing task split. When necessary, just-in-time (JIT) compilation can also be used to further optimize the computing graph. With a relatively small scheduling overhead, it is more suitable for application deployment.

However, predefining the computing graph also makes step-by-step debugging much more difficult as compared to the codes in Code 5.1, which is a big pain for developers. In addition, the symbolic program does not necessarily support the functions such as loop and branch, which will make it very hard to implement certain functions.

On the other hand, in Code 5.1, computation is performed instantly, and a computing graph can be generated dynamically. At the same time, various features of the advanced languages, such as debugging and loop, are supported, which brings great convenience to the developers. As a consequence, additional scheduling overhead is introduced, and a computing graph needs to be constructed for each running, while the performance of the graph is often not as good as that of a static graph.

In the current deep learning frameworks, both Caffe and TensorFlow are typical representatives of declarative programming. Although their programming languages, programming methods, and implementations are different, both the two frameworks essentially use the design idea of defining computing graph first before execution. On the contrary, another popular deep learning framework PyTorch has a typical imperative programming style, and its computing graph is built at runtime. In fact, different deep learning frameworks also learn from each other even if the programming styles are different. For example, TensorFlow introduces the dynamic graph mechanism (Eager Execution), while PyTorch introduces the JIT compilation to compile the computing graph at runtime to improve the computing performance. Moreover, MXNet has two mechanisms: dynamic computing graph and static computing graph.

So how do developers choose the deep learning framework? For deep learning researchers, choosing PyTorch would be a better option if the flexibility of development is more concerned. For developers who pursue performance or want to deploy deep learning applications, TensorFlow which is based on static graphs may be a better choice. The provided TensorFlow XLA and TensorFlow Lite can help deploy applications efficiently. In fact, in the industry, inference frameworks such as TensorRT are also introduced, focusing on the deep learning inference models. They often provide several times speed boost than inferencing in the deep learning frameworks and are more suitable for application deployment.

5.1.1.2 Caffe

Caffe is a typical deep learning framework with declarative programming style. It uses the prototxt file from Google's protobuf library [3] to store serialized structural data in the text file, which represents the neural network structure. The Code 5.3 displays the specific content of a pooling layer in the prototxt file, including the layer name, type, connection relationship with the upper layer and lower layer, and related parameters of the layer, such as the pooling type and stride. The data structure is defined in the caffe.proto file. After compiled by the proto compiler, the corresponding C++ source code can be generated to provide the serialization and parsing functions of different layers. After that, based on the command line input (training or inference), the application parses the prototxt file and generates a corresponding training computing graph or inference computing graph. Therefore, as long as Caffe supports the operators in the required deep learning model, developers only need to define the neural network structure in the prototxt file and add corresponding training or parameter configuration information to quickly train and infer with the deep learning model.

CODE 5.3 Description of the pooling layer parameters in prototxt.

```
layer {
   name: "pool1"
   type: "Pooling"
   bottom: "conv1"
   top: "pool1"
pooling_param {
 pool: MAX
 kernel_size: 2
 stride: 2
   }
 }
```

Developers do not need to know the calculation of each layer, which is implemented by the Caffe framework itself. Even now, although Caffe has stopped updating, it is still often used in real deep learning products, which is accredited from its declarative programming style and the use of C++ libraries.

5.1.1.3 TensorFlow

TensorFlow is another typical deep learning framework that supports Python frontend. When a beginner uses TensorFlow for the first time, he or she may often be confused by concepts such as Session, Graph, and Device. In fact, this is caused by the combination of TensorFlow's declarative programming and Python's imperative programming style. In Python, most libraries only provide a set of simple functions and data structures, but TensorFlow provides a whole set of new programming systems and runtime environments, leading it to an unusual Python library.

In the TensorFlow code displayed in Code 5.2, even if they are all written in Python, it is obvious to see the difference between the first half and the second half of the code. The first half of the code builds a computing graph as in Fig. 2.13 using the functions provided by TensorFlow. The second half of the code creates new NumPy arrays and sends data to A and B of the computing graph, and then returns the result of D. Such a graph is called a static computing graph. Once defined, the computing graph can perform computation based on a fixed calculation process, while other Python code is only to feed data to the graph or get the result.

5.1.1.4 Metaprogramming

TensorFlow's declarative programming style leads to a "lazy evaluation" style. The computing graph constructed by TensorFlow is more like a program, except that the specific computation is implemented and scheduled by TensorFlow. This programming way of "generating code with code" is called "Metaprogramming" [4]. The language used to generate code is called metalanguage, while the language of the operated program is called the target language. The metalanguage and target language can use the same language, e.g., the JavaScript code displayed in Code 5.4 implements the lazy evaluation of addition. They can also be entirely two different languages. For example, Code 5.5 shows using regular expressions in Python to perform complex string processing.

5.1.1.5 Domain-specific language

The feature of metaprogramming often leads to the emergence of a "domain-specific language (DSL)." That is, designing a language for the development of a program in a particular domain. This type of language is declarative programming. It focuses on the objective rather than the process and focuses on the description rather than implementation. It uses statements to directly describe the problem, focuses on the analysis and description of the problem, instead of

---

CODE 5.4 Lazy evaluation implemented in JavaScript for addition.

```
Function add(a,b) {
    return`${a}+${b}`;
}
x = 1
y = 2
z = add('x', 'y') // 'x+y'
eval(z) // Output:3
x = 4
eval(z) // Output:6
```

CODE 5.5 Using regular expressions for complex string processing.

```
import re
pattern = re.compile(r'hello')
match = pattern.match('hello world!')
if match:
    print(match.group()) # Output:hello
```

---

focusing on the processing logic and algorithm implementation process. The specific processing logic and algorithm implementation are done by the corresponding parsing engine.

However, due to the fixed processing logic of the parsing engine and the characteristics of its own design, such languages can only be used to solve problems in specific domains. For example, the regular expression in Code 5.5 is used to process character matching. The specific implementation logic is implemented by a dedicated program or library (e.g., the remodule in Python and the regex module in C++). For another example, the LaTeX language [5] focuses on text typesetting and there are dedicated LaTeX parsers for parsing the LaTeX language.

5.1.1.6 TensorFlow and domain-specific language

In TensorFlow, the code used to construct a computing graph can be regarded as a domain-specific language that is based on tensor calculation and focusing on deep learning domain. Even though TensorFlow uses Python to define a graph, many concepts, including Tensor, Node, and Variable, are different from Python. In fact, TensorFlow can be defined as a new language, similar as Caffe, i.e., prototxt, to represent the computing graph, and use Python to parse the graph and process the data before and afterwards, such that the two programming styles of Python code used for computing graph definition and evaluation could be decoupled. Currently, however, TensorFlow uses another solution by defining advanced programming interfaces, such as Estimator and Dataset, to separate the evaluation code from the code related to the computing graph definition.

Why do you have to create a domain-specific language for deep learning? The reason is simple. Deep learning has high requirements on computing power and requires a complete numerical library. For the deep learning operator library, there must be a very low interpreter overhead and good support for the hardware. These features are not satisfied by a general language like Python, while it is an easy job for domain-specific language for deep learning such as TensorFlow. However, there is one problem that cannot be ignored. The main reason why deep learning domain-specific language like TensorFlow can greatly optimize deep learning performance is based on some assumptions about deep learning calculation. For example, there is no decision-making and recursion in the feedforward neural network. In this case, the entire computing graph can be regarded as a directed acyclic graph as in Fig. 5.1, and the optimization of the entire network becomes very simple and straightforward. But once these restrictions are broken, such as when conditional branching, loops, and recursion exist, the deep learning framework is highly challenged.

In the future, a unified domain-specific language dedicated to deep learning may appear. It can be used to not only provide sufficient flexibility (such as imperative programming and branch jumping) but also provide sufficient performance (such as large-scale parallel computing), while various deep learning frameworks are only used as interpreters for this particular domain-specific language. This will be very friendly to developers. However, for now, although there are frameworks such as ONNX [6] and NNVM [7] that can provide general computing graph representations and their corresponding Python interfaces can be used for graph construction, they only support the inference, while the training process still needs to be done by each deep learning framework. Therefore, they cannot be considered as a true domain-specific language for deep learning. Development of such language will depend on the future development of the deep learning field and the efforts from the deep learning framework developers.

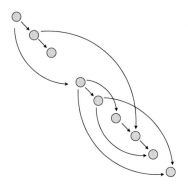

Fig. 5.1
Directed acyclic graph.

5.1.1.7 Turing completeness

The domain-specific language is not universal in most cases and is normally a nonturing complete language. In short, if a programming language can calculate all computable problems, it is Turing complete [8]. Currently, most programming languages are Turing complete, such as C++, C++ template, C++ constexpr, and Python. These languages support advanced features such as branch, jump, and recursion to support general computing. On the contrary, the domain-specific language focuses more on solving problems in specific tasks and domains, and basically does not have fancy features like recursion. For example, SQL, LaTeX, and regular expressions are not Turing complete.

5.1.1.8 Branch and jump in TensorFlow

The domain-specific language of TensorFlow is Turing complete, thanks to the ability of TensorFlow to provide functions such as tf.cond and tf.while_loop, in which the former can check conditions and the latter can process loop statements. However, it is important to note that when you actually define a graph, you must distinguish between TensorFlow and Python's loop and decision-making statements. The decision-making statement in the former is also a node in the computing graph. Therefore, the input of the decision-making condition is also a tensor in the graph. The value of the tensor is unknown when the network is defined. Thus, the decision-making statement cannot be used to check conditions as in Python. The decision-making condition in the latter is known when the computing graph is defined. Therefore, in the final computing graph, only a fixed branch is used for calculation.

Code 5.6 shows an example of incorrect use of the Python decision-making statement. As x and y are not actual numbers when defining the computing graph, the decision-making cannot be performed during definition. Code 5.7 displays a sample that correctly uses the TensorFlow decision-making syntax, and the decision-making node is added to the computing

---

CODE 5.6 Incorrect use of the Python decision-making statement.

```
import tensorflow as tf
a = tf.constant(2)
b = tf.constant(3)
x = tf.placeholder(tf.int32)
y = tf.placeholder(tf.int32)
# Incorrect code
if x < y :
    result = tf.multiply(a, b)
else:
    result = tf.add(a,b)
```

CODE 5.7 Using tf.cond for decision-making and branch.

```
import tensorflow as tf
a = tf.constant(2)
b = tf.constant(3)
x = tf.placeholder(tf.int32)
y = tf.placeholder(tf.int32)
result = tf.cond(x < y, lambda: tf.multiply(a, b), lambda:tf.add(a, b))
with tf.Session() as sess:
    print(sess.run(result, feed_dict={x: 1, y: 2})) # Output:6
    print(sess.run(result, feed_dict={x: 2, y: 1})) # Output:5
```

---

graph. Although the TensorFlow decision-making statement looks a bit complex, the good news is that TensorFlow provides the AutoGraph mechanism for a quick and easy graph manipulation process.

5.1.1.9 Collaboration between TensorFlow and python

In addition to decision-making nodes and loop nodes, TensorFlow has other interesting interfaces, such as file reader and writer, encoder and decoder. These interfaces will add the corresponding computation nodes in the computing graph. Therefore, TensorFlow can carry out the entire process of file reading, iterative training, and file writing by just defining the computing graph, which also means that the TensorFlow computing graph can run like a program.

In practice, not all operations are defined in the computing graph. In addition, Python and rich third-party libraries are also used for processing the input and output data. For example, developers can use Python to read image data, process the data using NumPy library, and send it to the computing graph. Also, Python loop can be used to implement the training loop. On the other hand, developers can also embed the file reading into the computing graph, and implement the training loop using the TensorFlow interface. In this case, only the file path needs to be provided to the computing graph as data input, and the computing graph can start the whole training process by itself. The specific way to choose for implementation depends on the developer's requirements of flexibility and computational efficiency.

5.1.1.10 Imperative programming and dynamic graph mechanism of PyTorch

Although the static graph mechanism of TensorFlow can provide very efficient implementation and support branch and loop to a certain extent, the mechanism of declarative programming and static graph make it difficult for using TensorFlow to implement some deep learning algorithms, such as word2vec [9] and recursive neural network [10]. In contrast, as PyTorch is

---

CODE 5.8 Implementation of decision-making and loop using PyTorch.

```
import torch
first_counter = torch.Tensor([0])
second_counter = torch.Tensor([10])
# Using Python's loop statement
while (first_counter < second_counter)[0]:
    first_counter += 2
    second_counter += 1
```

CODE 5.9 Implementation of decision-making and loop using TensorFlow.

```
import tensorflow as tf
first_counter = tf.constant(0)
second_counter = tf.constant(10)

# Decision making function
def cond(first_counter, second_counter):
    return first_counter < second_counters

# Body of loop function
def body(first_counter, second_counter):
    first_counter = tf.add(first_counter, 2)
    second_counter = tf.add(second_counter, 1)
    return first_counter, second_counter

# Using TensorFlow's loop interface
c1, c2 = tf.while_loop(cond, body, [first_counter, second_counter])
with tf.Session() as sess:
    counter_1_res, counter_2_res = sess.run([c1, c2])
```

closer to Python, it can directly use the decision-making and loop statements of Python to easily support the implementation of word2vec and recursive neural networks.

Codes 5.8 and 5.9 show, respectively, the use of PyTorch and TensorFlow for implementing a computation with the decision-making and loop. It can be seen that PyTorch is more like a Python library that provides data structures and functions for Python. The entire computation process seems like running Python code. For traditional Python programmers, there is no learning cost. In contrast, TensorFlow is relatively bloated. It cannot use the Python decision-making and loop statement but has to use the built-in tf. while interface. In addition, the corresponding decision-making subgraph (cond) and loop subgraph (body) need to be defined. The root cause of this problem is that the static graph feature of the TensorFlow requires the computing graph to support any input and any branch and loop conditions once the graph is constructed. In this way, after the TensorFlow computing graph is constructed, it acts like a compiled program with branch and loop conditions, so it can get the same results as of Code 5.8 which uses PyTorch for computation with decision-making and loop statements.

5.1.1.11 Difference between training and inference computing graph

Although the training process and the inference process of the deep learning model use the same neural network structure, the computing graphs are very different.

Firstly, the inference process only includes forward propagation, while the training process includes both forward and back propagation. Therefore, compared with inference, the training also reads the input data label, compares input data label and forward propagation output through Loss Function, and then obtains the training loss. Then, the gradient descent algorithm is used to propagate the training loss back layer by layer and update the parameters to be trained at each layer. Therefore, although the same language is used to define the computing graph, for example, using the tf.nn.conv2d of TensorFlow to define a convolutional layer, in the inference process, the weights and bias of the convolutional layer are only read as constants, while during the training process, with the optimizer, these values will be computed and updated.

Secondly, some functional layers have quite different computational characteristics in the training process and the inference process. For example, the dropout layer is only used during the training process and is not added or performs no operation during the inference process. The batch normalization (BN) processes the input data based on the statistical characteristics during the training, and trains additional parameters, while in the inference process, the fixed linear operation is performed.

Finally, many other computational nodes can be added to the computing graph. In the training computing graph, in addition to the computational subgraph of the neural network, there are also corresponding training computation nodes. Moreover, the computing graph may also have other computational nodes such as nodes for data reading and preprocessing.

Therefore, when developing deep learning programs, developers must clearly understand the nodes and operations in the computing graph. This is crucial not only for deep learning development but also for using and programming on Ascend AI processor introduced later in this chapter. During the development for deep learning, ensure that the following criteria are met:

(1) **Isolate the model definition from the program logic**
   - Use a function or class to define the model and ensure that the input and output follow the input and output formats of the model. For example, LeNet5 [11] can be defined by a specific function. The input parameter of the function is a tensor whose shape is [N, 28, 28, 1]. The return value is a tensor whose shape is [N, 10]. Here, N indicates the

number of samples to be processed at each time and needs to be fixed during the calculation. In this way, the computational subgraph of the model is defined.

- This design enables the model definition file to be reused in different projects. Therefore, each large deep learning framework can have a corresponding model library, which can be used to save popular models.

(2) **Set flags to distinguish between training and inference environments**
- Because functional layers such as dropout will have different computational characteristics in the training and inference phases, and sometimes additional operations need to be performed in the training stage, an additional flag is required to indicate whether the current environment is training or inference when defining the model.
- For example, in Caffe, the phase field is added to the prototxt to indicate whether training or inference phase is running currently, and the phase is used to determine whether to exclude some functional layers. In TensorFlow, a function parameter is used to specify the current phase, and a Python decision-making statement is used to determine whether to add the dropout layer to the computing graph.
- In addition, when the dropout ratio is 0, it is equivalent to that no operation is performed, in TensorFlow, the dropout ratio can be defined as a placeholder, so that the ratio in the dropout layer can be controlled during the training process, while the dropout layer does not perform any operation during the inference process.
- Such a design allows that in the model definition file, corresponding computing graph can be constructed based on simple flags.

(3) **Separate the training code and inference code**
Although the developer can write the training logic and the inference logic together, and determine current phase based on the input parameter because the program logic and the computing graph of the training and inference are different, the training and the inference code are usually written separately, and the weights are passed by using the model weight file. Generally, the final project contains the following files:
- model.py: Use the interfaces provided by the framework to define the neural network structure;
- train.py: Build a training computing graph based on the model.py, load the parameters of the pretrained model, train the model according to the program logic, and save the model parameters;
- test.py: Construct an inference computing graph based on model.py, load model parameters, perform inference prediction based on the inference code logic, and save the inference computing graph;
- Application code: Load the inference computing graph and model parameters for the application operations.

5.1.1.12 Model saving and loading

To make the model persistent, each deep learning framework provides a corresponding model saving and loading mechanism. Dedicated files are used to represent the computing graph structure and model parameters, such as the prototxt and caffemodel in Caffe and the meta, ckpt, and pb files in TensorFlow. Overall, the following files are often used to store different contents:

- Computing graph structure file: Store the structure of computing graph, which is serialized from the computing graph. For example, the meta file of the TensorFlow.
- Model parameter file: Store the model parameters, such as the parameters that can be trained in the model, including weights and biases, etc. The data is saved in the form of key-value. For example, the ckpt file in TensorFlow. It is also possible the file only saves the model parameters such as the pth file in PyTorch.
- Model file: Store computing graph structure and model parameters at the same time. Different frameworks have different implementations. For example, the pb file in TensorFlow.

Therefore, when saving a model, make sure to know what needs to be saved, and know what was saved when loading a model. Code 5.10 shows how to use the PyTorch to save and load models or model parameters.

5.1.1.13 Model conversion

While more and more deep learning frameworks (such as TensorFlow, Caffe2, MXNet, and PyTorch) and hardware acceleration platforms (such as CPU, GPU, FPGA, and ASIC) provide more choices for deep learning, it also brings troubles to deep learning model migration. For example, if someone wants to develop deep learning applications on the Amazon cloud, models from other frameworks must be converted into the MXNet format and retrained on the MXNet framework [12]. In most cases, the training result is inconsistent with the expected result due to different definitions of a common operator in different frameworks.

CODE 5.10 Model saving and loading methods in PyTorch.

```
# Save and load the entire model
torch.save(model, 'model.pth')
new_model = torch.load('model.pth')

# Only save and load model parameters
torch.save(model.state_dict(), 'params.pth')
model.load_state_dict(torch.load('params.pth'))
```

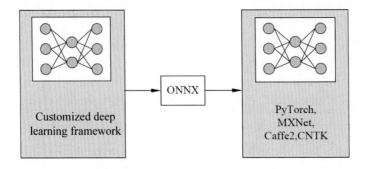

Fig. 5.2

Using ONNX for model conversion. *Image reference: https://onnx.ai/.*

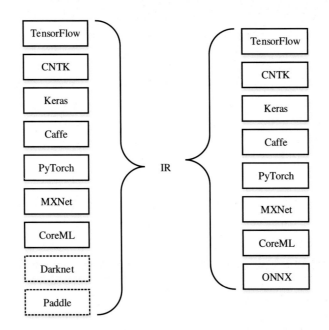

Fig. 5.3

MMdnn tool. *Image reference: https://github.com/microsoft/MMdnn.*

The emergence of ONNX (Open Neural Network Exchange format) [6] solves this problem to a certain degree. As shown in Fig. 5.2, ONNX provides an intermediate representation for converting different model. As long as the deep learning frameworks support ONNX in a unified manner, the conversion between one deep learning framework and others can be performed. In addition, there is another similar tool for deep learning model conversion, i.e., MMdnn proposed by Microsoft [13], as shown in Fig. 5.3. MMdnn aims to provide a model conversion tool that does not require other deep learning frameworks to support it like ONNX because MMdnn has already completed this part of the work. It provides a model format that adapts to each deep learning framework.

It should be noted that, although ONNX and MMdnn make it easy for migrating the deep learning model between different deep learning frameworks, they do not provide a running environment for the computing graph, which means that the model training, inference, and application deployment are still done by each deep learning framework.

5.1.1.14 Deep learning inference engine and computing graph

As mentioned earlier, with the development of the deep learning frameworks, the need for migrating the deep learning model between different frameworks promotes the emergence of ONNX and MMdnn. The demand for inferencing deep learning model efficiently on different hardware platforms promotes the emergence of deep learning Inference Engine.

Different from the deep learning framework, the deep learning Inference Engine does not support training. It is designed to use trained computing graphs from other deep learning frameworks, perform optimization, and efficiently run the computing graphs on different hardware platforms. Because the deep learning Inference Engine performs the end-to-end task from the deep learning model files to different hardware acceleration platforms, it does a similar job like the compiler which compiles and optimizes codes for different processors. Therefore, the deep learning Inference Engine is often referred to as the deep learning Compiler Stack.

For the deep learning Inference Engine, the input is model files from different deep learning frameworks, that is, the representation of computation graphs defined by each deep learning framework. Note that the ONNX is also one of the representations, but ONNX makes it much easier for the deep learning Inference Engine to support different frameworks so that there is no need to build the wheels repeatedly to support models from various frameworks. For developers of the deep learning Inference Engine, note the followings:

(1) The model file needs to contain both the computing graph structure and model parameters.
    For TensorFlow, only the pb file is required. For PyTorch, as the model parameters and model may be represented by a file with the same extension, it is important to know whether the model file contains the computing graph structure and model parameters at the same time.
(2) The computing graph should contain only the inference computing graph.
    As mentioned above, the training computing graph and the inference computing graph contain many different computational nodes. Even for the inference computing graph, it may also include some computational nodes that may not be supported by Inference Engine, such as the file reading and data preprocessing. Therefore, generally, the final inference graph should only include a subgraph for the neural network inference, that is,

the input of the computing graph is the input of the neural network, e.g., the image data whose shape is [32, 1, 28, 28] as input, and the output of the computing graph is the output of the neural network, e.g., the probability data whose shape is [32, 10].

According to actual requirements, for example, image pixel format conversion can be done using basic vector operations. In this case, this conversion can also be added selectively into the inference computing graph, as long as it is supported by the model file definition and the Inference Engine.

(3)   The unified model file format is recommended.

ONNX provides an intermediate representation of a unified computing graph for deep learning. It also defines a set of operators dedicated to deep learning inference. A unified model saving format (onnx file) which saves the computing graph structure and model parameters is also provided. In addition, various deep learning Inference Engines, such as TensorRT and TVM, support the ONNX format.

Therefore, converting other frameworks into ONNX and then passing them to the deep learning Inference Engine enables quick discovery of the problems mentioned above and these problems could be solved faster. Therefore, it can be better supported by the Inference Engine.

5.1.2 Deep learning inference optimization principle

Compared with the training phase, the computation process of the deep learning model inference phase is relatively fixed. So, there is often more space for optimization. In order to improve the inference performance of the deep learning application, various optimization methods are proposed. Some methods perform optimization from the aspect of algorithm implementation. For example, using FFT and Winograd convolution [14] can reduce the complexity of the algorithm. Some perform optimization from the aspect of computation scheduling. For example, using kernel fusion can reduce scheduling overheads. Some perform optimization from the aspect of hardware architecture. For example, TPU introduces systolic arrays to accelerate convolution calculation.

In combination with various optimization methods, the performance can be improved greatly. For example, a machine translation team introduced how they optimized the inference performance of a machine translation application, which is a very classic case. The team uses optimization methods such as kernel fusion and dedicated kernel to improve the performance and the optimized BatchMul kernel at the end runs 13 times faster than that of the cuBLAS library optimized by NVIDIA [15]. The performance can be further improved by 1.7 times through fusion of the batch matrix multiplication kernel. In fact, the optimization strategies adopted by major companies are roughly the same. The most classical optimization method is to fuse the three operators, namely, two-dimensional convolution, batch normalization, and ReLu activation function, to become the fused single kernel Fused-Conv2d-Bn-Relu. The trick was repeatedly used by many big companies, and it can even achieve higher performance than the manually optimized kernel in cuDNN, which is the deep learning accelerator library from NVIDIA.

Overall, deep learning inference optimization is divided into two levels of optimization. One is the computing graph optimization, which abstracts the common computations for deep learning at a high level, including memory allocation, kernel fusion, computation scheduling, and hardware-independent optimization. The other is kernel optimization, which abstracts the computing features of underlying hardware at the low level, including data arrangement, loop expansion, and other hardware-dependent optimization.

5.1.2.1 Inference process in the traditional deep learning framework

In the traditional deep learning framework, regardless of the programming style (declarative programming or imperative programming) and when the computing graph is constructed (static or dynamic), the input data is always processed based on the fixed calculation process once the inference computation of the deep learning model is started. Such a computation process can be regarded as a fixed program.

If the calculation of each operator in the inference phase is regarded as a function with parameters, e.g., the convolution operator performs different convolution operations according to the input parameter configuration, the inference computation of the entire deep learning model is equivalent to the function definition shown in Code 5.11. In the code, the computation process is constructed with functions corresponding to multiple operators like a TensorFlow static graph, and a simple control flow is also included.

In Code 5.11, conv, pooling, and fc represent the implementation of the convolutional, pooling, and fully connected layer operators, respectively. They can perform different operations on the

---

CODE 5.11 An abstraction of inference computing graph.

```
void inference(A, D, params)  // Model inference process
{
    if (condition) {    // Branch
        conv(A, B, params1); // convolution kernel function
    }
    else {
        conv(A, B, params2); // convolution kernel function
    }
    pooling(B, C, params3); // pooling kernel function
    fc(C, D, params4);   // full connection kernel
}
```

data (A, B, and C) based on different parameter configurations (params1, params2, and params3). Given the parameter configuration (params), the whole computation process starts with the input data (A) to get the output data (B).

Caffe is a deep learning framework that implements the abstraction of inference computing graph in Code 5.11 in a very direct way. Caffe defines a common set of operators. Each operator has a CPU or GPU implementation, while all of the implementations consider different parameter configurations. The operator is represented as Layer in the prototxt, and the connection relationship between the operators is defined by the bottom and top fields in the LayerParameter. In the actual inference process, the Caffe parses the connection between the operators needed by the model, finds the corresponding operator implementation in the operator library, and executes the operator implementations in a certain order, to process the input data.

In the above process, a function that implements operator computation on a specific hardware platform is referred to as kernel function, and the process in which the actual kernel function is invoked as in Code 5.11 is called execution graph. Of course, in a real system, the implementation of kernel invocation is more complicated, which includes complex operations such as memory management and data synchronization. For example, in a heterogeneous computing system consisting of CPU+GPU, normally, a GPU runs specific kernel functions to perform corresponding calculation, and the CPU is responsible for complex management such as memory management, data transfer, and computation scheduling.

No matter the static graph (e.g., TensorFlow) or the dynamic graph (e.g., PyTorch), the inference process needs to parse the inference computing graph, and construct the execution graph to invoke multiple kernel functions. Currently, most deep learning frameworks use kernel functions in acceleration libraries such as cuBLAS, cuDNN, and OpenBLAS when performing acceleration on a CPU or a GPU. Therefore, from the perspective of the compiler, the job of the current deep learning framework is more like the frontend of the compiler, while the difference is that different frameworks provide different domain-specific languages and flexibility for developers.

Understanding the abstraction of the inference graph in Code 5.11 and the implementation of different frameworks are essential for understanding the inference optimization methods and the principle of the Inference Engine.

5.1.2.2 Computing graph optimization

The computing graph optimization does not involve a specific hardware platform. The computing graph is mainly optimized from the perspectives of memory management, kernel invocation, and data synchronization.

Optimize the memory allocation mechanism

When performing inference using the deep learning model, a large amount of memory is needed for model parameters, input and output data, and intermediate representations. To avoid reallocating memory before each inference, before the inference task starts, deep learning frameworks generally allocates the memory for input and output of each node, and the memory for model parameters based on the shape. The same memory is reused for multiple inference processes. This is the approach that Caffe used. Therefore, Caffe requires that the shape of the input data must be specified in the prototxt file.

With the development and design iteration of the deep learning model, not only the shape of the input data may change, but also the model itself may change. Therefore, a one-time creation of the memory based on the fixed shape is not enough. Currently, the deep learning framework usually adopts the dynamic memory allocation mechanism. For example, in the TensorFlow code of Code 5.12, placeholders for input data can accept data of different shapes [N, 224, 224, 3], where N represents the dimension information which can only be determined at runtime. The shapes of all related tensors need to be calculated based on this dimension information at runtime.

This approach, while providing developers with sufficient flexibility so that the computation graph can be reused, also has serious overheads. On one hand, the shape of all following related tensors needs to be calculated at runtime. On the other hand, the memory of all related tensors needs to be dynamically allocated. To solve the above overheads, TensorFlow allocates a large memory space before running and uses a dedicated memory manager to manage the memory allocation of different tensors. However, the manager also has overheads and may not be able to achieve optimal memory management.

The input of the inference process of actual deep learning applications is often fixed. Therefore, a similar approach to Caffe's can be adopted. That is, allocating the required memory in a

---

CODE 5.12 The shape of the placeholder in TensorFlow is variable.

```
import numpy as np
import tensorflow as tf

# Define the placeholder
input_tensor = tf.placeholder(tf.float32, shape=(None, 224, 224, 3))
with tf.Session() as sess:
    input_data_0 = np.random.rand(16, 224, 224, 3)
    input_data_1 = np.random.rand(32, 224, 224, 3)
    print(sess.run(input_tensor, feed_dict={data_input:
input_data_0}).shape) # (16, 224, 224, 3)
    print(sess.run(input_tensor, feed_dict={data_input:
input_data_1}).shape) # (32, 224, 224, 3)
```

unified manner before the inference task starts, to avoid the overhead of dynamic memory allocation. Current deep learning Inference Engines, such as TVM and TensorRT, requires to specify the shape of the input data. Even for the model files which are dedicated to inference, such as ONNX and TFLite, the shape of input data also needs to be specified before the model conversion. All these approaches aim to reduce the memory allocation overhead.

Specify appropriate batch size

The selection of batch size can affect the model inference performance greatly. With the increase of batch size, the model inference performance increases gradually and reaches a peak. The reason for this phenomenon is that the small batch size does not make full use of the computing resources of the hardware. Taking the AICore Cube Unit in the Ascend AI processor described in this book as an example, if the matrix used for calculation is less than 16×16, the zero-padding policy is often used for filling up 16×16 unit. In this way, computing resources are wasted. With the increase of the batch size, the proportion of this computing resource waste gradually decreases, and the overall inference performance will reach a peak.

Currently, a lot of accelerator architecture research is in favor of comparing with GPU. However, since a proper batch size is not often selected, the memory bandwidth and computing resources of the GPU are not fully used. The computing performance of the GPU is far from the peak value. Therefore, it is not fair to compare in this situation.

Of course, in the actual deep learning inference task, it is not always good to choose a large batch size. On the one hand, the inference performance of the deep learning model on a specific hardware platform has a corresponding theoretical peak value of the computation performance, which is usually limited by memory bandwidth or computing resources. Generally, the peak value may be obtained through Roofline Model[b] analysis. On the other hand, increasing the batch size will increase the delay of the system processing. In scenarios such as autonomous driving, as the real-time requirement of the system often has a higher priority, a long delay is not acceptable. In the video field, although the system processing bandwidth is more important, it is also necessary to reduce the delay as much as possible when the peak computing performance is reached. Therefore, in a real scenario, the most appropriate batch size needs to be determined according to a trade-off between system delay and performance.

Reuse memory by fine memory management

With the development of deep learning, a variety of special structures of neural networks are emerging gradually, such as the residual block structure in Fig. 5.4, and the Inception block structure [16] in Fig. 5.5. Although these structures increase the complexity of computing graph, in actual inference, some operations can be eliminated through fine memory management.

---

[b] Refer to https://en.wikipedia.org/wiki/Roofline_model.

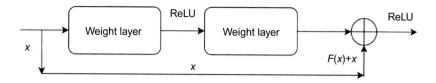

Fig. 5.4

Residual structure in ResNet. *Image adapted from H. Kaiming, et al. Deep residual learning for image recognition, in: Proceedings of the IEEE conference on computer vision and pattern recognition, 2016.*

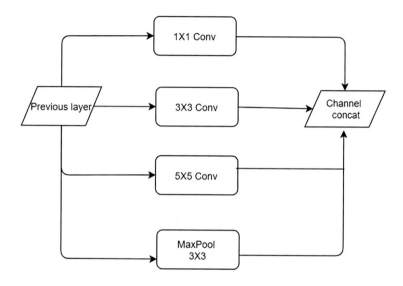

Fig. 5.5

Inception structure in GoogLeNet. *Image from S. Christian, et al. Going deeper with convolutions, in: Proceedings of the IEEE conference on computer vision and pattern recognition, 2015.*

For example, in the residual block structure in Fig. 5.4, the input data x needs to be kept in the memory until both convolutional layers are calculated, and added to the output $F(x)$ from the last convolutional layer to obtain the final output $F(x)+x$. The other example is the Inception structure [17] in Fig. 5.5. The output data of the upper layer serves as the input of the convolutional layers of 1×1, 3×3, 5×5 and max-pooling layer of 3×3 at the same time, and the outputs of the four operators are combined using the channel-wise feature map concatenation. Therefore, the memory can be allocated just for the output of the previous layer A and the final merged data B. On the one hand, the input of the four operators may share the memory of the A. On the other hand, the corresponding outputs may point to different positions in the B, respectively, by using accurate memory calculation. In this case, after the four operators finish the computation, the corresponding output data is assembled according to the required format without additional memory transfer.

Eliminate the control logic in the model as much as possible

From Code 5.11, the actual inference graph can have control logic such as if or while. Although these control operations are performed by the CPU which has a powerful logic control capability, they also introduce scheduling overheads. For example, the "if" statement requires the system to maintain the scheduling information about memory and kernel functions of two different branches at the same time, and the while statement introduces more complex kernel scheduling and memory management. In addition, if the control logic needs to be decided according to actual data, data transfer between different memory may also be involved, which introduces additional overheads.

The existence of the control logic may come from many reasons. For example, one may use control logic to control the computation flow during training and inference time, such as selectively avoiding certain computations during inference. Also, some are because the models themselves need to introduce these control logic, e.g., to support the parsing tree in natural language understanding. TensorFlow Fold implements the calculations that require dynamic graphs through a static graph with logic control. For the former, because the computation process is fixed in the actual application scenario, this control information is often known in advance, so that the control logic can be completely eliminated to reduce scheduling overheads. For the latter, because the control logic cannot be eliminated, the control flow and data flow need to be properly managed to minimize the overheads.

Use parallel computing in the model properly

In conventional convolutional neural networks such as LeNet-5 [11] and VGG [18], because the entire network is composed of multiple operators in sequence, the entire calculation process may be regarded as a serial execution of multiple kernel functions, and the serial execution process is referred to as Computing Stream. However, in the Inception block whose structure is shown in Fig. 5.5, because four operators in the middle share the input and no data dependency exists among the four operators, computation of the four operators may be regarded as four-independent Computing Streams, which brings a possibility of parallel computing.

For example, for GPU, different Computing Streams can run concurrently on the same GPU or run distributively on multiple GPUs. In the end, data is synchronized through a synchronization mechanism. Such method can improve the overall computing performance and reduces delay.

In an actual application scenario, it is not necessarily required that the model itself has a special structure that can be separated into independent Computing Streams. In fact, a kernel function or a Computing Stream may be split to obtain independent Computing Streams, which need a large amount of data synchronization accordingly. Therefore, the inference performance of the deep learning model can be improved as long as the parallel computing task split and data synchronization are performed properly. Of course, the actual distributed system is more complex, which involves communication between different devices and unified management of all devices. However, in essence, the goal is to improve the overall performance by parallel computing.

A magic optimization tool—Kernel fusion

To provide sufficient flexibility, most deep learning frameworks provide fine-grained algebraic operators, such as vector addition, subtraction, multiplication, division, and matrix multiplication. These operators are generally executed efficiently by invoking kernel functions in a dedicated linear algebraic library (such as cuBLAS [19] and OpenBLAS [20]). Although these fine-grained operators provide sufficient flexibility, because of the low level of abstraction, in actual inference calculations, hundreds of such operators are often used, which are then converted into hundreds of kernel calls. Frequent kernel calls can increase the system scheduling overhead and kernel startup overhead greatly. These overheads include memory reading and writing which are extremely expensive and affect the inference performance. For example, in batch normalization, the computation can be performed by a series of operations such as Broadcast, Reduce, and Element_wise, etc. In this case, an operator often includes multiple times of kernel scheduling, and intermediate data is frequently read back and forth between the register and the memory, so the corresponding overhead is very large.

The operation of fusing multiple kernel functions into one kernel function is called kernel fusion. Kernel fusion reduces the overhead of kernel invoking and improves the overall inference performance. The cuDNN library [21] from NVIDIA is an efficient implementation of common operators for deep learning, such as convolution and pooling. Since the kernel fusion is actually done manually, a lot of manual work is needed. Meanwhile, even if a common fusion kernel is implemented, there are still many unfused fine-grained kernels in the actual inference graph. Therefore, a manual fusion of kernel functions for each computing graph is not a method that can scale-up easily.

Normally, Kernel fusion has the following types:

As shown in Fig. 5.6, constant values and constant operations can be calculated directly during optimization instead of being calculated at runtime. This method is similar to the constexpr syntax in C++. In addition, anything that can be directly replaced by constants should be replaced by constants.

As shown in Fig. 5.7, simple fine-grained linear operations can be fused directly so that a kernel function can perform all operations. When necessary, an expression level optimization is needed for the corresponding calculation, such as common subexpression elimination.

As shown in Fig. 5.8, in the typical Inception block structure of the GoogLeNet network, the three operators Conv, BN, and ReLU appear multiple times. They can be combined into one

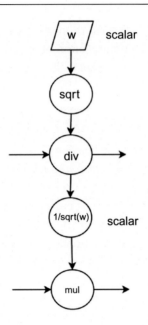

Fig. 5.6

Precalculation of constant operations. *Adapted from C. Tianqi, et al. TVM: end-to-end optimization stack for deep learning,* arXiv preprint arXiv:1802.04799 *(2018).*

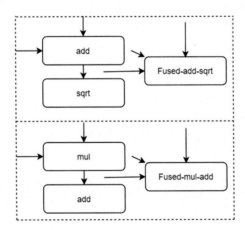

Fig. 5.7

Direct fusion of simple linear operations. *Adapted from C. Tianqi, et al. TVM: end-to-end optimization stack for deep learning,* arXiv preprint arXiv:1802.04799 *(2018).*

operator Fused-Conv-BN-ReLU (CBR). After fusion, the structure of the computing graph changes to the structure shown in Fig. 5.9, in which the previous six groups of {Conv, BN, ReLU} operators with a total of 18 kernel function calls are converted into 6 CBR fusion operators with only 6 kernel function calls required.

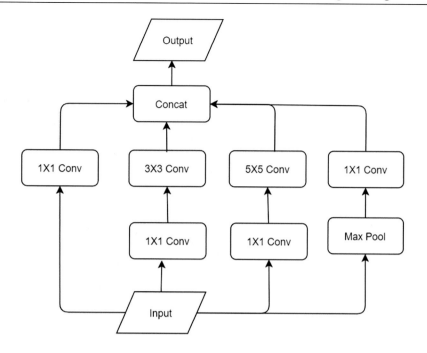

Fig. 5.8
GoogLeNet typical inception structure. *Adapted from S. Christian, et al. Going deeper with convolutions, Proceedings of the IEEE conference on computer vision and pattern recognition, 2015.*

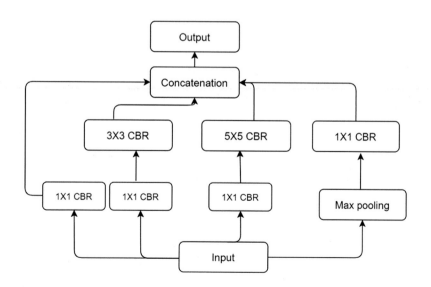

Fig. 5.9
Fusion of convolution, batch normalization, and ReLU activation. *Adapted from S. Christian, et al. Going deeper with convolutions, Proceedings of the IEEE conference on computer vision and pattern recognition, 2015.*

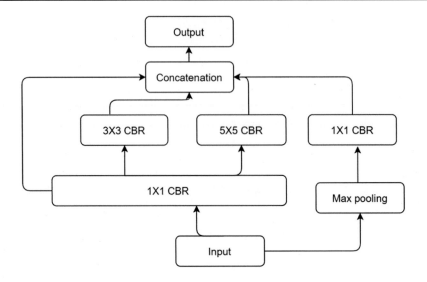

Fig. 5.10

Fusion of operators with the same configuration and same type. *Image adapted from: https://devblogs. nvidia.com/production-deep-learning-nvidia-gpu-inference-engine/network_horizontal_fusion/.*

If the operators with the same type and the same parameters have the same input, they can also be fused. As shown in Fig. 5.9, because the three 1*1 CBR fusion operators from the left to the right of the first three branches are the same operator and have the same parameter configuration (such as the size and stride of the convolution kernel), and share the same input data, then, the three fused CBR operators may be further fused into a CBR operator. As shown in Fig. 5.10, the three 1×1 CBR operators can be fused into a 1×1 CBR operator. So only one calculation is performed to further improve computing performance.

Normally, kernel fusion includes the following steps:

- perform basic optimization on the computing graph, including constant value calculation and expression optimization;
- detect nodes that can be fused in the computing graph. These nodes should be a continuous subgraph;
- generate the codes of corresponding kernel function for the given fused subgraph, which may be directly related to the hardware, or may be a universal intermediate representation, and finally, compile the codes into the instructions on the specific hardware using corresponding compiler to generate the fused kernel;
- replace the subgraph in the original computing graph with the fused kernel and invoke the fused kernel during the actual running.
- Replace existing nodes with a computational node that can be implemented more efficiently

Examples of this kind of optimization include model quantization, efficient implementation of FFT, and Winograd convolution, etc. The former uses the robustness of the neural network to convert the expensive high-precision floating-point arithmetic operations into low-precision integer operations, which improves the computing performance without losing much the precision of the algorithm. The latter transforms the original complex computations into relatively simple and highly hardware-optimized computations by spatial transformation, thus improving the computing performance.

In fact, this type of optimization should belong to algorithm level optimization and should be specified in the computing graph. However, because these optimizations often involve with the hardware architecture, following the trend of software and hardware collaborative design, this part of optimization is often performed by the Inference Engine. It is interesting that the deep learning acceleration library cuDNN provides a normal universal matrix computation version and a Winograd version for implementation of the convolution, and can dynamically select the implementation based on the shape of the input data, while the developer and framework cannot observe this optimization.

It is worth mentioning that the optimization of the algorithm will also affect the hardware architecture design. For example, the popularization of the model quantization causes the GPU to add a tensor core that uses the basic computing unit such as FP16 and INT8, and Winograd convolution also leads to the emergence of accelerator hardware architecture specifically designed for Winograd convolution. Therefore, how to fully utilize the advantages of the hardware architecture without affecting the algorithm implementation also brings challenges to the deep learning Inference Engine.

5.1.2.3 Kernel function optimization

The goal of kernel function optimization is to improve the performance of kernel functions, which involves the specific hardware architecture, storage hierarchy, and different parallel mechanisms. Kernel function optimization is optimized by data arrangement optimization, loop expansion, and data transformation.

Loop expansion and partitioned matrix

A kernel function of an operator is usually composed of a loop and a mathematical expression. For example, the convolution operation implemented with CPU consists of six layers of loops and multiplication operations. From the perspective of algorithms, GPU and TPU can accelerate the calculation of deep learning applications because they can perform parallel computing and use a single vector or tensor operation for a calculation which requires a loop implementation on the CPU. This is also the optimization method of various convolution kernel operations or two-dimensional matrix operations mentioned above, which uses the parallelism of computing resources in hardware to some extent.

CODE 5.13 Complexity of the matrix operations.

```
int A[M][K], B[K][N], C[M][N];
// Three loops for scalar operation
for (int i = 0; i < M; i++) {
    for (int j = 0; j < N; j++) {
        for (int k = 0; k < K; k++) {
            C[i][j] += A[i][k] * B[k][j];
        }
    }
}
// Two loops for vector operation
for (int i = 0; i < M; i++) {
    for (int j = 0; j < N; j++) {
        C[i][j] = mac(A[i][^], B[^][j]);
    }
}
// Zero loop for matrix operation
C = gemm(A, B);
```

As shown in Code 5.13, taking the matrix multiplication as an example, if the scalar operation is used, the matrix multiplication operation must be performed in the M, N, and K dimensions. The time complexity is O (N^3). If the vector operation is used (assuming that the vector array is wide enough), the loop on the K dimension can be converted into the multiplication-accumulate operation (MAC) of two vectors. In this case, only two loops are required for the calculation, and the time complexity is O (N^2). If the matrix operation is further used (assuming that the tensor array is large enough), the entire matrix operation may be converted into a second-order tensor operation, and the time complexity is O (1).

It can be seen that the hardware platform may reduce the time complexity of the algorithm by supporting specific computing resources which can perform a large amount of parallel computing. Some of these parallel computations are directly implemented in a hardware circuit (e.g., a systolic array in the TPU). And some requires the usage of some special instruction set (e.g., a vector operation instruction), and others are implemented in a kernel function, i.e., a combination of instruction sets (e.g., General Matrix Multiplication in the cuBLAS library). However, from the perspective of kernel computation, these parallel computations are considered as one highly optimized operation, such as Winograd and FFT, and do not involve actual hardware implementation.

Certainly, the calculation of the actual kernel function is not as simple as displayed in Code 5.13, because the degree of parallelism supported by the hardware is often limited. For example, the Cube Unit in the Ascend AI processor supports up to two 16 × 16 matrix

---

CODE 5.14 Expand the matrix operation based on the operation of the Cube Unit.

```
int M_dim = (M + 15) / 16;
int N_dim = (N + 15) / 16;
int K_dim = (K + 15) / 16;
int A_split[M_dim][K_dim][16][16];
int B_split[K_dim][N_dim][16][16];
int C_split[M_dim][N_dim][16][16];
for (int i = 0; i < M_dim; i++) {
    for (int j = 0; j < N_dim; j++) {
        for (int k = 0; k < K_dim; k++) {
            C_split[i][j] += gemm(A[i][k], B[k][j]);
        }
    }
}
C_split -> C
```

---

multiplication operations, while the dimension of the actual matrix may be greater than 16×16. In this case, the matrix needs to be partitioned to adapt to the computing capability of the actual hardware. Therefore, the loop in Code 5.13 needs to be properly expanded.

As shown in Code 5.14, by using a partitioned matrix, matrix multiplication with any size can be finally converted into 16×16 matrix operations that the Cube Unit can support. Using partitioned matrix in Code 5.14 is a kind of loop conversion. In addition, there are methods such as loop combination and loop reordering, whose purpose is to convert the loop body according to the characteristics of the hardware operation. For example, the loop combination in Code 5.15 can combine the calculation of the two loops into one loop, to reduce the overhead caused by the loop itself.

Optimization of the order of data storage

In the deep learning framework, multidimensional data is stored in multidimensional arrays. For example, the feature maps of convolutional neural networks are stored in four-dimensional arrays. The four dimensions are batch size (Batch, N), feature map height (Height, H), feature map width (Width, W), and feature map channels (Channels, C). However, because data can only be stored linearly, the order of the four dimensions matters. Therefore, there will be a problem if different deep learning frameworks store feature map data in different orders. For example, in Caffe, the order is [Batch, Channels, Height, Width], that is, NCHW. In TensorFlow, the order is [Batch, Height, Width, Channels], that is, NHWC. As shown in Fig. 5.11, for a picture in the RGB format, the NCHW actually stores in "RRRGGGBBB," where all pixel values of the same channel are stored in order, while the NHWC actually stores in "RGBRGBRGB," where the pixel values at the same position of multiple channels are stored in order.

CODE 5.15 Loop combination.

```
int A[N], B[N];
// before conversion
for (int i = 0; i < N; i++) {
    B[N] = A[N] * 2;
}
for (int i = 0; i < N; i++) {
    B[N] = B[N] + 1;
}
// after conversion
for (int i = 0; i < N; i++) {
    B[N] = A[N] * 2 + 1;
}
```

Fig. 5.11

NCHW and NHWC. *Image adapted from: https://mp.weixin.qq.com/s/I4Q1Bv7yecqYXUra49o7tw.*

Although the stored data is the same, different storage order will result in inconsistent data access features. Therefore, even if the same operation is performed, the corresponding computing performance will be different. For example, for the task of converting RGB to grayscale, Figs. 5.12 and 5.13 show the corresponding calculation methods of the two storage modes, respectively.

In Fig. 5.12, because all pixel values of the same channel are stored adjacently in the NCHW, only after all pixel values of each channel are multiplied by the corresponding factor, the accumulation may be performed. Since the results of all pixels can be obtained at the same time, the computation is strongly patterned and easy to control. However, since the final output result can only be calculated when the input data of all channels is ready, this storage mode requires a large amount of memory bandwidth and temporary memory space.

In Fig. 5.13, because pixel values of different channels adjacently in the NHWC and input data are formed by multiple groups of RGB pixel triplet, the output pixel values can be obtained by intragroup calculation from multiple pixel triplets, and the final output can be obtained by concatenating the values calculated from multiple pixel triplets. Because each triplet only needs three input data for calculation, the delay of calculating the first-pixel value is relatively

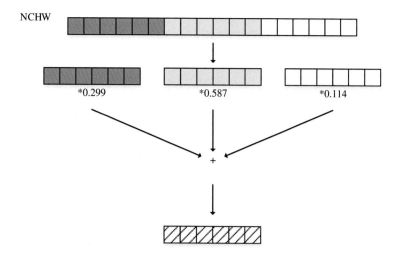

Fig. 5.12
RGB to grayscale conversion using NCHW. *Adapted from https://mp.weixin.qq.com/s/I4Q1Bv7yecqYXUra49o7tw.*

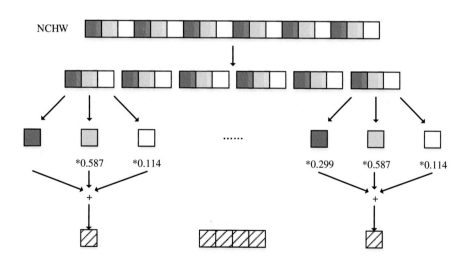

Fig. 5.13
RGB to grayscale conversion using NHWC. *Image adapted from: https://mp.weixin.qq.com/s/I4Q1Bv7yecqYXUra49o7tw.*

short, and only a small temporary space is required. In the implementation, the entire calculation process runs asynchronously by performing calculation while reading, to cover the memory reading time, and the requirement for the memory bandwidth is relatively small. However, because the start time of calculating each pixel triplet is different, it is complicated to control the whole calculation process.

The possible causes are as follows: on the one hand, data must be stored in the memory in a certain order; on the other hand, only linear access to the data in the memory can maximize the reading and writing bandwidth of the memory. Therefore, there is no generalized rule on the choice between NCHW and NHWC, while the decision needs to be determined according to specific requirements of the actual application. For example, NCHW is more suitable for operations that need to perform the calculation on each channel separately, e.g., the pooling layer in a neural network. The NHWC is more suitable for performing a certain operation on the same pixel of different channels, e.g., 1×1 convolution. Generally, NCHW is more suitable for GPU computation because it can use the large memory bandwidth of the GPU and the computation operation is strongly fixed. NHWC is more suitable for multicore CPU computation because the CPU memory bandwidth is relatively small, but the computation control is complex and flexible. Therefore, the deep learning acceleration library cuDNN uses the NCHW as the default format, while TensorFlow uses the NHWC because the TensorFlow uses the CPU for acceleration at its early stage.

The computing performance is affected not only by the order of the channel dimension but also by the order of the image height H and width W due to the same reason. This is why many operations care about whether the data is Row-Major or Column-Major.

Certainly, in many cases, data is not necessarily arranged in its natural format, and the storage format and data ordering often change based on the specific computation requirement. For example, the matrix A[M][K] in Code 5.14 is divided into A[M_dim][N_dim][16][16]. This is because the Cube Unit of the AI Core in the Ascend AI processor only supports the matrix operation with the size of 16×16. In addition, both input matrices need to be arranged in a very specific order because one matrix needs to be accessed by row-major, and the other one needs to be accessed by column-major. Therefore, before entering the Cube Unit, software or dedicated hardware is used to rearrange required data to achieve optimal computing efficiency, which is the most important focus of the deep learning engine.

Therefore, before performing inference with the deep learning model, the storage order of the model parameters may be converted based on the actual hardware structure and the computing resource. For the input data and the intermediate data, the transformation needs to be performed in the computation process. In the actual transformation process, the specific configuration and optimization strategies need to be considered, and this relates to the concept of the dedicated kernel below.

Dedicated kernel

Currently, the kernels invoked by the deep learning framework are all precompiled. For example, the computation of each layer in Caffe has the C++ and CUDA implementations. Once complied, the corresponding kernel can only perform the fixed computation logic. Therefore, to meet the computation requirements of different configurations, the corresponding kernel functions must be designed in a general manner and configured using different parameters. For example, a convolution kernel function needs to have multiple parameters such as an input data shape, a convolution kernel size, and a convolution stride. In the abstraction of the inference graph of Code 5.11, different convolution functions invoke the same kernel, but with different input parameters, so that the data can be processed differently.

Although such kernel can provide sufficient flexibility, it often fails to achieve the optimal performance. The reason is as follows: on the one hand, different parameter configurations inevitably bring a large number of online computing and online logic control, which affects the inference speed performance. On the other hand, to optimize the kernel calculation sufficiently, it often requires careful data arrangement and loop optimization. However, different configurations make this kind of optimization difficult. Although some proper rules can be used to automatically optimize the computation, there is still a big gap comparing to the manually optimized codes.

To some extent, the deep learning acceleration library cuDNN and linear computing library cuBLAS from NVIDIA want to solve this problem by using a dedicated kernel, i.e., manually optimized kernel versions for certain parameter configurations. cuDNN provides multiple well-optimized convolution implementations, including implementations of different precisions (FP32, FP16), different implementation methods (General Matrix Multiplication, Winograd convolution), and cuDNN automatically selects the optimal convolution algorithm based on the input parameter configurations. However, as such libraries themselves are precompiled, the optimal kernel version can only be selected with the best effort during the actual running process. In addition, even if the dedicated kernel is used, it can only be used for certain parameter configurations, such as the fixed convolution kernel size 3×3.

The problems caused by this customized kernel are shown in Table 5.1. The batch matrix multiplication kernel in the cuBLAS library performs dedicated optimization to a certain extent. However, to adapt to different matrix shapes, the system fills the matrix to a specific shape by zero padding. Therefore, regardless of the input shape, the calculation amount is constant, which will waste a lot of computing resources for a small matrix. Finally, a large number of engineers need to invest a lot of time to optimize libraries such as cuDNN and cuBLAS, while this task requires extremely rich practical experience. Therefore, it is impossible to achieve optimal optimization for each configuration and each case.

Table 5.1: Issues of batch matrix multiplication in cuBLAS[a].

Input shape [Batch, M, N, K]	Customized kernel	Theoretical calculation flops	Actual calculation flops	Theoretical/ actual flops (%)
[512, 17, 17, 128]	maxwell_sgemmBatched_128x128_raggedMn_tn	18,939,904	2,155,872,256	0.87
[512, 1, 17, 128]	maxwell_sgemmBatched_128x128_raggedMn_tn	1,114,112	2,155,872,256	0.052
[512, 17, 1128]	maxwell_sgemmBatched_128x128_raggedMn_tn	1,114,112	2,155,872,256	0.052
[512, 30, 30,128]	maxwell_sgemmBatched_128x128_raggedMn_tn	58,982,400	2,155,872,256	2.74

[a]https://tvm.apache.org/2018/03/23/nmt-transformer-optimize.

To solve the above issues, a popular method in the industry is to develop a dedicated kernel for the computation of the deep learning application. Because the common computing logic in the deep learning application is fixed, including the data shape and the configuration of various computational nodes, this information can be used to find the most time-consuming operations for designing a dedicated kernel. With enough optimization of these kernels, the inference performance can be improved greatly by calling these dedicated kernels during actual running. Actually, this method discards the precompiled kernel and introduces a new compilation process, which can provide more parameter information during the compilation and a better guide of optimization.

At present, many deep learning Inference Engines want to automate this process, i.e., with sufficient information, compile and automatically generate efficient dedicated kernels to replace manual optimization. With the development of the deep learning Inference Engine, these automatically generated kernels can reach 70%–80% performance of the manually optimized kernels. Therefore, by using the compiler of the deep learning Inference Engine, it is possible to implement the entire deep learning model using a dedicated kernel, thereby improve the overall inference performance. If this automated process is properly combined with the manual optimization, the performance of these automatically generated kernels may even exceed the performance of the manually only optimized kernels.

5.1.3 Deep learning inference engine

The deep learning Inference Engine only focuses on the inference process of the deep learning model. This tool has the following two purposes. On the one hand, the Inference Engine parses the computing graph structure and model parameters described in the model files and converts them into an intermediate representation of a unified computation graph. After that, this representation is converted into execution graphs for the supported hardware platforms, i.e., kernel invocations on specific hardware platforms. It provides capabilities for deploying models from various frameworks to various hardware platforms. On the other hand, based on the intermediate representation of the computing graph, the Inference Engine comprehensively adopts various optimization methods to improve the inference performance of the deep learning model in the actual hardware execution process.

At present, the deep learning Inference Engine is becoming more popular. Big companies and teams are "building the wheels" using their exclusive hardware support, such as DMLC's TVM, Intel's nGraph, NVIDIA's TensorRT for its GPU, Facebook's Tensor Comprehensions, Google's TensorFlow XLA, Baidu's Anakin, Ali's MNN and so on. Although the industry offers many different solutions, they all share similar basic design concepts, i.e., defining a set of intermediate representations that are dedicated to deep learning, developing a pipeline of DSL → Deep Learning IR → LLVM IR → Target, and adding various optimizations during the process. This development method actually can be referred to as the deep learning compiler.

Because different deep learning Inference Engines have different focuses and different abstraction levels and optimization strategies, they are often very different. For example, TensorRT only focuses on how to improve the inference performance of the deep learning model on the GPU architecture. Therefore, the GPU architecture is considered regardless of whether the computing graph is optimized or the low-level kernel is optimized. This is different from other inference engines. For another example, the TensorFlow XLA uses the LLVM intermediate representation to describe each operator and can reuse a series of frontend optimization methods of the LLVM. In contrast, Tensor Comprehensions is more aggressive and uses the Halide intermediate representation to describe underlying computation. By borrowing the optimization methods from various compiler theories, it transforms and optimizes the low-level computational loops for a specific hardware architecture.

This section focuses on the most famous TVM (Tensor Virtual Machine) in the industry, describing the abstraction level and optimization method of the TVM. Compared it with other deep learning inference engines, TVM not only has the intermediate representation of the computing graph level, i.e., NNVM and Relay, but also has the intermediate representation of Halide as the underlying computational support. On the one hand, this good abstraction level provides the capability to extend to other hardware architectures. On the other hand, developers can directly use the clearly defined domain-specific languages to describe all algorithms and can use the functional TVM primitives to define and schedule underlying computation. In addition, the TVM has the AutoTVM mechanism to provide the search algorithm so that developers can quickly find the best optimization solution for specific hardware architectures. In addition, the complete code generation mechanism of TVM can quickly generate the code for the specified hardware platform based on the computation definition and scheduling. To sum up, TVM makes the deep learning inference engine no longer a black box, which enables developers to quickly learn and participate in model optimization. Meanwhile, learning TVM helps understand the Ascend AI processor-related programming knowledge later in this book.

5.1.3.1 The first generation of computing graph intermediate representation of TVM—NNVM

NNVM is the earliest computing graph intermediate representation of TVM. Actually, the concept of NNVM is earlier than TVM. As early as 2016, Tianqi Chen and others found it unsustainable to make the deep learning framework to have good support for all hardware. Fortunately, the same problem once existed in the compiler field. At that time, programming languages were emerging and the CPU architecture was constantly being updated, it was difficult to make a compiler to support all the back ends well. The LLVM is an effective solution to this problem. It isolates the frontend and back end of the compiler by successfully dividing the module into different parts. Therefore, whenever a new programming language appears, it only needs to develop the corresponding frontend to convert the programming language into LLVM intermediate representation. In the case of new hardware architecture, the only need is to develop the corresponding back end for the LLVM intermediate representation. Inspired by the idea of LLVM, Tianqi Chen et al. proposed the concept of NNVM.

NNVM is equivalent to the LLVM in the deep learning field. It is a relatively advanced intermediate representation module in a neural network and is generally referred to as computing graph. The frontend framework only needs to express the computation in the intermediate representation of the NNVM, and then the NNVM uniformly performs operations and optimization that are irrelevant to the specific hardware and framework, including memory allocation, data type and shape derivation and operator fusion, and then use various compilation back ends to generate back-end hardware codes. By modularizing each component, the NNVM enables the deep learning framework to adapt to the rapid development of the frontend programming environment and back-end hardware. In the same era as NNVM, the computing graph intermediate representation also includes Intel's Nervana Graph (the predecessor of nGraph), which performs the same task.

However, the abstraction nature of NNVM determines it cannot be optimized at a very low level. Therefore, on the basis of NNVM, Tianqi Chen proposed the NNVM compiler in 2017 and introduced the TVM with the tensor optimization. The NNVM is used for the computing graph, whose objective is to convert a computing graph from a different deep learning framework into a unified computing graph intermediate representation, and then convert it into an execution graph after performing the computation graph optimization. TVM is used for the tensor operation. It provides an intermediate computational representation that is independent of hardware and adopts various methods (such as partitioning and caching) to optimize the corresponding calculation. Such a combined TVM/NNVM compiler stack is also described as "a complete optimization tool chain from deep learning to various hardware."

5.1.3.2 The TVM second generation of computing graph intermediate representation—Relay

In the current TVM version, NNVM has been replaced by its successor Relay. Relay is the second generation of NNVM and was introduced to the TVM compiler stack in 2018 with its own motivation.

The traditional deep learning framework uses the computing graph to represent the deep learning application. In addition, the computing graph is used as the data structure for input, intermediate representation, and execution. Following this idea, the NNVM proposed the unified computing graph representation.

A typical deep learning framework based on the computing graph is TensorFlow. TensorFlow uses a programming model which defines computing graph first before execution. This approach supports most number of the most advanced deep learning models, making TensorFlow widely used in the deep learning field. As mentioned earlier, TensorFlow essentially defines a high-level domain-specific language, so that the codes that define the graph are quite different from other Python codes and cannot directly use the various advanced language features of Python. Also, the computing graph is defined before execution, TensorFlow has the following defects:

- Cannot support control flow well, such as branch jump and loop.
- Cannot support those models which calculate the input shape depending on the input, such as word2vec.

Although TensorFlow has APIs such as tf.cond and tf.while_loop that can solve the first problem to some extent, and other tools such as TensorFlow Fold can solve the second problem, these methods are not particularly friendly to programmers who just start to learn the deep learning framework.

The dynamic graph-based frameworks represented by PyTorch solve the above problems. These frameworks discard the pattern of defining the computation graph before execution used in TensorFlow. Instead, they use the pattern of defining the computing graph at runtime. This computing graph is called a dynamic graph, and the corresponding programming method also becomes imperative programming. PyTorch embeds basic primitives into Python and can use various advanced features of Python. Therefore, the control flow of the computing graph is defined by the Python interpreter, and the specific calculation of the data flow is executed by the code of PyTorch framework which is based on Python.

However, there are still some problems with the dynamic graph mechanism of PyTorch:

- The control flow of the computing graph is controlled by the Python interpreter, so that the framework cannot optimize these control flows as well as TensorFlow Fold.
- The dynamic graph can only be defined at runtime. Therefore, if the topology structure of the computing graph changes, re-optimization is needed accordingly and the overhead of data migration is introduced.

Although the above problems can be resolved by changing the Python code, it makes no big differences from the static frameworks.

Relay solves the preceding problems. Specifically, Relay is not only an intermediate representation of a computing graph but also a domain-specific language dedicated to the field of automatic differentiation programming. Currently, TVM is a compiler for the Relay. For details about the Relay, please refer to the paper from Jared Roesch, the Relay: A New IR for Machine Learning Framework.

Relay provides the Python interfaces to convert the models of various frameworks into a unified computing graph intermediate representation. The specific interfaces are defined in the tvm. frontend.relay. Generally, the corresponding framework is used to load the model and then the corresponding interface in the Relay is invoked for conversion. Code 5.16 shows how to load the ONNX model and convert it to Relay intermediate representation. Some irrelevant codes

---

CODE 5.16 Import the ONNX model and convert it to Relay.

```
import onnx
import numpy as numpy
import tvm
import tvm.relay as relay

onnx_model = onnx.load(model_path) # import onnx model
x = np.array(img_y)[np.newaxis, np.newaxis, :, :] # Specify input
data shape
input_name = '1'
shape_dict = {input_name: x.shape}
mod, params = relay.frontend.from_onnx(onnx_model, shape_dict) #
Convert to Relay format
```

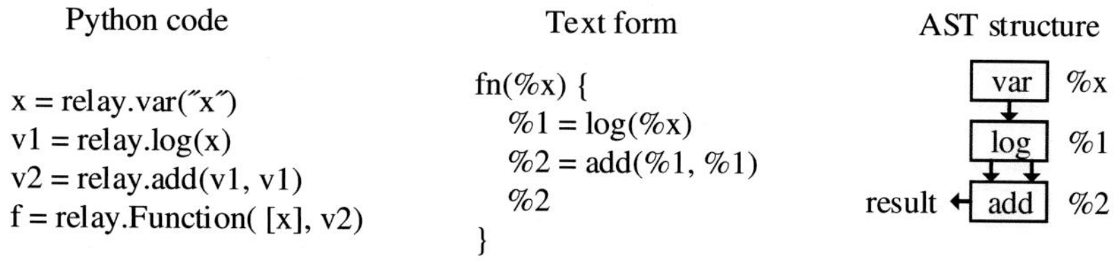

Python code	Text form	AST structure
x = relay.var("x")	fn(%x) {	var %x
v1 = relay.log(x)	%1 = log(%x)	log %1
v2 = relay.add(v1, v1)	%2 = add(%1, %1)	result ← add %2
f = relay.Function([x], v2)	%2	
	}	

Fig. 5.14

Construct a computing graph using Relay. *Image is referred to from TVM website: https://docs.tvm.ai/dev/relay_intro.html.*

have been omitted, and the last mod and params indicate the Relay module and parameter dictionary, respectively.

In addition, the Relay also supports the construction of a computing graph directly through the Python interface. Fig. 5.14 shows a use case from the official TVM. The Relay can either define a computing graph as in a traditional deep learning framework, or define a function as in a high-level language, and declare a variable so that it becomes a real differentiated language.

In the TVM code, the intermediate representation of the Relay computing graph can be compiled instantly by explicitly calling the compilation interface and run in the TVM runtime environment. Code 5.17 further performs the compilation and running operations based on Code 5.16.

5.1.3.3 Graph optimization in TVM

Normally, the deep learning Inference Engine is a black box that cannot be manipulated for developers. Generally speaking, the specified deep learning model only needs to be imported and converted into a unified intermediate representation as shown in Code 5.16. Then,

---

CODE 5.17 Compile and run the computing graph.

```
with relay.build_config(opt_level=1):
# Compile
intrp = relay.build_module.create_executor('graph', mod, tvm.cpu
(0), target)
dtype = 'float32'
# Run
tvm_output   =   intrp.evaluate()(tvm.nd.array(x.astype(dtype)),
**params).asnumpy()
```

---

the unified intermediate representation is compiled as in Code 5.17, so that it can run on a specific hardware platform. This is the pipeline of most deep learning inference engines. As a result, developers are often unaware of what optimizations have been made by the inference engine, and can only see some computational changes by printing some intermediate representation.

TVM Relay not only provides an automatic graph optimization mechanism but also allows developers to extend the features of the Relay by adding a CompilerPass.

The graph optimization part in TVM Relay is defined in the tvm.relay.transform. Code 5.18 shows the current optimization levels defined by TVM Relay. These optimizations have been mentioned in the preceding sections.

- SimplifyInference: Simple inference without any optimization.
- OpFusion: Operator fusion.
- FoldConstant: Fold the constant.
- CombineParallelConv2D: Combined parallel convolution and operation.
- FoldScaleAxis: Fold the scale axis.
- AlterOpLayout: Alter the operator arrangement.
- CanonicalizeOps: Canonicalize the operator.
- EliminateCommonSubexpr: Eliminates common subexpressions.

5.1.3.4 Low-level intermediate representation of TVM

The term TVM itself is used to define the intermediate representation of a low-level tensor computation. When presented as part of the NNVM compiler in 2017, it is at a different level from NNVM. However, with the development of TVM, the meaning of TVM is extended to the deep learning compiler stack for the CPU, GPU, and dedicated accelerator. The current meaning of TVM is as follows:

CODE 5.18 Graph optimization method provided by TVM Relay.

```
OPT_PASS_LEVEL = {
    "SimplifyInference": 0,
    "OpFusion": 1,
    "FoldConstant": 2,
    "CombineParallelConv2D": 3,
    "FoldScaleAxis": 3,
    "AlterOpLayout": 3,
    "CanonicalizeOps": 3,
    "EliminateCommonSubexpr": 3,
}
```

- Minimum invocable kernels to compile models from various frameworks to different hardware back ends
- Automatic generation and optimization of efficient kernels for different hardware back ends.

The purpose of the TVM tensor-level abstraction is to solve the optimization problems that the NNVM cannot handle. The graph optimization method introduced by NNVM can perform optimization effectively. For example, through memory optimization, NNVM allows developers to train the 1000 layer ImageNet ResNet model on a single GPU. However, it is not sufficient to efficiently support different back-end hardware by only using the computing graph level intermediate representation. For example, a convolution operator or a matrix multiplication operator may have different optimization methods on different hardware back ends, which involve memory arrangement, parallel method, caching method, and hardware primitive selection. However, these hardware-specific optimizations cannot be performed by using a computation graph level optimization. The emergence of TVM provides a low-level intermediate representation for optimizing specific operators on specific hardware.

5.1.3.5 Basis of the low-level intermediate representation of TVM—Halide

The design of the low-level intermediate representation of TVM learns a lot from the idea of Halide. Halide is a C++ based domain-specific language related to image processing. For example, in the traditional digital image processing, a vanilla C++ implementation of the local Laplacian Transform will be very slow. After manual optimization, 10 times boost of the acceleration performance can be achieved. However, it will take a lot of experienced engineers to spend a large amount of time on the optimization. If Halide is used, only a few lines of code can obtain the C++ code that is 20 times faster than the vanilla implementation. This greatly reduces the time for developers to manually optimize the underlying algorithm so that they can focus more on the algorithm design.

CODE 5.19 **Halide code.**

```
Func halide_blur(Func in) {
   Func tmp, blurred;
   Var x, y, xi, yi;
   // Algorithm implementation
   tmp(x, y) = (in(x - 1, y) + in(x, y) + in(x + 1, y)) / 3;
   blurred(x, y) = (tmp(x, y - 1) + tmp(x, y) + tmp(x, y + 1)) / 3;
   // Algorithm scheduling
   blurred.tile(x, y, xi, yi, 256, 32).vectorize(xi, 8).parallel
   (y);
   tmp.compute_at(blurred, x).vectorize(x, 8);
   return blurred;
}
```

The most important feature of Halide is that the algorithm implementation (Expression) is separated from the scheduling (Schedule), i.e., the algorithm description and performance optimization are decoupled. The former is simply an algorithm, and the latter is a method for executing the algorithm on specific hardware, such as memory allocation, parallelization method, and computing order. Code 5.19 shows the Halide code implementation of the Gaussian blurring algorithm. The tmp and blurred are two functions, respectively, which represent the specific calculation process of Gaussian blurring. It can be seen that the Gaussian module calculates the average pixel value of nine pixels, including the surrounding pixels and the center pixel. The following two lines of code are used to schedule the two functions. Tile, vectorize, and parallel are optimization methods introduced by Halide to optimize the loop in the algorithm. Also, interfaces such as inline, root, chunk, and reuse are used to define how data is cached. On a quad-core x86 architecture CPU, the C++ code generated by Halide in Code 5.19 can reach the speed of 0.9 ms/megapixel, while the directly implemented C++ code can only reach 9.96 ms/megapixel. The performance difference between the two is almost ten times.

In addition to separating algorithm implementation from scheduling, Halide also has several other highlighted features. For example, for the metaprogramming mentioned earlier, Halide is used to generate efficient C++ code. Halide can also automatically search for optimal optimization factors in the search space, such as loop expansion factors, to achieve automatic optimization.

5.1.3.6 *Features of low-level intermediate representation of TVM*

TVM not only absorbs the essence of Halide but also introduces the loop transformation tool and concepts from other deep learning frameworks. TVM mainly consists of the following features:

(1)   In order to simplify mathematical representations, HalideIR is used as its data structure.
(2)   Separate the operator implementation from the operator scheduling according to how Halide separates the algorithm implementation from the algorithm scheduling.
(3)   Similar to the automatic optimization used in Halide introducing, the AutoTVM is also introduced. Developers can customize the search space and use the search algorithm provided by TVM to find the optimal solution.
(4)   The low-level optimization strategy adopts the loopy tool for loop transformation and the idea of polyhedral model analysis, and uses loopy as loop transformation primitives.
(5)   A low-level domain-specific language is proposed for the deep learning models and Python is used as its host language to provide multiple primitives for algorithm implementation and algorithm scheduling.
(6)   The programming style uses the computing graph-based programming method in traditional deep learning framework, such as tensor and placeholder in TensorFlow.
(7)   For different hardware back ends, the same operator can be used for scheduling with different operators and generate corresponding code for different hardware.

5.1.3.7 TVM operator implementation

Take the commonly used operator, Reduction, as an example. It is used to reduce dimension of the data by summing or averaging. As shown in Code 5.20, the two-dimensional array A is reduced to the one-dimensional array B through summation for dimensionality reduction. Code 5.21 shows how the same function is implemented by invoking the TVM primitives.

As shown in Code 5.21, it can be seen that the programming style of the TVM code is very similar to that of TensorFlow, which are both declarative and static programming styles. The entire computation process is constructed by invoking the computation primitives provided by the TVM. Code 5.21 contains the following primitives:

- tvm.var.: Define a variable with the specified name and type. The default type is int.
- tvm.placeholder: As in TensorFlow, define the placeholder for input data, and the data is an empty tensor object.

CODE 5.20 C++ code for the sum reduction operator.

```
for (int i = 0; i < n; ++i) {
    B[i] = 0;
    for (int k = 0; k < m; ++k) {
        B[i] = B[i] + A[i][k];
    }
}
```

CODE 5.21 The calculation code (compute) for the sum Reduction operator.

```
import tvm
import numpy as np
n = tvm.var("n")
m = tvm.var("m")
A = tvm.placeholder((n, m), name='A')
k = tvm.reduce_axis((0, m), "k")
B = tvm.compute((n,), lambda i: tvm.sum(A[i, k], axis=k), name="B")
```

CODE 5.22 Print the default calculation scheduling.

```
s = tvm.create_schedule(B.op)
print(tvm.lower(s, [A, B], simple_mode=True))
```

- tvm.reduce_axis: The axis to define the iteration variable of a specified range and is dedicated to the loop.
- tvm.compute: Construct a tensor, which is calculated by a Lamda expression.
- tvm.sum: Construct a summation expression for a specified axis.

In the computation process, data input is through placeholders. After various calculations defined by primitives, developers can obtain output data from the output tensor B.

As shown in Code 5.22, by invoking the tvm.create_schedule interface, the default scheduling of the calculation process in Code 5.21 can be obtained. Generally, the default scheduling method uses the row-major serial calculation mode. The low-level intermediate representation of TVM, as shown in Code 5.23, can be printed. It can be seen that the corresponding intermediate representation style is very similar to the C language, and the implementation is the most direct implementation of the Reduction operator, which can be optimized by proper scheduling.

5.1.3.8 TVM operator scheduling

In the low-level intermediate representation of TVM, a proper transformation is mainly implemented by a loop. Similar to Halide, TVM provides multiple interfaces dedicated to operator scheduling. These scheduling interfaces focus to perform various transformations for the loops in the computation.

(1) split: Split the specified axis into two axes.
(2) tile: Execute the computing graph by tiling two axes.

CODE 5.23 Default calculation scheduling.

```
produce B {
  for (i, 0, n) {
      B[i] = 0.000000f
      for (k, 0, m) {
          B[i] = (B[i] + A[((i*m) + k)])
      }
  }
}
```

---

(3) fuse: Fuse two axes of a calculation.

(4) reorder: Rearrange the axis based on the specified order.

(5) bind: Bind the specified axis to the thread group, which is usually used in GPU programming.

(6) compute_at: For scheduling with multiple operators, TVM calculates the tensor from the root by default. compute_at can determine to move a computing phase to the specified axis of another computing phase.

(7) compute_inline: Mark a computing phase as inline, extend the computing body and insert it into the corresponding computing phase.

(8) compute_root: Move the computing graph of a computing phase to the root, which may be considered as an inverse process of the compute_at.

For the calculation in Code 5.21, the scheduling shown in Code 5.24 may be used, and the scheduling uses different factors to split the row axis and the column axis of the B. The corresponding code of the intermediate representation is complex and omitted here. The result will be a four-layer nested loop.

If developers want to build a GPU kernel, they can bind rows of B to the GPU thread group. The detailed codes are shown in Code 5.25. The code for corresponding intermediate representation is not shown here.

Code 5.26 shows the complete implementation of the sum Reduction code. For more operator scheduling examples and specific scheduling interface documents, please refer to the TVM official website.

5.1.3.9 Optimization method for TVM low-level intermediate representation

As described above, in the traditional deep learning framework, the kernel of each operator is precompiled, and a large number of branch jumps and dynamic memory allocation may be required. Therefore, the computing performance of the operators cannot be fully exploited. Although tools like TensorFlow XLA introduce instant compilation mechanisms, they do not

---

CODE 5.24 Implementation of the scheduling code for the sum reduction operator.

```
ko, ki = s[B].split(B.op.reduce_axis[0], factor=16)
xo, xi = s[B].split(B.op.axis[0], factor=32)
print(tvm.lower(s, [A, B], simple_mode=True))
```

CODE 5.25 Bind to the GPU thread.

```
s[B].bind(xo, tvm.thread_axis("blockIdx.x"))
s[B].bind(xi, tvm.thread_axis("threadIdx.x"))
print(tvm.lower(s, [A, B], simple_mode=True))
```

CODE 5.26 TVM code for the sum reduction.

```
import tvm
import numpy as np
# Define the computation
n = tvm.var("n")
m = tvm.var("m")
A = tvm.placeholder((n, m), name='A')
k = tvm.reduce_axis((0, m), "k")
B = tvm.compute((n,), lambdai: tvm.sum(A[i, k], axis=k), name="B")

# Define the scheduling
s = tvm.create_schedule(B.op)
ko, ki = s[B].split(B.op.reduce_axis[0], factor=16)
xo, xi = s[B].split(B.op.axis[0], factor=32)
s[B].bind(xo, tvm.thread_axis("blockIdx.x"))
s[B].bind(xi, tvm.thread_axis("threadIdx.x"))
```

---

essentially use dedicated kernels for specific operator configurations and specific hardware. Benefitting from the low-level abstraction and specialized compilation processes, TVM can solve above problems properly.

In Code 5.21, the input data is defined by placeholders. Although the shape of the placeholder is expressed by variables, in the actual compilation process, the specific shape can be determined based on the input data. Correspondingly, for a convolution operator, the operator configuration has information such as the input data shape, convolution kernel size, and stride. In the compilation process, these parameters are determined. Hence, for TVM, kernels for each convolution with a parameter configuration can be complied specifically for acceleration.

Therefore, for each dedicated convolution kernel, as it only accepts input of a specific shape, and runs a fixed calculation process to obtain the output of a specific shape, without branch jumping and dynamic memory allocation, TVM can perform sufficient optimization for the calculation of each kernel.

So now the question is what optimization strategy the compiler needs to use to ensure that each kernel is implemented efficiently? In TVM, the optimization of a specific operator is implemented by properly expanding the loops. In Code 5.24, the loop expansion factors 16 and 32 are predefined. This kind of expansion factor may be appropriate for one input configuration or hardware architecture, but not necessarily for all situations. A relatively simple solution is that, because the parameter of the operator and the specific hardware framework are known during compilation, it can follow the precompiler or template programming of the C++ to obtain an optimal expansion factor for the specific operator configuration and specific hardware by writing a template function and performing the computation during the compilation process. It is even possible to write a specialized operator scheduling. In this way, all kernels can be guaranteed to run efficiently. In fact, this is also one way that TVM provides to developers for manual tuning. In addition, TVM offers a more interesting mechanism—AutoTVM.

When searching for the optimal expansion operator, the developer actually wants to find the optimal solution from a search space during the compilation process. AutoTVM offers a way to achieve this. The code in Code 5.27 shows the use of AutoTVM.

Code 5.27 implements the calculation and scheduling of the multiplication of two matrices with shapes [N, L] and [L, M], respectively. In the scheduling, the two dimensions of the output matrix C is partitioned respectively, and the partitioning factors are (yo, yi) and (xo, xi), respectively. Now, the goal is to search for the optimal combination of factors to maximize the performance of the entire operator.

The AutoTVM mechanism can be represented by pseudo codes shown in Code 5.28.

Using the codes shown in Code 5.29, auto-tuning can be started and run sequentially on the actual hardware to find the optimal expansion factor.

Using the codes shown in Code 5.30, a dedicated kernel for specific operator configuration, specific hardware can be compiled, and its performance can be optimized.

In fact, the auto-tuning mechanism of TVM often needs to be combined with manual design to find the optimal solution in the search process. However, by using the predefined search space, TVM can automatically generate a dedicated kernel which has the close performance to the manually optimized kernel. Manual optimization is then performed to achieve higher performance. Also because TVM can automatically or semiautomatically generate efficient dedicated kernel quickly, it is widely used currently.

CODE 5.27 Use of the AutoTVM.

```python
@autotvm.template
def matmul(N, L, M, dtype):
    # Define input
    A = tvm.placeholder((N, L), name='A', dtype=dtype)
    B = tvm.placeholder((L, M), name='B', dtype=dtype)
    # Define computation
    k = tvm.reduce_axis((0, L), name='k')
    C = tvm.compute((N, M), lambdai, j: tvm.sum(A[i, k] * B[k, j],
axis=k), name='C')
    # Define scheduling
    s = tvm.create_schedule(C.op)
    y, x = s[C].op.axis
    k = s[C].op.reduce_axis[0]
    # Define search space
    cfg = autotvm.get_config()
    cfg.define_split("tile_y", y, num_outputs=2)
    cfg.define_split("tile_x", x, num_outputs=2)
    # Perform scheduling based on searching result
    yo, yi = cfg["tile_y"].apply(s, C, y)
    xo, xi = cfg["tile_x"].apply(s, C, x)
    s[C].reorder(yo, xo, k, yi, xi)

    return s, [A, B, C]
```

CODE 5.28 Pseudo code for AutoTVM.

```
ct = 0
while ct < max_number_of_trials:
    propose a batch of configs
    measure this batch of configs on real hardware and get results
    ct += batch_size
```

CODE 5.29 Use of AutoTVM.

```python
N, L, M = 512, 512, 512
task = autotvm.task.create(matmul, args=(N, L, M, 'float32'),
target='llvm')

# Two steps: construction and execution
measure_option = autotvm.measure_option(
builder='local',
runner=autotvm.LocalRunner(number=5))

# Start auto-tuning
tuner = autotvm.tuner.RandomTuner(task)
tuner.tune(n_trial=10,
measure_option=measure_option,
callbacks=[autotvm.callback.log_to_file('matmul.log')])
```

CODE 5.30 Use the optimal expansion factor to compile the corresponding kernel and verify the correctness.

```
# Select the expansion factor with best performance from the log
file and compile the corresponding kernel based on the factor
with autotvm.apply_history_best('matmul.log'):
with tvm.target.create("llvm"):
    s, arg_bufs = matmul(N, L, M, 'float32')
    func = tvm.build(s, arg_bufs)
# Verify the correctness
a_np = np.random.uniform(size=(N, L)).astype(np.float32)
b_np = np.random.uniform(size=(L, M)).astype(np.float32)
c_np = a_np.dot(b_np
c_tvm = tvm.nd.empty(c_np.shape)
func(tvm.nd.array(a_np), tvm.nd.array(b_np), c_tvm)
tvm.testing.assert_allclose(c_np, c_tvm.asnumpy(), rtol=1e-2)
```

5.1.3.10 TOPI mechanism

From the TVM code shown earlier, although TVM provides a complete mechanism for developers to perform fine scheduling of the computation, they also often need to be very familiar with the hardware architecture to perform the corresponding scheduling programming. In addition, even if developers are well aware of the various scheduling mechanisms and hardware architectures of TVM, it is also very difficult to schedule each computing task. Moreover, some scheduling codes repeat very often, and developers will perform a lot of repetitive work. In technical terms, such codes are called Boilerplate Code.

Boilerplate Code refers to the codes that are included in many places, but almost with no change. Such codes are needed but also not so important, and often only implement some secondary functions. In the scheduling code of TVM, thousands of lines of codes are often required to perform the scheduling of convolution, and many codes can be reused. Therefore, it is very painful for developers to write these Boilerplate Code over and over again.

To prevent developers from writing Boilerplate Code repeatedly, TVM introduced TOPI (TVM Operator Inventory) mechanism. As a Python module, TOPI provides developers with general operations and scheduling similar to the NumPy style. These operations and scheduling are abstracted from TVM.

Here, calculating the sum at a given axis is used as an example to describe the TOPI. This operation converts a two-dimensional array into a one-dimensional array by summing up the second axis. Code 5.31 shows the codes that implement the operations by using TVM primitives.

CODE 5.31 Use TVM for summing up specified axis of a two-dimensional array.

```
n = tvm.var("n")
m = tvm.var("m")
A = tvm.placeholder((n, m), name='A')
k = tvm.reduce_axis((0, m), "k")
B = tvm.compute((n,), lambdai: tvm.sum(A[i, k], axis=k), name="B")
s = tvm.create_schedule(B.op)
```

CODE 5.32 Use TOPI interface for sum operation.

```
C = topi.sum(A, axis=1)
ts = tvm.create_schedule(C.op)
```

CODE 5.33 Perform TVM scheduling on specific hardware platform.

```
x, y = 100, 10
a = tvm.placeholder((x, y, y), name="a")
b = tvm.placeholder((y, y), name="b")
c = a + b
d = a * b
e = topi.elemwise_sum([c, d])
f = e / 2.0
g = topi.sum(f)
with tvm.target.cuda():
    sg = topi.generic.schedule_reduce(g)
```

If someone wants to schedule the calculations for Code 5.31, scheduling primitives such as tvm. compute need to be explicitly used. For more complex computations, developers can imagine how complex it would be to write the corresponding scheduling. As shown in Code 5.32, similar to numpy.sum, TOPI provides the topi.sum interface, which has performed the scheduling by TVM.

In addition, as shown in Code 5.33, TOPI also optimizes scheduling based on the specified hardware platform, and also provides optimized scheduling for common neural network operators as in Code 5.34.

5.1.3.11 Code generation in TVM

After all levels of optimization are completed, the remaining task is to generate codes that can be deployed on the specified hardware platform. TVM does not involve the compiler development of any hardware platform. The task is to complete the conversion process of the

---

CODE 5.34 Automatic scheduling for Softmax on GPU.

```
tarray = tvm.placeholder((512, 512), name="tarray")
softmax_topi = topi.nn.softmax(tarray)
with tvm.target.create("cuda"):
    sst = topi.generic.schedule_softmax(softmax_topi)
    print(tvm.lower(sst, [tarray], simple_mode=True))
```

---

programming language from the low-level intermediate representation defined by TVM primitives to the specified hardware platform. The conversion process involves a lot of knowledge about the compiler and specific hardware architecture, which is not suitable to be expanded here. Readers can study the specialized conversion process on their own. Finally, TVM converts the low-level intermediate representation of multiple loops into corresponding codes such as LLVM, CUDA, Metal, and OpenCL based on the specified hardware platform.

It is worth mentioning that the good abstraction level of TVM makes it easy to extend to other hardware platforms, including those with customized deep learning accelerator architectures. Nowadays, more and more companies are developing their own deep learning acceleration processors, and have their own instruction sets and corresponding programming languages and compilers. If the company that designs processors wants to use TVM to develop an efficient kernel for its own processor, they can use the entire software stack just by performing the conversion from the low-level intermediate representation of TVM to the code for their own processor.

5.2 Techniques of Ascend AI software stack

The typical deep learning inference engines, such as TVM and nGraph, are designed to create a path from the deep learning frameworks to the existing hardware platforms and optimize according to the features of different hardware platforms as much as possible. The Ascend AI software stack is an Inference Engine developed by Huawei for its Ascend AI processor for developing applications in the deep learning domain. It serves a similar purpose as the TensorRT for the NVIDIA Corporation. Therefore, the software architecture design and optimization strategy of the Ascend AI software stack are closely coupled with the architecture and hardware platform of the Ascend AI processor.

Generally, with the help of the Ascend AI software stack, the development of the deep learning application based on the Ascend AI processor is simple, which includes the following processes. The development tools involved have been introduced in Chapter 4.

(1) **Model generation phase**

The offline model generator converts the model files of other deep learning frameworks and generates offline model files for specific Ascend AI processors. This process involves model parsing, computational graph optimization, and task scheduling. Developers only need to use the model conversion tool in MindStudio or the offline model generator in the DDK suite to complete this step.

(2) **Application compilation phase**

The Ascend AI software stack enables quick development of deep learning applications based on the specific Ascend AI hardware platform. This process involves the concatenation of computing engines and the compilation of the overall application. Developers can create a Mind project in the MindStudio or modify a sample project in the Command Line Interface.

(3) **Application deployment phase**

The applications are deployed on the Ascend AI hardware platform. This process is implemented by a dedicated general service process execution engine. Developers only need to run the application through the MindStudio or run the application on the corresponding device.

In most cases, the preceding processes do not require developers to perform specific programming. If the Ascend AI software stack is insufficient to support operators in the model, developers need to develop customized operators and applications. These contents will be described in Section 5.3.

5.2.1 Model generation phase

5.2.1.1 Model parsing

Like most deep learning inference engines, the Ascend AI software stack needs to parse the network structure and model parameters from the model files of other frameworks. This is done by the offline model generator. The operation is a black-box for developers.

The parsing logic of the offline model generator needs to refer to the parsing code of the corresponding deep learning framework. Take the Caffe framework as an example. The parsing rule of the prototxt used to describe the neural network structure is defined in the caffe.proto file. The corresponding parsing interfaces are obtained by compiling the file using the proto compiler. Based on these interfaces, the offline model generator is able to parse the network structure and model parameters. After parsing the network structure and model parameters, the offline model generator finds the operator implementation provided by the Ascend AI software stack based on the operator name, and then further construct the intermediate representation of the computational graph.

CODE 5.35 Offline model generator help document.

```
-framework    Framework type(0:Caffe; 3:Tensorflow)
```

CODE 5.36 The enumeration of the frameworks supported by the offline model generator.

```
enum FrameworkType
{
    CAFFE = 0,
    TENSORFLOW = 3,
    ANDROID_NN,
    FRAMEWORK_RESERVED,
};
```

As shown in Code 5.35, currently the offline model generator only supports the Caffe and TensorFlow frameworks, which must be specified during the conversion. Code 5.36 is the header file of DDK, which shows that the offline model generator is still being developed to support other deep learning frameworks. As for now, in order to use the model files of other deep learning frameworks, developers have to use conversion tools to convert the model files into the prototxt/caffemodel file of the Caffe framework or the pb file of the TensorFlow.

5.2.1.2 Intermediate representation in the computational graph

After the model is parsed, like most deep learning inference engines, the Ascend AI software stack converts the model into the intermediate representation of the customized computational graph. The work is also performed by the offline model generator, which is also a black-box operation.

The offline model generator has a set of intermediate data structures, which is called Graph Engine (GE). The data structures include Operator (operator node), TensorDesc (tensor description), and TensorPtr (tensor data). These data structures need to be used by developers during customized operator development.

The customized operator development may also involve the runtime tensor representation, which will be described in detail in Section 5.3.

5.2.1.3 Memory allocation

The Ascend AI software stack requires that the shape of the input data be specified when the offline model generator is converting a model. Therefore, during the model conversion, the shape of each tensor is determined, including the data tensor and weight tensor. In this case, we can allocate static memory for all tensors to avoid the overhead caused by dynamic allocation.

The conversion of each operator involves two functions: ParseParamsFn and InferShapeAndTypeFn. As shown in Code 5.37, ParseParamsFn is used to parse function parameters. Message is the message structure parsed from the prototxt. We can obtain parameters from the message structure and save the parameters to the internal Operator node. As shown in Code 5.38, InferShapeAndTypeFn is used to infer the output shape. According to the information in the Operator node, the input data shape and operator parameters can be obtained to determine the shape of the output data.

In addition to static memory allocation, the Ascend AI software stack can also reuse memory to reduce the total allocated memory.

5.2.1.4 Memory layout

As described before, tensor data is generally stored in the NHWC or NCHW format in the deep learning frameworks. In contrast, in the Ascend AI software stack, all tensor data is uniformly stored in a five-dimensional format of NC_1HWC_0 to improve data access efficiency. The C_0 is closely related to the micro architecture, and is equal to the size of the matrix calculation unit in the AI Core, which is 16 for the FP16 type and 32 for the INT8 type. This data needs to be continuously stored. C_1 is the number of C_0 that is contained in C, that is, $C_1 = C/C_0$. If C is not divisible by C_0, the last memory cell in data needs to be padded with zero.

The conversion process of the entire $NHWC \rightarrow NC_1HWC_0$ is as follows:

- Split the NHWC data from the C dimension into C_1 copies of $NHWC_0$.

CODE 5.37 An example of function parameter parsing.

```
Status ReductionParseParams(const Message* op_origin, ge::Operator&
op_des)
```

CODE 5.38 An example of shape inference function.

```
Status ReductionInferShapeAndType(constge::Operator& op,
vector<ge::TensorDesc>& v_output_desc)
```

CODE 5.39 Model weight transfer function.

```
Status ReductionTransWeight(intindex, constge::TensorPtr input,
ge::TensorPtr output)
```

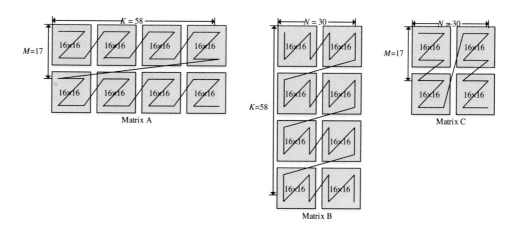

Fig. 5.15

Matrix block multiplication.

- The C_1 copies of $NHWC_0$ are continuously arranged in the memory, resulting in data with form NC_1HWC_0.

The conversion of input and output data needs to be performed online. The conversion of weight parameters can be performed when the offline model generator transforms the model, which mainly involves the TransWeightFn function. As shown in Code 5.39, two TensorPtrs indicate the weight data before and after the conversion.

In addition, when matrix multiplication is performed, the data arrangement format of the matrices needs special attention. An example of matrix block multiplication is shown in Fig. 5.15. The Matrix A of size 17×58 is multiplied by Matrix B of size 58×30, which results in Matrix C of 17×30. To fit matrices into the matrix computation unit of size 16×16, this matrix multiplication utilizes 8 units for each input matrix and 4 units for the output matrix. Because data needs to be stored linearly in memory, these matrices are stored in different sequences in memory, as shown in Fig. 5.15.

In Fig. 5.15, different storage sequences are used to meet a data reading order of matrix computation. For example, the row of the block matrix in matrix A and the column of the block matrix in matrix B are read sequentially. This design can greatly improve the read efficiency and computing performance.

5.2.1.5 Kernel fusion

Like most deep learning frameworks, the kernel fusion of the Ascend AI software stack is also a black-box operation, which is completed by the offline model generator. Therefore, developers are not aware of such operations and do not know what type of kernel fusion optimization is performed.

It is worth mentioning that, in addition to reducing the kernel scheduling overhead, kernel fusion is more important for the Ascend AI processor to fully utilize its advantages of the architecture design. Take the Conv, BN, and ReLU operators as an example. Based on the hardware architecture of the Ascend AI processor described in Chapter 3, the computing process of a typical kernel function is as follows: data is read from the memory to the AI Core, and then goes through multilevel cache, data format conversion, multiple operation units, finally, the data is written back to the memory. If the three operators are implemented by using separate kernel functions, each kernel function can only use some computing units. For example, the Conv uses only the matrix calculation unit, and the BN and ReLU use only the vector-computing unit. In addition, the entire process contains a large amount of memory migration, which leads to high overhead. Therefore, the kernel fusion can complete the matrix operation of the Conv and the vector operation of the BN and ReLU using only one data transmission process, to save the time for memory read/write and transfer, thereby improving inference performance.

5.2.1.6 Operator support

Similar to the cuDNN acceleration library of NVIDIA, the Ascend AI software stack has implemented most common operators. By combining these operators, most deep learning models can be implemented. During model conversion, the offline model generator traverses the operators in the computational graph, finds the corresponding operator implementation, and saves the corresponding kernel function calls. When the offline model is executed, the offline model executor directly calls the kernel function in the runtime library to perform corresponding functions.

Some of the operators are computationally intensive, which can be accelerated by using a matrix and a vector-computing unit, for example, a convolution or a fully connected layer. Such operators are implemented by AI Cores. However, the computation logic of some operators is complex and cannot be accelerated by parallel computing. These operators are implemented through AI CPUs.

5.2.1.7 Offline model file

The offline model file is the model file converted by the offline model generator and can be directly loaded and executed by the AI model manager. Previously, only the computational graph, the kernel function name corresponding to the operator, and the model parameters are saved in the offline model file. The scheduling is performed online by the CPU, which brings extra overhead. Currently, during the generation of the offline model, the computing scheduling is also performed in advance according to the specified hardware platform, including information such as memory allocation and kernel function calls. Therefore, the current offline model file further includes task scheduling information, which includes:

- Overall definition of the model, including the memory size occupied by the model, number of computation flows, number of events, operator list, and target platform information. The structure is defined by the davinci.proto file.
- Task list, which identifies the current task ID, type, flow ID, event ID, kernel function name, and function parameters.

The scheduling information of the model is determined in the offline model, which saves the overhead of online scheduling. However, the scheduling of the offline model is specific to the hardware platform and processor, and various optimization policies in the converted model are closely related to a specific architecture. Therefore, the offline model can only be used on the specific hardware platform and processor.

5.2.2 Application compilation and deployment phase

5.2.2.1 Computing engine

The Ascend AI software stack divides the deep learning applications into multiple computing engines. As shown in Fig. 5.16, an application is represented as a flowchart formed by multiple computing engines. A typical Ascend AI application includes four computing engines:

- Data engine: acquires data from data sources such as cameras and files.
- Preprocessing engine: directly uses the interfaces provided by the DVPP to preprocess media data, including video and image decoding, image cropping, and resizing.
- Model Inference engine: uses the interface provided by the AI model manager to load the offline model file to perform inference.
- Postprocessing engine: it is used to postprocess the output.

Flowchart

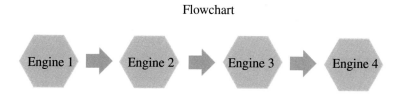

Fig. 5.16
Flowchart of computing engines.

Such a division of computing engines can decouple the computation of different tasks in the application so that each computing engine can independently complete its own functions. For example, the preprocessing engine is responsible for using the DVPP module to complete the preprocessing function, and the model inference engine is specifically responsible for loading and executing the offline model. The computing engine can be customized by the developers. The main functions that control the computing engine can also be developed by users. These contents are described in Section 5.3.

As mentioned in Chapter 4, the Ascend AI processor may come with different hardware platforms, such as the acceleration card and Atlas development board. On these two hardware platforms, the application may have different computing processes. As shown in Fig. 4.5, in the acceleration card setting, the data engine and postprocessing engine run on the host side. In contrast, as shown in Fig. 4.7, the Atlas developer board scenario, all computing engines run on the device. Therefore, dividing an application into computing engines according to different computing tasks can help shield details of a bottom-layer hardware platform, and let the Ascend AI software stack take care of the different compilation tools needed for different running ends.

5.2.2.2 Application development based on multiple devices and multiple processors

Take the accelerator card of the Ascend AI processor as an example. There are several possible scenarios, as follows:

- Multiple acceleration cards are mounted on the server. These acceleration cards need to complete an inference task together or each of them completes an inference task.
- One acceleration card is used to complete multiple inference tasks at the same time.
- Each accelerator card has multiple Ascend AI processors. These Ascend AI processors need to complete an inference task together or each processor completes an inference task.
- Multiple inference tasks need to be completed on one Ascend AI processor.

For the Ascend Atlas developer board, there is only one Ascend AI processor, and there is no collaborative computation among multiple developer boards. The possible scenario will be performing multiple offline model inference.

Considering all the aforementioned scenarios, the following things need to be considered during application development:

- Whether there is a single application or multiple applications needed to be run on the hardware platform.
- Single thread or multiple threads. Whether each application needs to start multiple threads to complete inference tasks.
- Whether a single processor is sufficient or multiple processors are required to complete the task.

For details, see the Ascend 310 Application Development Guide.

5.2.2.3 Operator scheduling

As mentioned previously, the operator may be executed on the AI Core or the AI CPU of the Ascend AI processor. When running an offline model, the CPU manages multiple AI Cores and AI CPUs, and delivers the operator kernel functions parsed from the offline model to the task scheduler. The task scheduler then delivers the data to the specific AI Core and AI CPU.

The CPU performs the following management:

- Memory management: after the model conversion is completed, all the memory can be statically allocated. The CPU manages the allocated memory addresses.
- Device management: manages the status of all computing devices (AI CPU and AI Core).
- Computing flow management: integrates kernel calls implemented by multiple operators into a computing flow. In a computing flow, multiple AI CPUs and AI Cores can be used to complete a task.
- Event management: manages messages such as data synchronization.

As mentioned in the previous chapters, the parallel structure and data synchronization in the model can be utilized to greatly improve the inferencing performance. For example, multiple branches of the Inception structure can be computed at the same time, by using multiple computing streams and then performing data synchronization. Therefore, the computing flow and event management are the key factors that determine whether the computing resources are properly utilized and the inferencing performance is optimized. This is determined by the offline model generator based on the specific processor and hardware platform when the model is converted.

In addition, no matter how many inference tasks are executed on a processor at the same time, the CPU only needs to manage the corresponding memory, device, computing flow, and event according to the requirements delivered by the model manager. The task scheduler only needs to deliver the operator kernel functions to the specific AI Core and AI CPU according to the CPU control. This design shields a specific scheduling process from an upper-layer application so that a developer can perform multiple inference tasks on the same processor at the same time.

5.2.2.4 Heterogeneous computing system

In the Ascend AI software stack, AI CPU and AI Core are used as heterogeneous devices to perform the entire computing process under the control of CPU scheduling. This is similar to that of the popular CPU+GPU heterogeneous computing system. For an operator kernel function, we need to start it at the host end, then specify its computing device and put it into a computing flow. After multiple such kernel functions are put into a computing flow, the computing flow can be started.

Codes 5.40 and 5.41 show the calling function on the CPU and the kernel function declaration on the AI CPU. The former uses a special mechanism to specify a computing flow to call the

---

CODE 5.40 The calling function on CPU.

```
voidopHost(...)
{
opKernel<<<1, NULL, stream>>>(...);
}
```

CODE 5.41 The kernel function on AI CPU.

```
__global__ __aicpu__ void opKernel(...);
```

---

kernel function of the AI CPU. In addition, the kernel function will specify the corresponding computing device. This is similar to CUDA.

5.2.2.5 Operator implementation-common kernel and customized kernel

The Ascend AI software stack provides the precompiled operator implementation, which are kernel functions developed by Huawei engineers using specific programming languages highly optimized for the DaVinci architecture. Developers are not given access to this level of programming at present.

These operators are compiled in advance and are implemented as common kernels to support universality. In order to improve inference performance, the Ascend AI software stack is inspired by the TVM design concept. When the offline model generator performs a model conversion, a customized kernel is provided for specific input data shapes and parameter configurations to improve inference performance.

The Ascend AI software stack incorporates the back-end code generation capability based on the existing TVM. That is, based on the existing TVM code, the back-end code can be quickly generated by adding computing scheduling for the DaVinci architecture feature. Therefore, the TVM mechanism can be used to quickly compile and generate the customized kernel functions on the Ascend AI processor.

Similar to the TOPI mechanism of TVM, the Ascend AI software stack encapsulates the scheduling code of the DaVinci architecture and provides operation interfaces, which are specific domain languages for the Ascend AI processor. By combining these specific domain languages, operators can be developed. These operators are usually called TBE operators. As shown in Code 5.42, similar to the development of the TVM operator, the specific domain language defined by the Ascend AI software stack can be called to quickly compile and generate a customized kernel for the DaVinci architecture.

CODE 5.42 An example of TBE operator.

```
data = tvm.placeholder(shape1, name="data_input", dtype=inp_dtype)
# For Ascend AI processor
with tvm.target.cce():
    # compute absolute value
    res = te.lang.cce.vabs(data)
    sch = generic.auto_schedule(res)
config = {...}
te.lang.cce.cce_build_code(sch, config)
```

The offline model generator compiles and generates a customized kernel based on the TBE operators and the existing function parameters. The customized kernel is used to replace the operators that are originally implemented by the Ascend AI software stack, thereby improving the overall inferencing performance.

5.3 Customized operator development

In the Ascend AI software stack, the internally implemented operators can be directly used. These operators are highly optimized by the Huawei engineers, which can adapt well to the underlying hardware architecture and have good performance.

In addition, the Ascend AI software stack allows developers to develop customized operators based on their own requirements. These operators can run on the AI CPU or AI Core. Developers can implement operators using C++ or the TVM mechanism.

5.3.1 Development procedure

5.3.1.1 Development motivation

In most cases, the Ascend AI software stack has the required operators implemented; therefore, developers do not need to implement the operator again. They only need to provide the deep learning model file, and the offline model generator will produce the offline model files. After that, the process orchestrator can generate specific applications. However, developers may need to develop customized operator in the following cases:

- The Ascend AI software stack does not have the operators in the model.
- The developer wants to modify the computation logic in the existing operator.
- The developer wants to develop operators to improve computational efficiency.

5.3.1.2 Development process

The customized operator development process includes the following steps:

> Step 1: create a customized operator development project. You can create a project in the integration development environment or modify the sample project provided by the DDK.
> Step 2: customized operator development. Develop different methods according to the operator type.
> Step 3: customized plug-in development. The plug-in is called by the offline model generator and provides functions such as parameter parsing, shape inference, and kernel compilation.
> Step 4: load the plug-in for model conversion. When the offline model generator converts the model, the plug-in is involved to parse parameters, infer the tensor shape, compile the operator provided in step 2 into the kernel function, and insert the kernel into the offline model.

Customized operator and plug-in development are required to be done by the developer.

5.3.1.3 Customized operator development

Operators can run on AI CPU and AI Core. The operators for the AI CPU and AI Core are developed in different ways.

The AI CPU itself is an ARM processor. Therefore, the development based on the AI CPU is the same as programming in C++, which only requires to comply with the established data format. The Code 5.43 shows the function declaration of an AI CPU customized operator, which is explained as follows:

(1) __global__:
Similar to the function prefix of CUDA, it indicates that the function is a kernel function that is called by the CPU and runs on AI CPU or AI Core.
(2) __aicpu__:
Similar to the function prefix of CUDA, it indicates that the kernel function runs on AI CPU.
(3) inputDesc and outputDesc:

CODE 5.43 AI CPU operator function.

```
__global____aicpu__voidoperator(opTensor_t*inputDesc,constvoid**
inputArray, opTensor_t * outputDesc, void ** outputArray, void *
opAttrHandle)
```

opTensor_t structure type, which is used to describe the information about input and output tensors, including the tensor type and dimension information.

(4) inputArray and outputArray:

void ** pointers to the address that stores the actual tensor data.

(5) opattr_handle:

Pointer to the address of the structure that stores the parameters of the kernel function. Although the source file that contains this function definition has a Huawei internal format suffix, it does not actually contain any features related to the DaVinci architecture.

In contrast, the AI Core operator development is more complex, which includes the following two methods:

Development using the TVM primitives

The Ascend AI software stack adds back-end code generation based on TVM. Therefore, this development is essentially the same as that of TVM. For details, see Code 5.26. However, the computation scheduling needs to take into consideration the specific DaVinci architecture, it requires to master the use of the scheduling primitive to complete the data tiling to achieve good performance. Therefore, this method is recommended only for developers who are very familiar with TVM programming as well as the DaVinci architecture.

Domain-specific language development

To facilitate the development of customized operator, the Ascend AI software stack uses the mechanism similar to TOPI of TVM to provide some common computing scheduling and encapsulate them into interfaces, which are called domain-specific languages dedicated for AI Core operations. For example, in the TBE operator example shown in Code 5.42, the developer only needs to use the domain-specific language to declare the computation process and then use the automatic scheduling (auto_schedule) mechanism to specify the target code generation, which can be further compiled into a customized kernel.

The entire computation may be represented as a process in which multiple input tensors are used by one computing node to output multiple tensors. In fact, the development process of the TVM primitive is similar to that of the domain-specific language, but the abstraction level of the development is different. The operators developed by using the two methods are both called TBE operators. The customized kernel is generated by using the offline model generator.

5.3.1.4 Customized plug-in development

The plug-in is developed by the C++ code and compiled into a dynamic link library (DLL). The DLL is used by the offline model generator. The key is to define functions such as parameter parsing and shape inference and to register the customized operator through the registration mechanism provided by the offline model generator.

CODE 5.44 **Customized operator registration for AI CPU.**

```
REGISTER_CUSTOM_OP("test_layer")
    .FrameworkType(CAFFE)
    .OriginOpType("Test")
    .ParseParamsFn(ParseParams)
    .InferShapeAndTypeFn(InferShapeAndType)
    .UpdateOpDescFn(UpdateOpDesc)
    .ImplyType(ImplyType::AI_CPU);
```

CODE 5.45 **Customized operator registration for AI Core.**

```
REGISTER_CUSTOM_OP("test_layer")
    .FrameworkType(CAFFE)
    .OriginOpType("Test")
    .ParseParamsFn(ParseParams)
    .InferShapeAndTypeFn(InferShapeAndType)
    .TEBinBuildFn(BuildTeBin)
    .ImplyType(ImplyType::TVM);
```

Codes 5.44 and 5.45 show the customized operator registration codes of AI CPU and AI Core, respectively.

Some explanation of the codes is as follows. Note that the data structure such as Operator and TensorDesc indicates the intermediate node of the graph during the conversion of the model and the opTensor_t in the kernel function parameter in the Code 5.43 is the tensor type during actual running.

(1) REGISTER_CUSTOM_OP: Register customized operator. "test_layer" is the operator name in the offline model file. It can be any name as long as it does not conflict with an existing operator name.
(2) FrameworkType: Different parsing logic is needed for different frameworks. The plug-in registration code must indicate the corresponding framework. Currently, only Caffe and TensorFlow are supported.
(3) OriginOpType: The operator name must be the same as the one defined in Caffe Prototxt or TensorFlow. Otherwise, the operator name cannot be parsed.
(4) ParseParamsFn: This step is used to register the function that parses model parameters. This step is required only when the plug-in is developed for the Caffe framework. The parameter parsing of the TensorFlow is completed by the framework.
The function definition is shown in Code 5.46. The Message is the message structure of the protobuf used in Caffe. The parameter of the customized operator is defined by the

---

CODE 5.46 **Parameter parsing function.**

```
Status ParseParams(const Message* op_origin, ge::Operator& op_dest)
```

CODE 5.47 **Shape and type inference function.**

```
Status ReductionInferShapeAndType(const  ge::Operator&  op,
vector<ge::TensorDesc>& v_output_desc)
```

---

developer. Therefore, the developer needs to parse the parameter according to the format they define in the caffe.proto. op_origin is the definition of computing node in the Ascend AI software stack. The entire function parses parameters and saves the parameters to op_dest node.

(5) InferShapeAndTypeFn: This function is used to register shape and type inference functions.

The function definition is shown in Code 5.47. op is a computing node, which stores the input tensor description and various operator parameters. v_output_desc stores all output tensor descriptions of the computing node. This function determines the output tensor description, including the tensor shape, type, and data arrangement format, based on the input tensor description, operator logic, and operator parameters.

(6) UpdateOpDescFn: This is used to register the function that updates the customized operator description and is used only in the development of the AI CPU operator. The function definition is shown in Code 5.48. This function gets the parameter information in the op and saves it in the parameter structure OpAttr defined by the developer.

(7) TEBinBuildFn: This is used to register the compilation function of the TBE operator. It is used only in the development of the AI Core operator. It uses C++ to call Python and uses the TVM backend code generation mechanism to generate the specific kernel.

The function definition is shown in Code 5.49, where op stores various information of the operator, and tb_bin_info stores the compiled kernel path and JSON file path.

(8) ImplyType: This specifies the implementation mode of the operator. ImplyType::AI_CPU indicates that the operator is implemented for the AI CPU, and ImplyType::TVM indicates that the operator is implemented for the AI Core.

5.3.1.5 *Load the plug-in for model conversion*

When the offline model generator loads plug-ins for model conversion, the AI CPU and AI Core operators have slightly different procedures. The difference is whether to load the binary file generated by compiling the customized operator or not.

CODE 5.48 Operator description update function.

```
Status ReductionUpdateOpDesc(ge::Operator& op)
```

CODE 5.49 Operator compiling function.

```
Status BuildTeBin(const ge::Operator& op, TEBinInfo& te_bin_info)
```

As shown in Fig. 5.17, for the development of customized operator for the AI CPU, we need to compile both the plug-in code and the operator code into binary files. When converting the model, the offline model generator first loads the binary file of the plug-in to register operators, perform operations such as parameter parsing, shape, and type inference. Then the offline model generator loads the customized operator binary file to the offline model file, which is called during model inference.

As shown in Fig. 5.18, for the development of customized operator for AI Core, only the customized plug-in code is compiled into a binary file for the AI Core development. Therefore, when converting the model, the offline model generator loads a binary file of the plug-in to register an operator and performs operations such as parameter parsing, shape, and type inference. After that, the generator converts the custom operator into a unified intermediate representation and compiles the customized operator according to the parsed information. The compiled kernel is a customized kernel, which is put into the offline model file and called during model inference.

5.3.2 AI CPU operator development

5.3.2.1 Features of the reduction operator

Reduction is an operator in Caffe. It performs the reduction operation on the specified axis and the subsequent axis of the multidimensional array data. Reduction contains the following parameters to be parsed.

Parameter parsing

(1) ReductionOp: Reduction options supported by the operator, including four types (see Table 5.2).
(2) axis: An axis needs to be specified. The reduction is performed on the axis and its subsequent axis. For example, suppose that the input tensor shape is [5, 6, 7, 8].
    If the specified axis is 3, the shape of the output tensor is [5, 6, 7].
    If the specified axis is 2, the shape of the output tensor is [5, 6].

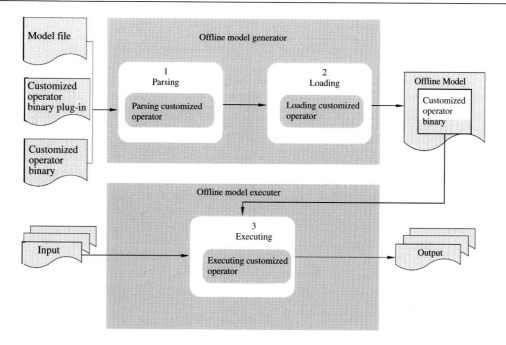

Fig. 5.17
Offline model generator loads the binary files for AI CPU.

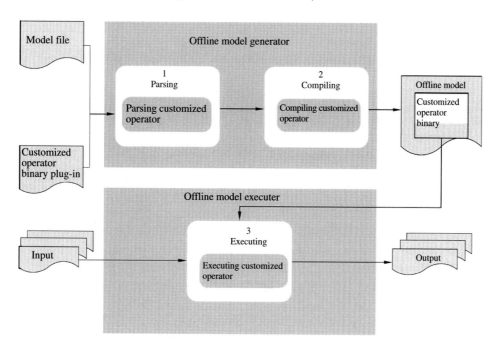

Fig. 5.18
Offline model generator loads the binary files for AI Core.

Table 5.2: Reduction operations.

Option	Description
SUM	Sum up all the numbers that need to be reduced
ASUM	Sum up the absolute values of the numbers
SUMSQ	Sum up the squared values of the numbers
MEAN	Reduction using the mean value

Table 5.3: Reduction operator inputs.

Input	Description
x	Input data, its size defined by shape
shape	N dimensional tensor
dtype	Data type, e.g., float16, float32
axis	The specified reduction axis, in $[-N, N-1]$.
op	Reduction operation: SUM, ASUM, SUMSQ, MEAN
coeff	Scalar

If the specified axis is 1, the shape of the output tensor is [5].

If the specified axis is 0, the shape of the output tensor is [1].

(3)   coeff: A scalar, which is used to scale the result.

Input and output parameters

The input and output of the Reduction operator are as follows:

(1)   Input parameter (see Table 5.3).

(2)   Output parameter:

y: its data type is the same as the input data x, while its shape is determined by the input shape and the specified axis.

5.3.2.2 Create a customized operator project

Table 5.4 lists the core source code in a project of a customized operator of AI CPU.

(1)   Reduction.cce, Reduction.h, operator.cce, and op_attr.h are responsible for the operator computation logic. Reduction.cce and op_attr.h need to be modified by developers.

(2)   The Reduction_parser.cpp is responsible for the plug-in computation logic and needs to be modified by developers.

5.3.2.3 Operator logic development

Fig. 5.19 shows the computation logic of the customized operator.

operator.cce

Table 5.4: Core source code for AI CPU operator.

Directory	File	Description
operator (Customized operator folder)	Reduction.cce	Operator source code
	Reduction.h	Head file for the operator
	operator.cce	Shared codes for operators
	Makefile	Compile rules
Reduction_plugin (Customized plug-in folder)	Reduction_parser.cpp	Parameter parsing code
	Makefile	Compile rules
common (parameter configuration folder)	custom_op.cfg	Definition of input/output
	op_attr.cpp	Parameter assignment file
	op_attr.h	Head file for parameter structure

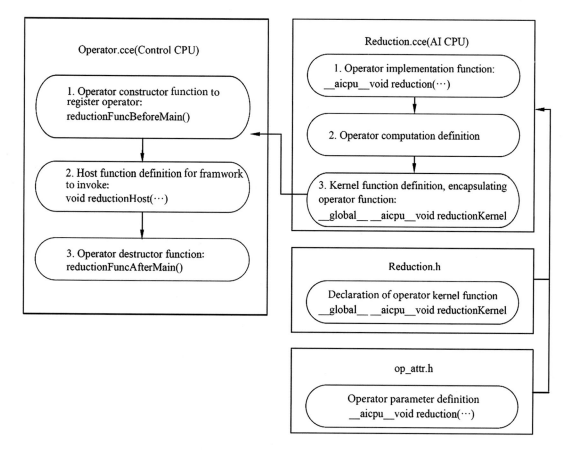

Fig. 5.19
AI CPU operator computation logic.

CODE 5.50 Operator constructor.

```
void __attribute__((constructor)) reductionFuncBeforeMain()
{
    char opetype[50] = "reduction_layer";
    RegisterAicpuRunFunc(opetype, reductionHost);
}
```

CODE 5.51 The declaration of the RegisterAicpuRunFunc function.

```
extern "C"
{
    extern void RegisterAicpuRunFunc(const char * om_optype,
aicpu_run_func op_runner_func);
}
```

The file contains three functions: operator constructors, operator destructors, and functions called by the operator host.

The operator constructor function is shown in Code 5.50. First, the name "reduction_layer" of the customized operator must be defined. This name must match the name used for plug-in registration. Second, RegisterAicpuRunFunc function is used to register the operator. Opetype is the operator name, and reductionHost is the function called by the operator host. The RegisterAicpuRunFunc function declaration is shown in Code 5.51. This function is implemented by the model manager.

In Code 5.51, aicpu_run_func is the type of the function called by the operator host, which is defined in Code 5.52. The parameter list indicates the input tensor description, input tensor data, input data size, output tensor description, output tensor data, output data size, operator parameters, and computation flow.

The function which calls the Reduction operator on the host is shown in Code 5.53. The function parameters are omitted here. Most importantly, reductionKernel is a kernel function that actually runs on AI CPU. The CPU uses a mechanism similar to CUDA to start the kernel function. In <<<>>>, 1 indicates the number of started AI CPUs, and stream specifies the computing stream where the current kernel is located.

The operator destructor does not perform any operations. Developers can add any operations as required.

CODE 5.52 Definition of the function called by the HOST.

```
typedef void (*aicpu_run_func)(opTensor_t **, void **, int32_t,
opTensor_t **, void **, int32_t, void *, rtStream_t);
```

CODE 5.53 The host function which calls the reduction operator.

```
void reductionHost(...)
{
    reductionKernel<<<1, NULL, stream>>>(...);
}
```

CODE 5.54 Definition of the parameter structure.

```
typedef struct {
    char operation[ATRPARAMNAMESIZE];
    int64_t axis;
    float coeff;
} OpAttr;
```

op_attr.h

As shown in Code 5.54, this header file is used to define the operator parameter structure, which is used by both the operator development code and the plug-in code.

Reduction.h

The function declaration is shown in Code 5.55:

- __global__: similar to the prefix of the CUDA function, it indicates that this is a kernel function.
- __aicpu__: similar to the prefix of the CUDA function, it indicates that the kernel function runs on the AI CPU.
- inputDesc: input data description;
- inputArray: input data array;
- outputDesc: output data description;
- outputArray: output data array;
- opattr_handle: pointer to the structure of the operator parameter. The corresponding structure is defined in the op_attr.h file.

CODE 5.55 The declaration of the operator kernel function.

```
__global__ __aicpu__ void reductionKernel(opTensor_t ** input-
Desc, constvoid ** inputArray, opTensor_t ** outputDesc, void**
outputArray, void * opattr_handle);
```

Reduction.cce

The source code needs to be programmed by developers, which includes two functions: operator kernel function and operator function. The parameters of the two functions are the same, and the operator kernel function is used to encapsulate the operator function.

This example only shows some of the implementations of the summation operation in the Reduction operator. Other operations can be modified accordingly.

The operator parameters can be obtained as shown in Code 5.56.

Code 5.57 demonstrates how to obtain the data of the first input tensor and the first output tensor. Similarly, other tensor data may be obtained by specifying the index of the inputArray and the outputArray.

As shown in Code 5.58, the dimensions, shapes, and types of input and output tensors can be obtained using inputDesc and outputDesc.

The Code 5.59 shows the implementation of the summation function of the Reduction operator, which sums up the elements of the array based on the specified axis.

5.3.2.4 Operator plug-in development

Operator plug-in development involves the implementation of Reduction_parser.cpp. The most important components are the operator registration function, operator parameter parsing function, the function that obtains the operator output description, and the function that update the operator description.

Operator registration

As shown in Code 5.60, the "reduction_layer" is the customized operator name, which must be the same as the operator name declared in operator.cce. The framework is Caffe, and the corresponding operator is Reduction, and the operator is implemented for AI CPU.

ReductionParseParams: This function is used for parsing operator parameters

The function declaration is the same as that in the Code 5.46. The core code is shown in Code 5.61, which converts the Message class to the LayerParameter subclass, which is used to store layer parameters in Caffe. After that, the function parameters can be obtained by calling

---

CODE 5.56 **The code for obtaining operator parameter.**

```
int64_t axis = ((OpAttr *) opAttrHandle)->axis;
```

CODE 5.57 **The code for obtaining input and output data.**

```
constvoid *x = inputArray[0];
void *y = outputArray[0];
```

CODE 5.58 **The code for obtaining the input and output tensors information.**

```
int in_dim_cnt = inputDesc[0]->dim_cnt;
int out_dim_cnt = outputDesc[0]->dim_cnt;
```

---

the reduction_param function. ReductionParameter is the parameter obtained from the caffe.proto. Based on the parameters, we can set parameters for the computing node defined in the Ascend AI software stack.

InferShapeAndTypeFn: This function is used for inferring output shapes and types

The function declaration is the same as that in the Code 5.47. The core code is shown in Code 5.62. First, op is used to obtain the input tensor description, and the function parameter is obtained. Then the output tensor description is modified according to the function parameter, which is saved to the v_output_desc output tensor description array.

UpdateOpDescFn: This function is used to update the operator description

The function declaration is the same as that in the Code 5.48. The core code is shown in Code 5.63. This function is used to obtain various parameters from the computing node and write the data to the op node according to the structure defined by the op_attr.h, so that the operator can directly obtain operator parameters from the function parameter opAttrHandle.

5.3.3 AI Core operator development

5.3.3.1 Reduction operator features

The Reduction operator feature is the same as that in Section 5.3.2.

CODE 5.59 The implementation of the summation option of the reduction operator.

```
int dimAxisInner = 1;
int dimAxisOuter = 1;
T sum = 0;
T* pDst = (T*) y;
const T* pSrc = (const T*) x;

// Compute the number of entries after summation
for (int i = 0; i < axis; i++) {
    dimAxisInner = dimAxisInner * inputDesc->dim[i];
}
// Compute the number of entries that need to be summed up
for (int i = axis + 1; i < inputDesc->dim_cnt; i++) {
    dimAxisOuter = dimAxisOuter * inputDesc->dim[i];
}
// compute the summation
for (int idxDimOuter = 0; idxDimOuter < dimAxisOuter; idxDimOuter
++) {
    const T* pSrcOuter = (const T*) x + idxDimOuter * dimAxisInner
* inputDesc->dim[axis];
 for (int idxAxisInner = 0; idxAxisInner < dimAxisInner; idxAxi-
sInner++) {
    sum = 0;
    pSrc = pSrcOuter + idxAxisInner;
    for (int j = 0; j < inputDesc->dim[axis]; j++) {
     T value = *(pSrc + j * dimAxisInner);
     sum = sum + value;
    }
    *pDst = sum;
    pDst++;
 }
}
```

CODE 5.60 Reduction operator registration (AI CPU).

```
REGISTER_CUSTOM_OP("reduction_layer")
    .FrameworkType(CAFFE)
    .OriginOpType("Reduction")
    .ParseParamsFn(ReductionParseParams)
    .InferShapeAndTypeFn(ReductionInferShapeAndType)
    .UpdateOpDescFn(ReductionUpdateOpDesc)
    .ImplyType(ImplyType::AI_CPU);
```

CODE 5.61 Core code of the parameter parsing function.

```
const              caffe::LayerParameter*          layer          =
dynamic_cast<constcaffe::LayerParameter*>(op_origin);
const caffe::ReductionParameter& param = layer->reduction_param();
op_dest.SetAttr("axis",
AttrValue::CreateFrom<AttrValue::INT>(param.axis()));
```

CODE 5.62 Core code for shape and type inference.

```
auto tensorDesc = op.GetInputDesc(0);
auto shape = tensorDesc.GetShape();
ge::AttrValue axisAttrValue;
op.GetAttr("axis", axisAttrValue);
axisAttrValue.GetValue<AttrValue::INT>(axis);
// Modify tensorDesc according to function parameters
tensorDesc.SetShape(shape);
v_output_desc.push_back(tensorDesc);
```

CODE 5.63 Core code for updating operator description.

```
OpAttr op_attr;

int64_t axis = 0;
ge::AttrValue axisAttrValue;
op.GetAttr("axis", axisAttrValue)
axisAttrValue.GetValue<AttrValue::INT>(axis))
op_attr.axis = axis;

std::string key = "opattr";
Buffer bytes = Buffer::CopyFrom((uint8_t *)&op_attr, sizeof(OpAttr));
op.SetAttr(key, AttrValue::CreateFrom<AttrValue::BYTES>(bytes));
```

5.3.3.2 Create an operator project

Table 5.5 shows the core source code for an AI Core operator project. In comparison to the AI CPU operator project, the AI Core operator project is simpler, the most important of which are the following two files.

- reduction.py: this file is the Python program based on the domain-specific language, which implements the operator computation logic and needs to be completed by developers.

Table 5.5: Source code for AI Core project.

Directory	File	Description
operator Plug-in	reduction.py caffe_reduction_layer.cpp Makefile	Operator source code Plug-in source code Compile rules

- caffe_reduction_layer.cpp: developers need to implement the operator plug-in logic in this file.

5.3.3.3 Operator logic development

The development process of the AI Core operator based on the domain-specific language is the same as that of the TVM development. The development process is described as follows.

Import the Python module

Code 5.64 shows the Python module provided by the Ascend AI software stack. The te.lang.cce includes the specific domain language interfaces of common operations such as vmuls, vadds, and matmul. te.tvm introduces the TVM back-end code generation mechanism. Topi.generic provides interfaces for automatic operator scheduling. Topi.cce.util provides tools such as data shape and category verification.

Definition of the operator function

As shown in Code 5.65, the function of an operator contains the shape, type, operator parameters, operator kernel name, and compilation and printing configuration of the input tensor. This function is called by the plug-in code through the Python interface of C++ and executed when the offline model generator performs the model conversion.

Operator logic implementation

A typical Reduction summation computation logic is shown in Code 5.66. It can be seen that this is consistent with the TVM development. The tensor placeholders for the input data need to be defined, and then the various specific domain language interfaces in the te.lang.cce can be used. As shown in the code, data is the input tensor, res is the output tensor, and vmuls (vector multiplication), sum (sum), and cast (type conversion) are used to generate the result.

Operator scheduling and compilation

After the computing logic is defined, the corresponding scheduling can be automatically generated by using the auto_schedule mechanism, as shown in Code 5.67. Here, the intermediate representation can be seen by using the printing mechanism of the TVM. The "config" includes information about whether to print, build, and also includes operator kernel names, and input and output tensor list.

CODE 5.64 Import python modules.

```
import te.lang.cce
from te import tvm
from topi import generic
from topi.cce import util
```

CODE 5.65 Operator function.

```
def reduction(shape, dtype, axis, op, coeff, kernel_name="Reduction",
need_build=True, need_print=False)
```

CODE 5.66 The implementation of operator computing logic.

```
data = tvm.placeholder(shape1, name="data_input", dtype=inp_dtype)
with tvm.target.cce():
    cof = coeff
    data_tmp_input = te.lang.cce.vmuls(data, cof)
    tmp = data_tmp_input
    res_tmp = te.lang.cce.sum(tmp, axis=axis)
    res = te.lang.cce.cast_to(res_tmp, inp_dtype, f1628IntegerFlag=True)
```

CODE 5.67 Operator compilation.

```
sch = generic.auto_schedule(res)
config = {
    "print_ir": need_print,
    "need_build": need_build,
    "name": kernel_name,
    "tensor_list": [data, res]
}
te.lang.cce.cce_build_code(sch, config)
```

Note that the input and output tensors are saved in the tensor list. The order must be arranged according to the input and output data sequence of the operator.

Finally, the cce_build_code interface provided by the te.lang.cce can be used to compile the operator based on the scheduling and configuration. The customized operator kernel is generated based on the input data shape, category, and operator parameters. This process occurs when the offline model generator converts the model.

5.3.3.4 Operator plug-in development

The development process of the operator plug-in is similar to that in Section 5.3.2. The most important components of the AI Core operator plug-in development are operator registration, operator parameter parsing function, operator output description inference function, and the TBE operator compilation function.

The parameter parsing function and the output description inference function of the AI Core plug-in are the same as those of the AI CPU plug-in. The AI Core operator does not need to update the operator description function, instead, it must have the TBE compilation function.

Operator registration

The registration code of the Reduction operator is shown in Code 5.68. In the code, "custom_reduction" can be specified in a way that it does not conflict with the existing operator name in the offline model file. The plug-in code is for the Caffe framework. The corresponding operators are implemented by the TVM for the AI Core.

TEBinBuildFn: This function is used to compile operators

The function declaration is the same as that in Code 5.49. This function is called when the offline model generator performs a model conversion. It mainly completes the following processes:

Obtain all tensor information, including shape, type, and various operator parameters. This information has been determined during the model conversion.
Specify the operator implementation file, operator function, and kernel name.
Specify the file path for the generated kernel and the JSON file containing kernel information.
Call the te::BuildCustomop function to use the Python function to compile the operator.

CODE 5.68 Reduction operator registration (AI Core).

```
REGISTER_CUSTOM_OP("custom_reduction")
     .FrameworkType(CAFFE)
     .OriginOpType("Reduction")
     .ParseParamsFn(CaffeReductionParseParams)
     .InferShapeAndTypeFn(CaffeReductionInferShapeAndType)
     .TEBinBuildFn(CaffeReductionBuildTeBin)
     .ImplyType(ImplyType::TVM);
```

CODE 5.69 Compile customized TBE operator.

```
te::BuildTeCustomOp(..., "(i,i,i,i), s, i, s, f, s", ...);
```

The BuildCustomop function is shown in Code 5.69. For details about the function declaration, see the "include/inc/custom/custom_op.h" file under the DDK installation path. The parameters that are omitted are its own configuration parameters, including the version of the DDK. The "(i, i, i, i), s, i, s, f, s" is the same as the definition of the operator implementation function in Code 5.65. i represents integer data, s represents the string type, f represents the single-precision floating-point type, and the rest of the parameters indicate the corresponding parameter values. The BuildCustomop calls the operator implementation function based on these parameters, generates the kernel using the TVM mechanism, and then saves the kernel in the specified path.

5.4 Customized application development

The Ascend AI software stack allows users to develop computing engines based on their own requirements. In addition, it allows the user to configure the serial and parallel computing modes among computing engines according to the actual application scenarios and device conditions.

5.4.1 Development motivations

The Ascend AI software stack has many predefined computing engines, which can be used to resize images or load offline model files for inference. However, developers may need to develop computing engines based on the actual application requirements. Several such scenarios are listed as follows:

(1) The application has a special requirement for reading data. For example, acquiring data from a camera, reading data from a local file, or obtaining data from a network flow. In this case, the user may need to develop a data engine based on the specific requirements.
(2) The data needs to be preprocessed, for example, the video or image needs to be decoded, or the image needs to be cropped and resized. In this case, the preprocessing engine needs to be developed based on the requirements.
(3) The model requires a special input data format. For example, the image data is no longer the 224×224 size, or the data is not RGB but YUV. In this case, the user needs to develop the model inference engine based on the requirements.

(4) The data needs to be postprocessed, for example, saving the model inference result to files, or showing the category and probability information on the corresponding image. In this case, a postprocessing engine needs to be developed.

(5) Sometimes additional processing flows need to be added according to requirements. In this case, a new computing engine needs to be defined to complete the corresponding work.

5.4.2 Development process

The customized application development process based on the Ascend AI processor generally includes the following steps:

(1) Create an application development project, inside of which create a source file and a header file for each computing engine, and develop corresponding functions for them.

(2) Create a configuration file for the flowchart and configure the connection among the computing engines.

(3) Create a main function source file to control the logic of the entire application, including the construction, running, and destruction of the flow chart.

(4) Select the compiler tool based on the configuration of the computing engine to build the application.

5.4.3 Serial configuration of the computing engine

In an application project, the flow chart of the application is stored in a prototxt file, where the configuration of the computing engine and the connection among them are specified. Similar to the prototxt file of Caffe, the configuration information is stored using the protobuf library. The parameter format is defined in the proto file. For detailed example about the prototxt file, see the "./sample/hiaiengine/test_data/config/sample.prototxt" file in the DDK installation path. The corresponding proto file is "include/inc/proto/graph_config.proto" in the DDK installation path.

The typical configuration file of a flowchart contains three types of messages:

(1) Flowchart message, the graphs, as shown in Code 5.70. A flowchart message contains the graph ID, priority, device ID, multiple computing engines, and connection messages (connects). In this example code, there are three computing engines and two connections. It should be noted that a flowchart may be run on one or more processors, and may also be run on multiple PCIe cards. In order to run on different processors, a device ID needs to be specified. By default, only the processor whose ID is 0 is used.

(2) Computing engine message, the engines, as shown in Code 5.71. A computing engine message contains information such as the ID, engine name, running side, and number of threads.

```
CODE 5.70  Flowchart message.

graphs {
    graph_id: 100
    priority: 1
    device_id: 0
    engines {...}
    engines {...}
    engines {...}
    connects {...}
    connects {...}
}
```

```
CODE 5.71  Computing engine message.

engines {
    id: 1000
    engine_name: "SrcEngine"
    side: HOST
    thread_num: 1
}
```

It should be noted that the running side determines whether the engine runs on the host or the device. The digital vision preprocessing (DVPP) engine and the inference engine must run on the device, which is the Ascend AI processor. While the running side of the data preparation engine and data postprocessing engine need to be determined based on the hardware platform. For example, for the Atlas 200 development board which has the Ubuntu system, the data preparation engine and data postprocessing engine run on the device. On the PCIe accelerator card, the data preparation engine and data postprocessing engine usually run on the host.

(3) Engine connection message, the connects. As shown in Code 5.72, the ID of the two engines and the ID of the engine port are included.

5.4.4 Computing engine development

Code 5.73 shows a declaration template for a customized engine. All header files related to the computing engine are defined in "include/inc/hiaiengine" of DDK. In Code 5.73:

(1) The customized computing engine class inherits the Engine parent class. The name of the computing engine subclass can be specified.

CODE 5.72 Engine connection message.

```
connects {
     src_engine_id: 1000
     src_port_id: 0
     target_engine_id: 1001
     target_port_id: 0
}
```

CODE 5.73 Declaration template for a customized engine.

```
#include "hiaiengine/api.h"
#define ENGINE_INPUT_SIZE 1
#define ENGINE_OUTPUT_SIZE 1
using hiai::Engine;

class CustomEngine : public Engine {
public:
     // only model inference engine needs to overload this function
     HIAI_StatusT Init(consthiai::AIConfig& config, const
std::vector<hiai::AIModelDescription>& model_desc) {};
     CustomEngine() {};
     ~CustomEngine() {};
     HIAI_DEFINE_PROCESS(ENGINE_INPUT_SIZE, ENGINE_OUTPUT_SIZE)
};
```

(2) The Init function is an initialization function. Generally, the Init function is used only in the model inference engine. It starts the AI model manager based on the input parameters, and further loads the offline model file. Other engines do not need to have the Init function overloaded.

(3) The developer can modify the constructor and destructor of the computing engine subclass.

(4) The HIAI_DEFINE_PROCESS statement indicates that the computing engine has one input port and one output port.

Code 5.74 shows a customized engine definition template, where.

(1) HIAI_IMPL_ENGINE_PROCESS is used to register the computing engine, we need to specify the engine name (corresponding to the engine name in the flowchart configuration file), the corresponding class, and the number of input ports of the engine.

(2) The data is obtained by using the void type pointer arg0, arg1, and arg2. The number of such pointers is the same as the number of input ports of the computing engine.

CODE 5.74 Definition template for a customized engine.

```
#include <memory>
#include "custom_engine.h"

HIAI_IMPL_ENGINE_PROCESS("CustomEngine", CustomEngine, ENGINE_
INPUT_SIZE)
{
    // receive data
    std::shared_ptr<custom_type> input_arg =
std::static_pointer_cast<custom_type>(arg0);
    // some function
    func(input_arg)
    // send data
    SendData(0, "custom_type", std::static_pointer_cast<void>
(input_arg));
    return HIAI_OK;
}
```

---

(3) Because the arg0 is of the void type, it needs to be converted into the pointer of the required type. The custom_type is a customized type defined by the developer.

(4) After some operations are performed on the input data. The data needs to be converted back to the void type and transmitted using the SendData function. 0 indicates the output port index, custom_type is the data type, and input_arg is the processed data.

5.4.5 The computing engine is connected in series

With the control of the main function, all computing engines will be initialized, and then begin to accept, process, and transfer data. A typical implementation process is shown in Fig. 5.20, which includes:

Step 1: the main function uses HIAI_Init to initialize the entire HiAi environment.
Step 2: the main function calls CreateGraph to obtain the flowchart configuration file and creates a flowchart object. During this process, the computing engine object is created and the corresponding Init function is called. Multiple flowchart objects can be created at the same time in a process, and different flowcharts can run on different devices (processors) independently.
Step 3: the main function calls GetInstance to obtain the flowchart object.
Step 4: the main function calls SetDataRecvFunctor to set the callback function to receive data.
Step 5: the main function reads data and sends the data to the data preparation engine by calling SendData.

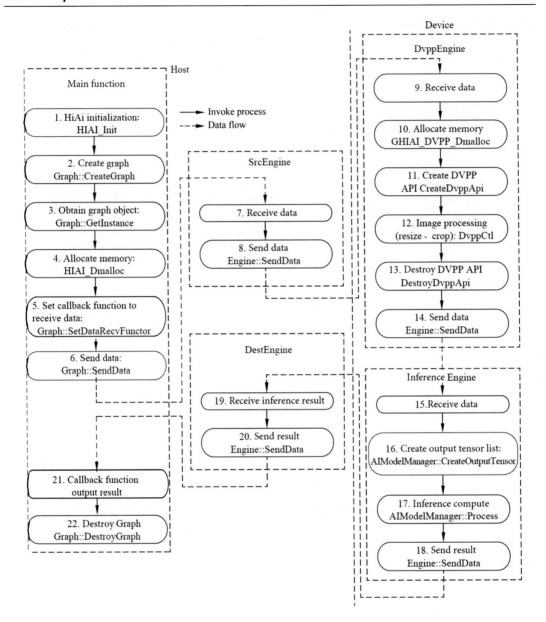

Fig. 5.20
A typical flowchart implementation.

Step 6: the source engine receives data, processes the data, and transmits the data to the DVPP engine.

Step 7: the DVPP engine receives data, uses the interface provided by the DVPP to process data, such as image resizing and cropping, and then transfers the data to the inference engine.

Step 8: when a computing engine object is created, the Inference Engine has already loaded the offline model file through the AI model manager. After receiving data from the DVPP, the Inference Engine calls the Process function of the AI model manager to perform specific model inference and then transfer the result to the data postprocessing engine.

Step 9: after receiving the data, the data postprocessing engine processes the data and sends the data back to the main function.

Step 10: the main function obtains data through the callback function and outputs the result.

Step 11: the main function calls DestroyGraph to destroy the flow chart object.

Project codes described in this chapter and more detailed development process can be found in the 'Ascend Developer Zone' website https://www.huaweicloud.com/intl/en-us/ascend/home.html.

References

[1] XLA: Optimizing Compiler for Machine Learning. Google. https://www.tensorflow.org/xla (Accessed 2020).
[2] TensorRT. Nvidia. https://developer.nvidia.com/tensorrt (Accessed 2020).
[3] Protocol Buffers. Wikipedia. https://en.wikipedia.org/wiki/Protocol_Buffers (Accessed 2020).
[4] Meta Programming. Wikipedia. https://en.wikipedia.org/wiki/Metaprogramming (Accessed 2020).
[5] LaTex. Wikipedia. https://en.wikipedia.org/wiki/LaTeX (Accessed 2020).
[6] Open Neural Network Exchange. https://onnx.ai/ (Accessed 2020).
[7] NNVM Compiler: Open Compiler for AI Frameworks. https://tvm.apache.org/2017/10/06/nnvm-compiler-announcement (Accessed 2020).
[8] Turing completeness. Wikipedia. https://en.wikipedia.org/wiki/Turing_completeness (Accessed 2020).
[9] Word2vec. Wikipedia. https://en.wikipedia.org/wiki/Word2vec (Accessed 2020).
[10] Recursive neural network. Wikipedia. https://en.wikipedia.org/wiki/Recursive_neural_network (Accessed 2020).
[11] Y. LeCun, et al., Backpropagation applied to handwritten zip code recognition. Neural Comput. 1 (4) (1989) 541–551, https://doi.org/10.1162/neco.1989.1.4.541.
[12] MXNET: A flexible and efficient library for deep learning. https://mxnet.apache.org/ (Accessed 2020).
[13] MMdnn. Microsoft. https://github.com/microsoft/MMdnn (Accessed 2020).
[14] A. Lavin, S. Gray, Fast algorithms for convolutional neural networks, in: Proceedings of the IEEE Conference on Computer Vision and Pattern Recognition, 2016, pp. 4013–4021.
[15] Bringing TVM into TensorFlow for Optimizing Neural Machine Translation on GPU. TVM. https://tvm.apache.org/2018/03/23/nmt-transformer-optimize (Accessed).
[16] K. He, X. Zhang, S. Ren, J. Sun, Deep residual learning for image recognition, in: Proceedings of the IEEE Conference on Computer Vision and Pattern Recognition, 2016, pp. 770–778.
[17] C. Szegedy, et al., Going deeper with convolutions, in: Proceedings of the IEEE Conference on Computer Vision and Pattern Recognition, 2015, pp. 1–9.

[18] K. Simonyan, A. Zisserman, Very deep convolutional networks for large-scale image recognition, arXiv preprint arXiv:1409 1556 (2014).

[19] Dense Linear Algebra on GPUs. Nvidia. https://developer.nvidia.com/cublas (Accessed).

[20] OpenBLAS: An optimized BLAS Library. https://www.openblas.net/ (Accessed).

[21] Nvidia cuDNN. Nvidia. https://developer.nvidia.com/cudnn (Accessed).

## CHAPTER 6

Case studies

The transformation of Artificial Intelligence (AI) from theoretical research to industrial practice depends on three factors: improvements in algorithms, computing power, and data. This chapter focuses on the data and algorithms to run AI, based on the computation power of the Ascend AI processor. This chapter is divided into two sections. In the first section, the standard evaluation criteria for image classification and video-based object detection algorithms are introduced followed by the criteria to evaluate the hardware's inferencing performance. In the second section, examples of image recognition and video object detection are used; their datasets and typical algorithms used, to illustrate how to develop customized operators and end-to-end applications on Ascend AI processors.

When considering machine learning as a storybook, there are two different storylines known as training and inference and the major characters of each differ slightly. The former is fulfilled by the algorithm scientists, the other is based on the work of algorithm engineers. As shown in Fig. 6.1, more users generate more data. To better characterize the data, algorithm scientists develop bigger models to improve accuracy. However, this causes the structure of the model to become more complicated, and as a result, more powerful training hardware is needed. As a result, more engineers work on deploying in richer scenarios, which attracts more users and generates more data. This series of "more" form a closed cycle in the research and application, which promotes the development of artificial intelligence.

Developers of artificial intelligence or algorithm scientists emphasize more on the training process. They design various complex or concise operators, training parameters, and fine-tuning hyperparameters of networks and verify the algorithm performance on given datasets. For the convolution operator, whose implementation has been introduced previously, as scientists are not satisfied with how it characterizes the data, a series of extended convolutions are proposed. For example, dilated convolution [1] can have a larger receptive field and deformable convolution [2] can describe the target object better with the same amount of weights.

Implementers of artificial intelligence focus more on the aspect of inference. A production-level system often requires real-time processing of dozens or even hundreds of HD images per second. For example, a company that specializes in video object detection for drones is unlikely to accept a network with hundreds of layers. A model with hundreds of megabytes and the electricity consumption of tens of watts are quite challenging for the weight-limited

Ascend AI Processor Architecture and Programming. https://doi.org/10.1016/B978-0-12-823488-4.00006-0

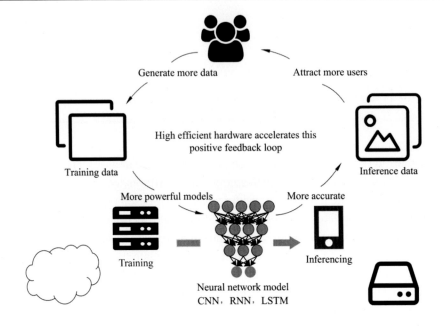

Fig. 6.1

Pipeline of deep learning: From academic research to industry practice.

low-cost drones. Recently, more attention is given on researching algorithms that are more computationally efficient and require less memory. From MobileNet [3] to ShuffleNet [4], based on Group Convolution and Depth-wise Convolution, these compressed networks obtain a similar performance comparing to the original large networks such as GoogleNet and VGG16, with much fewer parameters and decreased model size.

For this reason, Huawei has launched the full-stack and full-scenario intelligent solutions from on-device (Fig. 6.2) to on-cloud (Fig. 6.3). From the perspective of technology, Huawei has a full-stack solution that includes IP and processor, processor enablement, training and inference frameworks, and application enablement. From the perspective of business, Huawei can provide services for full-scenario deployment environments including public and private cloud, edge computing, IoT, and consumer terminals.

To provide the computing power for AI, the Ascend processors are developed into five series including Max, Mini, Lite, Tiny, and Nano, to satisfy the diverse requirements of different scenarios. On the top of the hardware, a highly automated processor enablement software stack CANN is also provided, including the aforementioned offline model conversion tool, offline model running tool, and tensor boost engine, to help R&D workers fully utilize the computing power of the Ascend processor. At the same time, as a unified training and inference framework which can work on-device, on-edge, and on-cloud independently or collaboratively, Huawei's MindSpore is very friendly to AI researchers, so that the performance of the

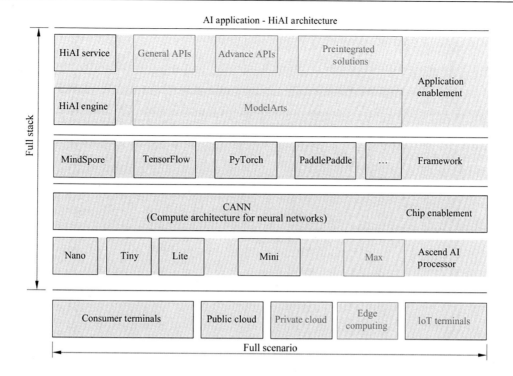

Fig. 6.2
Overview of Huawei's on-device solution HiAI.

model can be further improved. At the application layer, ModelArts, which can provide services for the entire pipeline, offers layered APIs and preintegrated solutions for users with different requirements.

As a typical inference processor, Ascend 310 takes the advantages of its low power consumption and high performance and targets at efficient on-device deep neural network inference. It aims to use a simple and complete toolchain to achieve efficient network implementation and migration, from automatic quantization to process layout. Due to space limitations, details on how to design a neural network will not be discussed in this book. More descriptions are focused on the support of Ascend AI processors for various networks, illustrating how to migrate appropriate networks to the Ascend development platform.

6.1 Evaluation criteria

This section will briefly introduce the standard evaluation criteria for image classification and video object detection (accuracy, precision, recall, F1 score, IoU, mean average precision, etc.), as well as for hardware (throughput, latency, energy efficiency ratio, etc.).

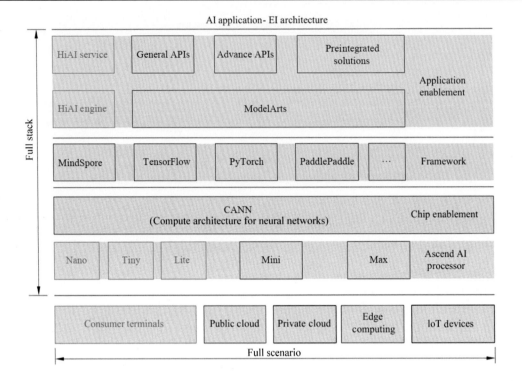

Fig. 6.3

Overview of Huawei's cloud solution EI.

6.1.1 Accuracy

For classification problems, accuracy is an intuitive evaluation measure, which refers to the percentage of correctly classified samples in the total samples.

$$\text{Accuracy} = \frac{\text{Number of correct prediction}}{\text{Number of total samples}}$$

Let's start with the following example:

Dataset 1: Apples and Pears

There are 100 apples and 100 pears in the warehouse. They are all round. There are 90 yellow and 10 green apples, 95 green, and 5 yellow pears.

Please design a classifier to classify apples and pears.

A feasible solution for the classifier is to let {"yellow = apple" and "green = pear"}, which means that all yellow fruits are apples and all greens are pears. The shape of the fruits can be ignored at this moment because both fruits have the same shape (round) and hence this feature cannot differentiate between the two fruits.

The Accuracy of this classifier is:

$$\text{Accuracy} = \frac{\text{Number of correct prediction}}{\text{Number of total samples}} = \frac{(90+95)}{(100+100)} = 92.5\%$$

It looks not bad, does it?

Next, let's modify the data set slightly:

Dataset 2: Apples and Pears.

There are 10,000 apples and 100 pears in the warehouse. They are all round. There are 9000 yellow and 1000 green apples, 95 green, and 5 yellow pears.

Please design a classifier to classify apples and pears.

It seems that there are little changes from dataset1 to dataset2 as 90% of apples are yellow and 95% of pears are green. The only change is the number of each fruit. Accuracy for the same classifier, {"yellow = apple", "green = pear"} is:

$$\text{Accuracy} = \frac{\text{Number of correct prediction}}{\text{Number of total samples}} = \frac{9000+95}{10,000+100} = 90.5\%$$

It doesn't seem to be a problem, but what about creating a classifier based on shape, such as {"circle = apple", "square = pear"}? The "square" attribute does not appear in the data. It can be replaced by any attribute that is not round, such as "triangle." Then all round fruits are considered as apples, which also means all pears are classified as apples. Take a look at the performance of this classifier:

$$\text{Accuracy} = \frac{\text{Number of correct prediction}}{\text{Number of total samples}} = \frac{10,000}{10,000+100} = 99.01\%$$

The classification based on shapes seems very unreasonable, since all fruits will be classified into one category, and this classifier is useless in a strict sense. However, based on the accuracy score as above, it seems much better than the classifier which is based on colors, and it is worth thinking about. In some applications, simply taking accuracy as the only evaluation measure may cause problems with serious consequences. Taking the earthquake prediction scenario as an extreme example, if a sample is taken every second, there will be 86,400 data points each day, and there is usually NO single positive sample for the nearly 2.6 million data points collected in a month. If the accuracy is taken as the measurement, the model will undoubtedly choose to classify the category of each test case into 0 (no earthquake) and achieve an accuracy of over 99.9999%. As a result, in the event of an earthquake, the model will not predict it correctly, resulting in huge losses. Researchers would like to choose to report false positives to capture such rare samples. The same situation applies to rare disease recognition tasks. It is better to give more tests to a suspected patient instead of failing to identify the rare disease.

The classification on a dataset with imbalanced data size of different categories is generally referred to as an imbalanced data classification problem. To evaluate this kind of problem better, some new evaluation concepts need to be introduced.

As shown in Table 6.1, if the prediction result is a pear (positive) and the ground-truth label is also a pear, then the prediction belongs to true positive (TP). If the predicted value is 'pear', but the real ground-truth value is 'apple', the prediction is false positive (FP). If the predicted value is apple (negative) and the ground-truth value is also apple, the prediction belongs to true negative (TN). If the predicted value is an apple, but the ground-truth value is a pear, the prediction is a false negative (FN).

Based on the above description, we can give the definitions as:

$$\text{Precision} = \frac{\text{Number of true positive}}{\text{Number of positives in predictions}} = \frac{\text{TP}}{\text{TP} + \text{FP}}$$

$$\text{Recall} = \frac{\text{Number of true positive}}{\text{Number of positives in the ground truth}} = \frac{\text{TP}}{\text{TP} + \text{FN}}$$

The performance of the above classifier {"round" = apple, "square" = pear}, can be given as Table 6.2:

$$\text{Precision} = \frac{\text{TP}}{\text{TP} + \text{FP}} = 0$$

$$\text{Recall} = \frac{\text{TP}}{\text{TP} + \text{FN}} = 0$$

Table 6.1 Classification result.

Prediction\ground truth	Pears: Positive	Apples: Negative
Pears: Positive	True positive (TP)	False positive (FP)
Apples: Negative	False negative (FN)	True negative (TN)

Table 6.2 Result of the classifier.

Prediction\ground truth	Pears: Positive	Apples: Negative
Pears: Positive	0	0
Apples: Negative	100	10,000

For this given problem, if precision and recall are used as evaluation metrics, the results of the shape classifier will not be misleading. For specific cases, evaluation criteria should be set reasonably in accordance with the data distribution and data characteristics. If the goal is to design a relatively balanced classifier, the F1 score is a good evaluation measure to use:

$$\text{F1 score} = \frac{2 \times \text{Precision} \times \text{Recall}}{\text{Precision} + \text{Recall}} = \frac{2\text{TP}}{2\text{TP} + \text{FP} + \text{FN}}$$

Once the evaluation criteria are determined, let's look back to the original dataset. Can 200 fruits in the warehouse represent all the apples and pears? Are there other fruits? How many different colors are there for apples in the real world? What are their percentages? Will it misclassify red apples from yellow apricots? How about round oranges from star carambolas? The list goes on and on. Sufficient data collection and preparation is the prerequisite for the success of any intelligent model. With the increased capability of current AI models, existing algorithms can deal with more types of features, while the demand for data also increases as well. To train a high-performance model, it is essential to make the right assumption on scope and type of sampled data, based on the context of the actual task. Various data modeling details including overfitting and underfitting will not go into detail here due to space limitation. For those interested please read [5] by Ian Goodfellow, Bengio, and Aaron Courville, three pioneers of deep learning.

To summarize, the accuracy metric does not consider the objective of the classification, since it only focuses on calculating the percentage of correct predictions on each category. The use of accuracy as an evaluation measure should be with great caution, especially for classification tasks, in which the data has imbalanced categories. On the contrary, precision, recall, and F1 score are practical evaluation measures for real applications, and the selection of the evaluation measure for the classifier should be based on the data and label characteristics of the actual cases.

6.1.2 IoU

Based on image classification, a series of more complex tasks can be extended according to different application scenarios, such as object detection, object localization, image segmentation, etc. Object detection is a practical and challenging computer vision task, which can be regarded as a combination of image classification and localization. Given an image, the object detection system should be able to identify the objects in the image and provide their location. Comparing to image classification tasks, as the number of objects in an image is uncertain and the accurate location of each object should also be provided, the task of object detection is more complex and its evaluation criteria are more controversial.

As shown in Fig. 6.4, an object detection system can output several rectangular boxes and labels. Each rectangular box represents the boundary of the predicted object, as well as its category and position information. Both of these outputs are needed to be evaluated by

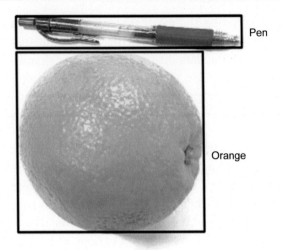

Fig. 6.4
An example of object detection.

developers. To evaluate the accuracy of the predicted boundary, the Intersection over Union (IoU) metric is introduced. To evaluate the correctness of the predicted category labels, the mean Average Precision (mAP) metric is introduced.

The concept of IoU is very intuitive; it illustrates the intersection of the predicted boundary and the ground-truth boundary. The bigger the IoU is, the higher is the performance of the prediction. If both intersections overlap entirely, the result is perfect.

$$IoU = \frac{\text{Predicted boundary} \cap \text{Ground} - \text{truth boundary}}{\text{Predicted boundary} \cup \text{Ground} - \text{truth boundary}}$$

In Fig. 6.5, a solid border indicates the ground-truth boundary of the object "orange" and a dashed border indicates the predicted boundary. In general, a matrix can be defined with the coordinates of the upper left corner and the lower right corner of the matrix, namely:

$$\text{Predicted boundary} = \{(xp1, yp1), (xp2, yp2)\}$$

$$\text{Ground} - \text{truth boundary} = \{(xt1, yt1), (xt2, yt2)\}$$

The concept of IoU is not difficult to understand, but how is it calculated? Will the relative position between the predicated boundary and the ground-truth boundary affect the calculation? Should we discuss whether the two boundaries intersect on a case by case basis? Do any intersections contain the cases of nested overlap?

At first glance, it seems that it is necessary to discuss the relative positions and intersection types of the predicted boundary and the ground-truth boundary case by case and make decisions

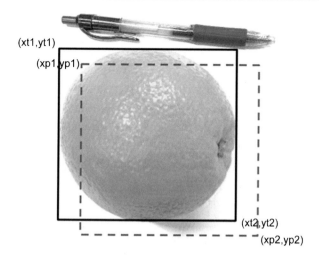

Fig. 6.5
Illustration of IoU.

based on various coordinates situations. However, the calculation of IoU is not so complicated. For calculating the intersection, the position of the predicted border and the ground-truth border can be swapped arbitrarily, and the coordinates of the intersected bounding box of the two borders need to be calculated only. If the two borders do not intersect, the output of IoU must be zero.

Code 6.1 is the code for calculating the IoU. Take the top left corner of the image as the origin $(0,0)$, and let the x-axis extends to the right and the y-axis extends downward. The input parameters are the coordinates of the upper left and lower right corners of the predicted and the ground-truth borders. The output IoU score is a floating-point number between $[0,1]$. Assuming

CODE 6.1 Code for computing the IoU.

```
def get_IoU(xp1, yp1, xp2,yp2,xt1, yt1, xt2,yt2):
    inter_xmin = max(xp1, xt1)
    inter_ymin = max(yp1, yt1)
    inter_xmax = min(xp2, yt2)
    inter_ymax = min(yp2, yt2)
    inter_area = np.maximum(inter_xmax - inter_xmin, 0.) *
np.maximum(inter_ymax - inter_ymin, 0.)
    pred_area = (xp2 - xp1) * (yp2 - yp1)
    truth_area = (xt2 - xt1) * (yt2 - yt1)
    union_area = pred_area + truth_area - inter_area
    return inter_area / union_area
```

that the overlapping area of the two borders in Fig. 6.5 is the case of inter, the x coordinate inter_xmin of the upper left corner is the min value between {xp1 and xt1}, and the y coordinate inter_ymin is the max one between {yp1 and yt1}. Similarly, we can get the x and y coordinates (inter_xmax, inter_ymax) of the lower right corner. Worth noting here is that if the borders do not overlap at all, the value of inter_xmax - inter_xmin may be negative, which needs to be set to zero using the np.maximum function as Code 6.1. If either of the *x* and *y* axis does not overlap, the predicted and ground-truth borders do not overlap. The area of the intersection between the predicted border and the ground-truth border can be calculated using the coordinates of the inserted points on the diagonal direction. The area of the union can be obtained by adding the area of the two borders. Then the IoU ratio can be obtained by dividing the intersection area by the union area.

If you are interested, you can build your own sample to test it. In actual programming, it is common to add 1 to the length and width when calculating the area.

6.1.3 Mean average precision

As the name implies, mean Average Precision (mAP) refers to the mean value of the average precision of each category. The average precision here refers to the area under the Precision-Recall curve (PR curve).

For most algorithms, given a data sample, the prediction of a model is based on its derived confidence value between [0, 1]. If the confidence is higher than a threshold, the corresponding sample will be classified as positive, otherwise negative. It is obvious that the threshold value directly affects the results of prediction. In practice, precision and recall of the model can be controlled by adjusting the threshold. Generally, a higher precision will result in a lower recall or vice versa. Briefly, precision indicates the percentage of true positives in the predicted positives, and recall shows what percentage of the ground-truth positives is predicted as positive. Different tasks have different preferences for precision and recall. Efforts are often made to improve the performance on one of precision and recall without sacrificing the other. For example, given a requirement of at least 70% of ground-truth positives to be detected, it allows improving the precision as much as possible while keeping the recall value not lower than 0.7.

The precision-recall curve can be drawn intuitively as Fig. 6.6,[a] where the vertical axis P represents the precision and the horizontal axis R represents the recall. It is easy to draw a typical precision-recall curve using the automatically generated classification data from sklearn. When recall increases, the precision decreases gradually. In practice, it is usually difficult to calculate the accurate area under the PR curve. Usually, the approximate average

---

[a] Image reference https://machinelearningmastery.com/roc-curves-and-precision-recall-curves-for-classification-inpython/.

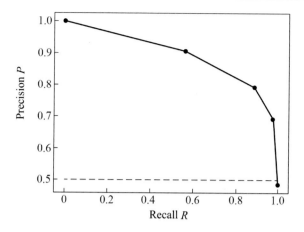

Fig. 6.6
Example of the precision-recall curve (PR curve).

precision is computed by changing the value of recall from 0 to 1 gradually with a fixed step size (e.g., 0.01).

In the problem of object detection, the mAP is often used as a unified indicator for considering the two kinds of errors from precision and recall. Because of the special requirement for object detection, the IoU is used to determine whether an object of a particular category is accurately detected or not. The value of the threshold can be set based on the actual applications. The typical threshold value is usually 0.5. In practice, a detection model may output multiple predicted boundaries (more than the number of ground-truth boundaries) for each image. If the IoU of the predicted and ground-truth bounding boxes is larger than 0.5, the predicted bounding box is considered to be correct, otherwise, the predicted bounding box is considered to be wrong. With more bounding boxes predicted, the recall increases as well. By averaging the precision at different recall rates, the corresponding average precision value can be obtained. The final mean average precision can be obtained by computing the mean value of the average precision of all object classes.

One problem that can be easily ignored is how to set the threshold of the IoU when calculating the mAP. If the threshold is set too low, even the erroneous bounding box detections can get excellent scores. As shown in Fig. 6.7, we designed two object detectors, both of which are considered to perform perfect predictions of the object boundary under the measurement of mAP, while the performance of detector 2 was actually far from the ground-truth label. In the article "Best of both worlds: human-machine collaboration for object annotation", it is also mentioned that it is actually difficult for human eyes to distinguish the object boundary corresponding to IoU$=0.3$ and IoU$=0.5$. Needless to say, this situation may cause some problems in the development of practical applications. The ways to evaluate object detectors

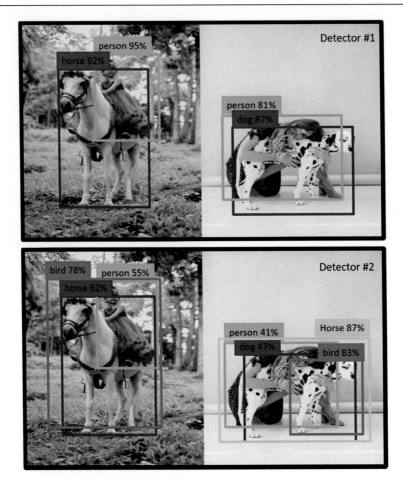

Fig. 6.7
Example of using mAP to evaluate two models. *Image reference https://www.pexels.com/.*

can vary from each other, depending on the context of the actual application. In practice, the average precision corresponding to different IoU thresholds (0.5–0.95, with 0.05 as the step size) is often calculated. With further average computation, the average precision of objects of different sizes also can be obtained. This is how the object detector is evaluated on the MS COCO dataset [6] in the following section.

6.1.4 Throughput and latency

The training process usually involves massive training data and complex neural networks. To train the parameters in the model, it requires a huge amount of computation and the processor requirements are quite high in terms of computing power, accuracy, and expansibility. The inference process involves testing the trained models on new data. For example, a video monitoring device determines whether a captured face is suspicious based on the backend deep neural network model. Although the inference process has much fewer operations than training, it still involves a lot of matrix operations.

During training, accuracy is more critical, while performance such as real-time and speed are more important during inference. Throughput is one of the easiest measures to evaluate the overall performance of inference, i.e., the number of images that can be processed per second when running a model. Latency (reciprocal of the throughput) is the average time spent to infer each image and is one of the important metrics to measure performance. Generally, the unit of latency is milliseconds (ms) and the time used to process the first frame is often excluded when calculating the average latency. The throughput can be computed by dividing 1000 (number of milliseconds per second) by the latency.

$$\text{Throughput} = \frac{1000}{\text{Latency}}$$

As mentioned previously, the computing power of a processor is commonly measured by TOPS, which is the number of operating basic deep learning operators per second. If the computing power of a processor is used as a measurement for hardware, throughput is the performance measurement based on the integration of hardware and software. It is highly related to the data structure, model architecture, and even the batch size for batch processing. In general, given data with the same type and size, the model which has fewer parameters has a faster absolute processing speed and higher throughput. Of course, as the complexity and number of parameters of the deep learning model increase, it shows more advantages of the high computing power and low energy consumption of specialized processors such as the Ascend AI processor.

It is important to note that the operands defined in a processor may vary depending on the type and precision of the computation, which will result in different throughput. Therefore, when stating the performance of a processor (including computing power, energy efficiency ratio, throughput, etc.), some detailed information, such as the computing type and precision (such as FP16 or INT8), should be provided. Sometimes the neural network architecture of the computational model should also be provided to facilitate a relatively fair comparison. By quantization, the model trained with FP32 precision can be compressed into FP16 or INT8 version for inference. Typically, the lower the data quantization precision is, the worse is the accuracy of the inference. A proper quantization technique can improve throughput while avoiding the loss of precision for inference.

6.1.5 Energy efficiency ratio

The unit of the energy efficiency ratio is TFLOPS/W, which is defined as average computing power when the processor consumes 1-Watt electricity power. In practice, given the precision, batch size, model architecture, and data characteristics, Watt/Image is also often used to measure the average power consumption per image.

As mentioned previously, the higher the TFLOPS is, the faster is the processor and therefore, theoretically, the processor can provide a larger throughput with the same algorithm and data. However, in engineering practices, larger throughput is not always the best choice. The selection of computing power should be based on the context of the practical application. Taking the power of the light bulbs as an example, a bulb is often brighter if it has a larger watt. However, there is no need for 300 W searchlights everywhere, and the high-watt bulb will not even glow if the local power system is not strong enough. The choice of light bulbs is limited by the power supply and environment, so as the choice of artificial intelligence processors.

The application scenarios of AI are rather complicated. To achieve the same computing power, the electricity power consumed may vary due to different processor architectures or different model structures. Meanwhile, more advanced deep learning models usually work with more parameters, and hence the requirement for computing power is higher. Although companies can design processors with different computing power for different scenarios, it is definitely more desirable to achieve a higher computing power for the same application scenario or with the same power consumption limit.

With the recent rapid development of deep learning, the vast energy consumption of data computation has attracted more and more attention. To save energy costs, Facebook chose to build its data center in Sweden, not far from the Arctic Circle. The average winter temperature there is about −20°C, and cold air enters the central building and naturally cools the servers by exchanging with the generated hot air. Subsequently, a joint venture between the United States and Norway, Kolos, also proposed to construct the world's largest data center in the Norwegian town of Barnes, which also located in the Arctic Circle. The power consumption of this proposed data center is 70 MW, with 1000 MW as its peak value.

On average, training a deep learning model produces 284 tons of carbon emissions, which is equivalent to one-year carbon emissions of 5 vehicles. Therefore, the energy efficiency ratio becomes more and more critical when evaluating the deep learning platform. The design of the dedicated neural network processors can be customized based on the algorithm to reduce excessive power consumption and improve the computation efficiency. With improved performance, these processors will have a bright future in applications on mobile devices, which require high-performance and low energy consumption.

6.2 Image classification

Considering the maturity of deep neural networks in computer vision, this chapter explains how to create a typical application with Ascend AI processor using image classification and video object detection as examples. In the image classification example, a command-line-based end-to-end development pipeline is explained, and the model quantification method is also briefly introduced. The video object detection example focuses on how to customize the operators in the network and then discusses the factors that affect the performance of inference.

6.2.1 Dataset: ImageNet

In this chapter, the ImageNet dataset [7] is selected for image classification because of its richness of data composition and its popularity in computer vision. Being the largest image dataset in the world now, it has about 15 M images covering more than 20,000 categories. It is also known as the first dataset that is annotated based on the WordNet semantic hierarchy. As in Fig. 6.8, the semantic hierarchy of ImageNet from top to bottom level is shown from left to right. For example, "husky" is a subset of the "working dog," "working dog" is a subset of the "dog," "dog" is a subset of the "canine," "canine" is a subset of to the "carnivore," and "carnivore" belongs to "placental" which is a subset of "mammal." Although there are ambiguous labels in ImageNet dataset at some levels, it is much better than other datasets in which "female" and "human" are classified into completely distinct categories. The directed acyclic semantic structure itself provides a good reference for extracting the semantic feature from various images. At the same time, the tree-structure organization also facilitates researchers to extract the desired information and select certain specific nodes to train the classifier based on their application needs. It can be imagined that the features that distinguish "cats" from "dogs" are not the same as those features which distinguish "trucks" from "cars."

There are three types of tasks defined on ImageNet: image classification, single object detection, and multiple object detection. The most popular one is image classification, in which the model only needs to classify the object in the image into a particular predefined category. Most images of this task come from Flickr and other search engines. Each image was manually labeled into one of 1000 categories, and each image is supposed to have just one object of a particular category. The number of images for each category may be from one to several, and their sizes and shapes may vary as well. In the paper, "ImageNet Large Scale Visual Recognition Challenge" [8], the authors summarize the ImageNet dataset from eight dimensions, including scale, the number of instances, texture type, etc., ensuring the diverse and representativeness of the dataset. At the same time, the granularity of categories of ImageNet is finer than that of a similar dataset PASCAL [9]. The class of "birds" in the

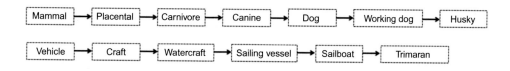

Fig. 6.8

ImageNet image classification based on semantic levels. *Figure inspired from D. Jia, et al. Imagenet: a large-scale hierarchical image database, in: 2009 IEEE conference on computer vision and pattern recognition.*

PASCAL dataset will be subdivided into several categories including flamingo, cock, ruffed grouse, quail, and partridge in ImageNet (Fig. 6.9). It is worth mentioning that this type of fine-grained classification also causes difficulties for people who do not have sufficient prior knowledge. The human classification error rate on the dataset reached 5.1%, partly because the image quality is low and the target object is not prominent. Some volunteers gave feedbacks that they labeled incorrectly because they could not accurately classify "quail" from "partridge", both of which are not popular birds. To some extent, this is one of the reasons why the classification accuracy of the recent models on ImageNet is higher than that of humans, while it still cannot prove that machine learning is more intelligent than a human.

Along with the birth and development of ImageNet, the world-famous "ImageNet Large Scale Visual Recognition Challenge (ILSVRC)" [7] began in 2010. In the competition, two evaluation measures are used: Top-1 error rate (for a certain image, whether the label with top one probability predicted by the algorithm is the same to the ground-truth label) and Top-5 error rate (whether the labels with top five probabilities predicted by the algorithm is the same as the ground-truth label). In 2012, AlexNet, the winner of ILSVRC competition, marked the first time that the convolutional neural network is able to classify with a top-5 error rate of 15.4%, while the top-5 error rate of the second-ranked model is 26.2%. The whole community of computer vision was shocked by the performance and deep learning became popular since then. GoogleNet and VGGNet in 2014 and ResNet in 2015 are subsequent impressive models because of their great achievements. Since then, "model trained on ImageNet" means that the model is trained and evaluated on the data provided by a particular year of ILSVRC (the data of ILSVRC 2012 is most commonly used). At the same time, researchers are surprised to find that the model trained on ImageNet (pretrained model) can be used as the basis for fine-tuning parameters of other image classification tasks, which is especially useful when the training data is insufficient. By using the intermediate result of a specific layer before the fully connected layer, this first part of the model can become an excellent image feature extractor. The second part of the model can be designed based on the requirement of the application. After fine tuning with a certain amount of data, a good result can usually be obtained. Fig. 6.10 briefly summarizes some suggestions for using the pretrained model and transfer learning for image classification, w.r.t. the data size of the target application, and its similarity to ImageNet.

When looking back, ImageNet was only published as a poster at a corner of CVPR2009. While 10 years later, in CVPR2019, it won the "PAMI Longuet-Higgins Prize," which shows its significant contribution to computer vision research. Many people regard ImageNet challenge as a catalyst for the current wave of artificial intelligence, and the participating companies from various areas of the tech industry spread all over the world. From 2010 to 2017, in just several years, the classification rate of the winners increased from 71.8% to 97.3%, which has surpassed the performance of a human. It also demonstrates that more data can lead to better learning results. "ImageNet has changed people's understanding of datasets in the field of

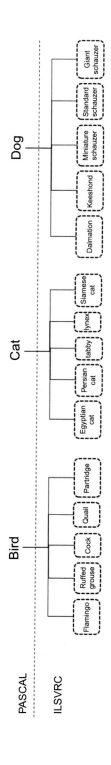

Fig. 6.9

Example of fine-grained image classification on ImageNet: "bird," "cat," "dog" in PASCAL are subdivided into subcategories. *Figure inspired from R. Olga, et al., Imagenet large scale visual recognition challenge, Int. J. Comput. Vis. 115(3) (2015) 211–252.*

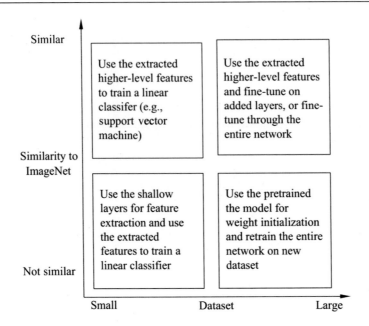

Fig. 6.10
Suggestions for using the pretrained model and transfer learning for image classification.

artificial intelligence. People begin to realize that datasets are as important as algorithms in research", said by Professor Fei-Fei Li from Stanford University.

6.2.2 Algorithm: ResNet18

The key to deep learning is probably the "deep" layers. The technique that transforms networks from two or three dozens of layers, such as the VGG and GoogleNet, to hundreds of layers is the residual block. As one of the top performed networks for image classification on ImageNet dataset, Deep Residual Net (ResNet) ranked first place in ILSVRC 2015. It outperformed the second-ranked system with a big gap in all three tasks of image classification, object detection, and object localization. Their top-5 error rate was as low as 3.57%, which refreshed the record of precision of CNNs on ImageNet. The residual block, proposed by Kaiming He et al., provided a solution to resolve the difficulties of training networks with deep structures, and it became a milestone in the history of deep learning.

To understand ResNet, let us first look at the Degradation problem is solved. Degradation is the phenomenon that the performance of the neural network decreases while the number of layers increases. Generally speaking, for the deep learning networks with convolutional layers, theoretically, with the increasing number of network layers, there should be richer feature extraction and the accuracy of the network should increase as well. However, when the number of network layers reaches a certain level, its performance will be saturated, and further adding new layers will lead to a degraded of the overall performance. Surprisingly, this degradation is not due to overfitting, because the performance decline on both the test and the training set, which differs from the obvious characteristics of overfitting, i.e., the performance decreases on the test while the performance increases on the training set.

To some extent, this is even counterintuitive—how could a deeper network be less effective than a shallow one? In the worst case, the later layer only needs to make an identity mapping for the incoming signal, i.e., the output signal of the previous layer does not change after flowing through the current layer, and the error rate after the information passing through current layer should be equal. In the actual training process, due to the limitations of the optimizer (such as stochastic gradient descent) and data, the convolution kernel is difficult to converge to the impulse signal, which means the convolutional layer is actually difficult to achieve the identity mapping. Therefore, the model cannot converge to the theoretical optimal result after the network depth becomes deeper. Although the Batch Normalization technique can solve a part of the gradient loss problem caused by back propagation, the problem of network performance degradation with increased depth still exists and it has become one of the bottlenecks that restrict the performance of deep learning.

In order to solve this problem, ResNet proposed the residual block (Fig. 6.11[b]). Given input as x, the goal to learn a mapping $H(x)$ as the output of the neural networks. In the figure, $F(x)$ is the learned mapping from the weight layer. In addition to the output of the weight layer, another connection directly connects x to the output. The final output is obtained by adding x to $F(x)$, which uses the entire residual block to fit the mapping:

$$H(x) = F(x) + x$$

It is easy to see that if $F(x)$ is zero (i.e., all parameters in the weight layer are zero), then $H(x)$ is the identity mapping, as mentioned above. By adding the Shortcut structure, the residual block provides a way for the network to converge to identity mapping quickly and tries to solve the

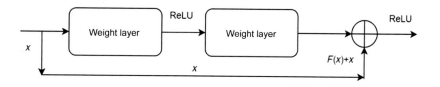

Fig. 6.11

Shortcut in the residual network. *Figure adapted from H, Kaiming, et al., Deep residual learning for image recognition, in: Proceedings of the IEEE conference on computer vision and pattern recognition, 2016.*

---

[b] *Re*-reference of figure in Chapter 5 for convenience of readers.

problem of performance degradation when the depth goes deeper. This simple idea really provides a solution for the difficult problem of fitting identical mapping using convolutional layers, which makes it easy for the optimizer to find the perturbations on the identical mapping instead of learning the mapping as a new function. Because of these characteristics, ResNet achieves an outstanding performance on various computer vision datasets, including ImageNet.

To illustrate the performance of residual networks with different depths, the author designed 18-, 34-, 50-, 101-, and 152-layer residual networks, respectively. In practice, ResNetN is often used to represent n-layer residual networks. In order to reduce the number of parameters and computation, when using deeper networks, the high-dimensional input, e.g., 256 dimensions, is first reduced to 64 using 1×1 convolution, and to use 1×1 convolution to recover back afterward. The details are shown in Fig. 6.12, and the top figure is a residual block of ResNet18/34, and the bottom is the residual block of ResNet50/101/152, which is also called as a Bottleneck Design. It is a good practice to compare the difference of parameters numbers between residual block with bottleneck design and conventional residual block.

Experiments show that the residual network can effectively solve the problem of performance degradation when the depth goes deeper. In general, a conventional CNN suffers the aforementioned degradation issue, however, with residual network architecture, the performance continues to be improved along with the depth of the network, i.e., a 34-layer version consistently outperforms than its 18-layer counterpart in both training and validation set.

It is easy to get the implementation of the residual network on the official website of TensorFlow [11]. To note here is that the description in this chapter is based on the publication "Deep Residual Learning for Image Recognition" [10] in 2015 and it corresponds to the v1 version of TensorFlow's official implementation. The author, Kaiming He, in the following

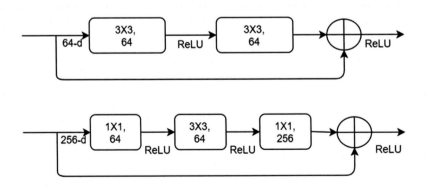

Fig. 6.12
The top is the residual block in ResNet18 and 35; the bottom is the residual block in deeper networks (ResNet50/101/152) [10].

year (2016) published another article "Identity Mappings in Deep Residual Networks" [12], and it includes details about the relative positions of activation function and batch normalization which are ignored here. The corresponding code is available as v2 version of the implementation.

6.2.3 Model migration practice

The Ascend AI processor provides two ways to migrate trained models onto the processor. One is the integrated development environment, Mind Studio, and the other is the digital developer suite. Both methods are based on the same set of artificial intelligence full-stack development platforms developed by Huawei. The former provides the drag-and-drop style visual programming, which is suitable for the beginners for a quick start. The latter offers a command-line development suite, which is suitable for advanced developers for customized development.

This section takes the reader through the deployment process of applications on the Ascend AI platform using the command line (DDK). The reader is supposed to finish the installation of the DDK (for details on installation, see "Ascend 310 DDK sample usage guide (command mode)" or "Ascend 310 Mind Studio installation guide"), and the DDK installation directory is $HOME/tools/che/DDK, where $HOME represents the user's home directory.

Generally, several steps are involved to migrate a model. This section will introduce each of them:

- Model preparation: Get the model weight file and convert it into the DaVinci offline model file which is supported by Ascend AI Processor.
- Image processing: Process images using DVPP/AIPP for decoding, cropping, etc.
- Project compilation and execution: Modify the configuration file, set the install folder for DDK, path to the model file, and runtime environment parameters and compile the code to the executable file.
- Result verification: Verify the inference result of the model.

6.2.3.1 Model preparation

We assume that the network has been trained on the host side and the corresponding weight file has been computed. For this example, you can download the trained weight file from the home page of Kaiming He,[c] the main contributor to ResNet. As mentioned above, a residual network has implementations for different depths. The provided link contains models for ResNet-50, ResNet-101, ResNet-152, etc., with their corresponding weight file (caffemodel) and prototxt file. Here, the 50-layer ResNet50 is used as an example.

---

[c] https://github.com/KaimingHe/deep-residual-networks.

CODE 6.2 **An example of data layer definition in prototxt.**

```
name:  "ResNet-50"
input:  "data"
input_dim:  1
input_dim:  3
input_dim:  224
input_dim:  224
```

Interested readers can learn about the operators and network structure of ResNet from its configuration document, such as prototxt/ResNet-50-deploy.prototxt. For example, Code 6.2 prototxt defines the input parameters for this sample case, and it shows that the input data is a three-channel image with a size of 224*224 pixels. The reader can prepare the test data according to the input parameters in this file.

To understand the configuration of specific layer in the neural network, the convolutional layer in Code 6.3 can be used as an example.

Based on what you have learned in the previous chapters of this book, it is easy to see that "bottom" refers to the input of the current layer and "top" is the output of the current layer. The "type" indicates the characteristics of the current layer and the value "Convolution" here means the current layer is a convolutional layer. The field "name" refers to the name of the current layer and is free to be defined by the reader, but note that this name is used as a reference to the relative position of the layer in the network, so this value needs to be unique.

CODE 6.3 **An example of the convolutional layer in prototxt.**

```
layer {
    bottom:  "data"
    top:  "conv1"
    name:  "conv1"
    type:  "Convolution"
    convolution_param {
        num_output:  64
        kernel_size:  7
        pad:  3
        stride:  2
    }
}
```

Fig. 6.13
Illustration of zero padding.

Next comes the parameter setting for the convolutional layer, which has 64 convolution kernels (the "num_output" field in the code) of size 7*7 (i.e., the "kernel_size" field in the code). The field "pad" refers to the amount of padding at image edges, and the default value is 0, which means no padding. The padding needs to be symmetric in the up, down, left, and right directions. Here, the size of the convolution kernel is 7*7, as shown in the following Fig. 6.13 (nonreal pixel ratio). The number 3 here means that all 4 edges of the image have been expanded with $(7-1)/2=3$ pixels to extract features from the pixels at the image edge successfully. The field "stride" refers to the step length of the convolution kernel, whose default value is 1. Here, the stride value is set to 2, i.e., the convolution is calculated every two pixels; stride_h and stride_w can also be used to set the vertical and horizontal stride values, respectively.

When the model file is ready, it needs to be converted into the offline model file supported by the Ascend AI processor. During the process of model migration, any unsupported operators are required to be customized by the user themselves. The customized operators can be added to the operator library to make it possible for the model migration. The process for customizing operators will be introduced in the following section, the implementation of object detection, in detail. All operators of ResNet, in this section, are supported by the built-in framework of the Ascend AI platform. The user can directly migrate the model using the following commands (Code 6.4). After executing the command, a model file with the extension .om is generated, e.g., the resnet50.om file.

CODE 6.4 **An example of command for migrating the OMG model.**

```
$HOME/tools/che/ddk/ddk/uihost/bin/omg -model=resnet50.prototxt -
weight=resnet50.caffemodel -framework=0 -output=resnet50
```

Here:

- model: relative path to the model configuration file resnet50.prototxt
- weight: relative path to the weight file resnet50.caffemodel
- framework: the type of backend framework
  - 0:Caffe
  - 3:Tensorflow
- output: name of the output model file, defined by the user

6.2.3.2 Image processing

With the development of IoT technology, the demand for on-device image processing of edge computing has increased. Hence, the required number of image frames to be processed per second and the number of codec operations increased as well. To speed up image data processing, a DVPP module, which is dedicated to image processing, is provided on the Ascend AI platform. Taking Ascend 310 as an example, its dual-core VDEC can process real-time dual-channel 4 K HD video at 60 frames per second, and its 4-core VPC can speed up to 90 frames per second, for real-time 4-channel 4 K HD video. With a higher compression rate such as H.264/H.265 and a large amount of computation for the codec, implementing the encoding and decoding operations on the hardware can effectively release CPU resources, so that data can be processed efficiently on the device.

In order to better represent and store images, the DVPP module supports two image formats including YUV and RGB/RGBA. As shown in Fig. 6.14, the YUV format is divided into three components. "Y" refers to Luminance or Luma, namely the gray value. "U" and "V" represent Chrominance, or Chroma, which describes the color saturation of an image, i.e., the pixel colors. The mainstream YUV formats are YUV444 (each pixel has Y, U, V values), YUV422 (each pixel has a Y value and two pixels share the same U, V values), YUV420 (each pixel has a Y value and four pixels share the same U, V values), and YUV400 (only Y value, i.e., black or white). The RGB format is more familiar to us, which can produce a wide variety of colors by changing the channels of red (R), green (G), and blue (B) and combining them with each other. The A in RGBA represents Alpha (transparency). RGB/RGBA format is defined according to the color identified by human eyes, which can represent most colors and is a friendly way to display on the hardware side, but it requires higher storage and transmission costs than YUV.

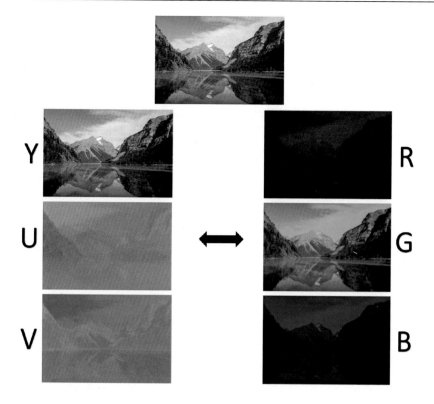

Fig. 6.14
Comparison on channels of YUV format and RGB format.

In this example, the preprocessing of images is already supported internally by the framework. Users can also call DVPP for image processing according to actual needs. There are mainly two methods to call DVPP, which are calling through the interface and calling through the executor. Due to the space limitation of this book, please refer to the attachment "Ascend 310 DVPP API reference" for detail.

6.2.3.3 Project compilation

In the local DDK installation directory, you can find a folder named sample, which contains a series of development cases for Ascend AI processors. Due to factors such as version upgrade and algorithm iteration, you are advised to obtain the reference samples of the classification network from the Ascend official website.[c] For typical scenarios such as image classification and object recognition, the corresponding code can be found there. Here, ResNet50 belongs to the image classification model. After the model conversion is done, you can start the local project compilation and execution based on the built-in image classification reference samples (classify_net/).

Considering that the context of the compilation environment is different, the compilation procedure is divided into two steps. It is recommended that the executable file and the dynamic link library file on the device side should be compiled separately. For the Atlas development board which is a computation platform with the independent processor for executing the inference, the environment for compiling executable files is on the device side. For the environment where the PCIe card or accelerator card is controlled by the central processing unit on the host side, the environment for compiling executable files should be set on the host side. For all types of Ascend platforms, the environment for compiling the link library and the scenario where the project is running should be consistent with itself.

Modify the "classify_net/Makefile_main" file according to the actual situation and compile the executable file. Modify the following items:

> DDK_HOME: ddk installation directory. The default value is "../../che/ddk/ddk/".
> CC_SIDE: Indicates the side where the file is compiled. The default value is host. When the Atlas development board is used, set this parameter to device. Note that the value is in lowercase.
> CC_PATTERN: Indicate the scenario where the project is running, the default value is ASIC. In the Atlas scenario, the value is changed to Atlas.

After the modification, run the "classify_net/Makefile_main" file. You can generate a series of executable files in the "out" folder of the current path. The differences may vary depending on the software version and scenario of the reference samples. Modify the "classify_net/Makefile_device" file[d] to change the value of CC_PATTERN. The default value is ASIC. In the Atlas scenario, the value is changed to Atlas. After the execution is successful, a series of link library files including libai_engine.so are generated in the "classify_net/out" folder. So far, all the files required to execute the inference on the Ascend platform are ready.

After the compilation is completed, insert the ResNet50.om and ResNet50.prototxt that are successfully converted in the previous step into the "classify_net/model" path on the device side, and modify the corresponding path of the inference engine in "graph_sample.txt" according to the path described in the previous chapter.

The code in Code 6.5 is a typical sample of the basic definition of the inference engine. In the code, "id" indicates the ID of the current engine, "engine_name" can be determined by the reader, and "side" indicates the position where the program is executed (DEVICE indicates the device side and HOST indicates the host side). "so_name" refers to the dynamic link library file generated in the previous step. In "ai_config", you can use the "model_path" field to configure the path of the model. In this example, the path is changed to the om path generated by the conversion.

---

[d] Note here, please use chmod 755 * to modify the permission if needed.

CODE 6.5 **An example of the inference engine definition.**

```
engines {
   id: 1003
   engine_name: "ClassifyNetEngine"
   side: DEVICE
   so_name: "./libai_engine.so"
   thread_num: 1
ai_config{
   items{
     name: "model_path"
     value: "./test_data/resnet-50/model/ResNet50.om"
   }
   }
}
```

6.2.3.4 Analysis of results

Based on the abovementioned evaluation criteria in this chapter, it is easy to know that the dataset commonly used by the ImageNet 2012 has 1000 class labels in the image classification task, and the prediction result provided by the model is also a 1000-dimension vector. As shown below, each horizontal row represents one dimension in the label vector. The first column indicates the ID of the corresponding label, and the second column indicates the probability that the label is true.

```
rank: 1 dim: 1000 data:
label:1      value:5.36442e-07
label:2      value:4.76837e-07
label:3      value:5.96046e-07
label:4      value:1.01328e-06
label:5      value:8.9407e-07
...
```

Generally speaking, the Top-1 prediction selects that the label with the highest value as the output label. The image input here is the Australian Kelpie dog, which is predicted accurately with the confidence of 99.8%. If you select MindStudio as the integrated development environment, which has built-in visualization function, you can right-click the resulting engine to view the result shown in Fig. 6.15.

Finally, let us take a look at the pipeline of processing the input image by the Ascend AI processor in this case. As shown in Fig. 6.16, the DVPP module completes image transcoding, segmentation, and deformation. Next, the AIPP completes a series of preprocessing, including

Fig. 6.15
An example of image classification result: Kelpie. *Picture from: https://commons.wikimedia.org/wiki/ File:Kelpie1.jpg.*

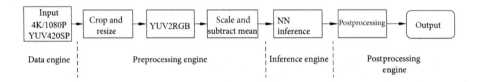

Fig. 6.16
Inference pipeline of the Ascend AI processor.

regularization, for input data. The DaVinci architecture processing core, which is the AI Core, processes the core inference. The operation result is sent to the CPU for postprocessing, and the postprocessing result is the output. The implementation and execution sequence of operators has been completed on the host side. You only need to perform offline inference calculations on the device side.

In the evaluation criteria section, the FP32 model is often quantified to FP16 or even INT8 precision in order to provide higher throughput and reduce the cost of energy consumption per image. The following section uses the residual network as an example to describe the general algorithm and performance of the quantization.

6.2.3.5 Quantification methodology

Compared with the FP32 type, the low-precision types such as FP16 and INT8 occupy less space. Therefore, the corresponding storage space and transmission time can be significantly reduced. To provide more human-centric and intelligent services, more and more operating systems and applications are integrated with the deep learning function. Naturally, a large number of models and weight files are required. Considering the classic AlexNet as an example, the size of the original weight file exceeds 200 MB, and the structure of recent newer models is becoming even more complex with a higher number of parameters. Obviously, the space benefit of low-precision type is quite prominent. As the computing performance of low bits is higher, INT8 runs three or even more times faster than FP32.

During inference, the Ascend AI processor collectively refers to the actions for the quantization process to the quantization Calibration, which is responsible for completing the following functions:

- Calibrating the input data of the operator, determining a value range [d_min, d_max] of the data to be quantized, and calculating an optimal scaling ratio and a quantization offset of the data;
- The weight of the operator is quantized to INT8, and the scaling ratio and quantization offset of the weight are calculated.
- The offset of the operator is changed to INT32.

As shown in Fig. 6.17, when the offline model generator generates an offline model, the quantized weight and the offset quantity can be combined into the offline model by using the quantization calibration module (Calibrator). In the DaVinci architecture, the quantization from FP32 to INT8 is used as an example to describe the quantization principle.

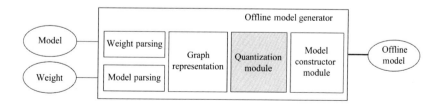

Fig. 6.17
Quantization module in the offline model generator.

To determine the two constants of the resizing ratio and the quantization offset, the following formula is used. For simplification, it may be assumed that the high-precision floating-point data may be linearly fitted by using low-precision data.

$$d\_float = scale * (q\_uint8 + offset)$$

d_float is the original high-precision floating-point data, the scale is an FP32 floating-point number, and q_uint8 is the quantization result. In practice, the 8-bit unsigned integer (UINT8) is used for q_uint8. A value that needs to be determined by the quantization algorithm is a constant scale and an offset. Because the structure of the neural network is divided by layers, the quantization of the weight and the data may also be performed in the unit of the layer, and the parameters and data of each layer are quantized separately.

After the scaling ratio and the quantization offset are determined, the conversion of the UINT8 data obtained by calculation using the original high-precision data is shown in the following formula.

$$q_{\text{int8}} = \text{round}\left(\frac{d_{\text{float}}}{\text{scale}}\right) - \text{offset}$$

In the formula, round() is the rounding function, scale is a FP32 floating-point number, q_uint8 is an unsigned 8-bit integer, and offset is an INT32 number. The data range is [scale*offset, scale*(255+offset)]. If the value range of the data to be quantized is [d_min, d_max], the scale and the offset are calculated as follows:

$$scale = (d\_max - d\_min)/255$$

$$offset = round(d\_min / scale)$$

The weight value and the data are both quantized by using the solution of the aforementioned formula, and d_min and d_max are the minimum value and the maximum value of the to-be-quantized parameter.

For the quantization of the weight value, because the weight value is determined when the inference acceleration is performed, the weight value does not need to be calibrated. In the algorithm, d_max and d_min can directly use the maximum value and minimum value of the weight value. According to the algorithm verification result, for the convolutional layer, each convolution kernel adopts one independent quantization coefficient, and the precision of inference is high after quantization. Therefore, the quantization of the convolutional layer weight value is performed according to the number of convolution kernels, and the calculated scaling ratio and the number of the quantization offset are the same as the number of the convolution kernels. For the fully connected layer, the weight value quantization usually uses one set of scaling ratios and quantization offset.

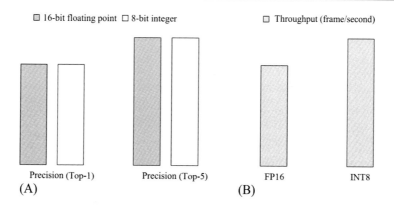

Fig. 6.18

ResNet152 performance on the ImageNet dataset: (A) precision comparison between 16-bit floating-point number (FP16) and 8-bit integer (INT8); (B) comparison between the throughputs of 16-bit floating-point number (FP16) and 8-bit integer (INT8).

Data quantization is to collect statistics on input data of each layer to be quantized, and each layer calculates an optimal set of scaling ratios and quantization offset. Because data is an intermediate result of inference calculation, the range of data is related to input, and a group of reference (the dataset used for inference) input needs to be used as an example to obtain the input data of each layer to determine d_max and d_min for quantization. In practice, the test dataset is often sampled to obtain a small batch of the dataset for quantization. Because the range of the data is related to the input, to make the determined [d_min, d_max] better robust when the network has different input data, a solution of determining the [d_min, d_max] based on the statistical distribution is proposed. The difference between the statistical distribution of the quantized data and the one of the original high-precision data is calculated and the optimal [d_min, d_max] is calculated by minimizing the difference, which leads to the optimal [d_min, d_max], and the offset and scale can be computed thereafter based on the calculation result.

In this case, for the residual network of 152 layers, as shown in Fig. 6.18, a throughput increase of about 50% may be obtained by using a precision cost of less than 0.5%. Quantification plays a significant and practical role in typical industrial application scenarios.

6.3 Object detection

6.3.1 Dataset: COCO

Although ImageNet provides tags for object detection and localization tasks, the most commonly used dataset in this area is the COCO dataset sponsored by Microsoft Corporation, which consists of a large number of daily scene images containing everyday objects. It provides

(A)   (B)   (C)

Fig. 6.19

(A) Iconic object images; (B) iconic scene images; (C) noniconic images. *Picture from: https://www. pexels.com/photo/man-and-woman-wearing-black-and-white-striped-aprons-2696064/; https://www.pexels. com/photo/photo-of-man-doing-rodeo-2664938/; https://www.pexels.com/photo/brown-wooden-center-table- 584399/; https://www.pexels.com/photo/worm-s-eyeview-of-tall-tree-under-a-gray-sky-618608/; https://www. pexels.com/photo/tiger-lying-on-green-grass-2649841/; https://www.pexels.com/photo/nature-animal-dog- pet-33053/.*

richer data for object detection, semantic segmentation, and text annotation with pixel-level annotations, which facilitates training and evaluation of object detection and segmentation algorithms. Every year, this dataset is used for a competition, which covers typical machine vision applications such as object detection, semantic segmentation, key point estimation, and image captioning (the contextual relationship between objects). It is one of the most influential academic competitions since the ILSVRC.

Compared to ImageNet, COCO consists of images, which contain objects with the scene background, i.e., noniconic images. As shown in Fig. 6.19, such an image can better reflect the visual semantics and is more in line with the requirements of image understanding. In contrast, most images in the ImageNet dataset are iconic images, and these are more suitable for image classification, as it is less affected by the semantics.

The COCO object detection task consists of 80 object categories and 20 semantic categories. The 2014 version of the COCO dataset includes 82,783 training images, 40,504 validation images, and 40,775 testing images. The basic format of the dataset is shown in the following table, where the instance segmentation annotates the exact coordinates of each control point on the boundary with a precision of two decimal places. For example, we "segmentation":[180.83, 73.21, 164.07, 44.99, 137.6, 27.34, 107.61, 37.05, 105.85, 54.69, 77.62, 43.22, 50.28, 67.92, 29.99, 93.5, 38.81, 115.55, 59.98, 130.55, 87.33, 133.19, 119.96, 135.84, 134.08, 127.9, 151.72, 109.38, 166.71, 96.15, 181.71, 74.09]

Fig. 6.20
Broccoli boundary points (in (*x*, *y*) pairs) illustration.

randomly select an image[e] from COCO dataset which can be described using the text "Two black food boxes with a variety of cooked foods." To illustrate the polygon segmentation annotation, Fig. 6.20 shows a sequence of boundary points, each in (*x*, *y*) pair, which belongs to the "Broccoli" object in the image. Note that a single object that is occluded may require multiple polygons to represent it. There are also data labeled by traditional bounding boxes (corresponding to the "bbox" field in the image annotation *json* file). The meaning of the four numbers is the top left horizontal coordinate, the top left vertical coordinate, the width, and the height (the unit is pixel). More descriptions and data downloading instructions can be found in the COCO dataset official website.[f]

As mentioned in the first section of this chapter, the evaluation criteria for object detection is more complicated than image classification. The COCO dataset provides more refined criteria, which not only facilitates the data visualization and evaluation but can also help analyze the underlying reasons for typical model errors and identify any shortcomings of the algorithms.

For example, the evaluation criteria provided by COCO includes the mean Average Precision (mAP) based on different Intersection over Union (IoU) thresholds. In terms of the mAP, the evaluation metrics used by COCO are as follows:

- AP: The IoU starts from 0.5, with a step size of 0.05, to 0.95. The mean of the average precision of all 80 categories is computed at each of the 10 IoU thresholds. This is the major evaluation metric for the COCO object detection challenge.
- $AP^{0.5}$: When the IoU is 0.5, the mean average precision of all categories, which is the same as the PASCAL VOC evaluation metrics.
- $AP^{0.75}$: When the IoU is 0.75, the mean of the average precision of all categories, which is stricter than the previous one.

Compared with ImageNet, which focuses on single object localization, the objects to be detected in COCO are smaller and more complex. The "small object" with an area of 32*32 square pixels or less accounts for 41% of the objects. The "medium object" with an area between 32*32 and 96*96 square pixels accounts for 34%, and the rest 24% is "large object"

---

[e] http://cocodataset.org/#explore?id=495090

[f] http://cocodataset.org/#detection-2018.

with an area over 96*96 square pixels. To better evaluate the algorithms, COCO also uses the mean average precision based on the size of the object as follows:

- AP^S: Mean average precision on the "small object": the area is within 32*32 square pixels.
- AP^M: Mean average precision on the "medium object": the area is between 32*32 and 96*96 square pixels.
- AP^L: Mean average precision on the "large object": the area is above 96*96 square pixels.

Besides, the recall rate in the field of object detection describes the number of objects detected out of all the objects in the image. For example, if there are five birds in the image, and the model only detects one, then the recall rate is 20%. For the average precision, COCO also considers the number of repeated calls of the algorithm (repeated detection of each image or 1 time, 10 times, and 100 times) and the different scales of the object, and uses the average recall rate as an important evaluation criterion. These standards established by COCO have gradually been recognized by the academic community and became a universal evaluation standard. It can also be seen in Table 6.2 that the small objects (APS) have lower mean average precision than the large object (APL). In general, smaller objects are more challenging to detect. In addition, when the IoU is 0.5, the mean average precision is higher. It is largely because the mAPs of all 80 categories obtained at the three IoU thresholds of [0.85, 0.90, 0.95] are significantly lower. Especially for small objects, it is generally difficult to achieve a 90% IoU.

Ever since ResNet achieved milestone results on ImageNet in 2015, the subsequent image recognition competitions are no longer as attractive for major companies and universities as it was before. The reason is that after the performance of the algorithm gradually approaches or even surpasses the performance of human, it is difficult for researchers to make subversive improvements in the algorithm. Therefore, the organizing committee chose to end the competition, and researchers moved to the MS-COCO object detection task. As shown in Table 6.3, the best algorithm utilizing the MS-COCO has a mean average precision of only about 53%. Therefore, there are significant rooms for improving state-of-the-art algorithms in object detection. Furthermore, complex object detection algorithms are widely used in the

Table 6.3 Ranking of object detection on COCO Dataset 2017.

Team	AP	AP50	AP75	APS	APM	APL
Megvii (Face++)	0.526	0.73	0.585	0.343	0.556	0.66
UCenter	0.51	0.705	0.558	0.326	0.539	0.648
MSRA	0.507	0.717	0.566	0.343	0.529	0.627
FAIR Mask R-CNN	0.503	0.72	0.558	0.328	0.537	0.627
Trimps-Soushen+QINIU	0.482	0.681	0.534	0.31	0.512	0.61
bharat_umd	0.482	0.694	0.536	0.312	0.514	0.606
DANet	0.459	0.676	0.509	0.283	0.483	0.591
BUPT-Priv	0.435	0.659	0.475	0.251	0.477	0.566
DL61	0.424	0.633	0.471	0.246	0.458	0.551

industry, to enable applications such as autonomous driving, smart security, smart city, and many other areas that need to parse and analyze complex scenes in images for abstraction and analysis. Also, the demand for real-time object detection is very high. Considering autonomous driving as an example, limited by the transmission bandwidth of the internet and environmental conditions, hundreds of image frames and sensor data need to be processed and analyzed per second on the device side. Only when decisions can be made within milliseconds in such systems, the safety of the passengers can be guaranteed.

6.3.2 Algorithm: YoloV3

In the previous section, the residual block was explained and the focus was mostly given on explaining the depth and precision of neural networks. In this section, the Yolo model is demonstrated, and the attention is given more on the speed of network inference. From the first version of Yolo (named from You Only Look Once, meaning "you just have to look at it once," only one convolution block is required) to the third version, the primary objective is to make the object detection as fast as possible. The low precision for small object detection, which is the shortcomings of the previous versions, has been well overcome in YoloV3, and it has become the most cost-effective algorithm so far.

As shown in Table 6.4, under similar hardware configurations, YoloV3 is 100 times faster than the Region-based Convolution Neuron Network [13] (RCNN) and 4 times faster than the Fast Region Convolutional Neural Network [14] (FastRCNN). Furthermore, YoloV3 is 3 times faster than the similar algorithm Single Shot Multibox Detection [15] (SSD) and even more accurate. YoloV3 provides a cost-effective solution for commercial applications with its ability to perform real-time video analysis based on lower-cost hardware, making it one of the most commonly used models for video processing in industrial practices.

Table 6.4 The amazing performance of YoloV3 at IoU = 0.5.

Method	mAP	Inference time (ms)
SSD321	28.0	61
DSSD321	28.0	85
R-FCN	29.9	85
SSD513	31.2	125
DSSD513	33.2	156
FPN FRCN	36.2	172
RetinaNet-50-500	32.5	73
RetinaNet-101-500	34.4	90
RetinaNet101-800	37.8	198
YOLOv3-320	28.2	22
YOLOv3-416	31.0	29
YOLOv3-608	33.0	51

The performance data in the figure is based on the NVIDIA M40 or Titan X graphics card (recreated).

Based on the article "Focal Loss for Dense Object Detection" [16], the commonly used algorithms for object detection can be roughly classified into three categories. The first is the traditional object detection algorithm. Based on the sliding window theory, windows of different sizes and aspect ratios are used to slide across the whole image with certain step size, and then the areas corresponding to these windows are classified. The Histograms of Oriented Gradients [17] (HOG) published in 2005 and the Deformable Part Model [18] (DPM) proposed later are representatives of traditional object detection algorithms. Based on the carefully designed feature extraction method, these algorithms obtain excellent results in certain fields such as human pose detection. After the emergence of deep learning, the traditional image processing algorithms gradually fade out due to the lack of competitiveness in accuracy.

Deep-learning based object detection models can be divided into two groups. The first group is two-stage models. The core idea is similar to the traditional object detection algorithms. The first step is to select multiple high-quality region proposals from the image that probably corresponds to real objects. The next step is to select a pretrained convolutional neural network (such as VGG or ResNet as described above), "cut the waist" at a layer before the fully connected layer and take out the "front half" of the network (layers starting from the input image and to the selected layer) as the feature extractor. The features extracted with the feature extractor for each region proposal are then resized into fixed size required by the successive layers. Based on these features, the successive layers predict the categories and bounding boxes, which are further compared with the ground-truth categories and bounding boxes to train the classifier and the regression model. For example, if the object to detect is "cat," the network is trained to predict the category of the region proposal to be "cat" and regress the bounding box to fit the ground-truth boundary box of "cat." The two-stage models have developed for years from "Selective Search for Object Recognition" [19] and recently evolved to the R-CNN series, while the first stage mostly involves a selective search to extract the region proposals which contain important information of the target objects, and the second stage is to perform classification and regression based on the features extracted upon the region proposals. However, because such algorithms require extracting the features for each region individually, overlapping regions can cause a large amount of redundant computation. A major improvement of Fast R-CNN over R-CNN is that, based on the shift invariance of the convolution operator, the forward inference of the convolutional neural network is only needed to perform once on the image to map the positions of objects from the original image to the convolutional feature map. In addition, Faster R-CNN further improves the efficiency of selective search by using the neural network to predict the candidate object boundary. However, there is still a gap in real-time video analysis.

The second group is one-stage algorithms that use only one network to predict the categories and locations of objects. Algorithms such as SSD and Yolo belong to one-stage methods. The general pipeline of the algorithm is shown in Fig. 6.21. First, the image is resized, and then features are extracted by the convolutional neural network. Then the results are filtered by

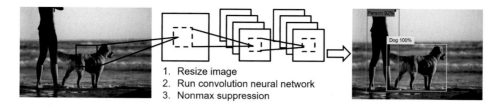

1. Resize image
2. Run convolution neural network
3. Nonmax suppression

Fig. 6.21

The pipeline of the "one-shot" algorithm in Yolo. *Test image is from https://www.pexels.com/photo/animal-beach-clouds-dog-313979.*

nonmaximum suppression, and the bounding boxes, as well as the categories, can be obtained at one shot. In short, it treats the object detection as a regression problem and predicts the labels directly from the image. As can be seen in Fig. 6.21, the two-stage methods are relatively complex and slower, but it has high precision. The one-stage techniques are simple and straightforward with a faster speed, but the mean average precision is relatively lower. In practice, developers can choose the optimal algorithm and hardware architectures based on their business needs and scenarios.

In the first Yolo model, which was published in 2015, the author borrowed the network structures from the popular GoogleNet at the time and attached two fully connected layers to the 24-layer convolutional network, using 1*1 convolution to control the feature dimensions. At the last layer, the author used a linear activation function to predict a 7*7*30 vector matrix. The meaning of 7*7 here is simple and clear. You can refer to the leftmost image in Fig. 6.22. The image is divided into 7*7 small squares (feature maps) and each square region corresponds to its detection result, which is represented as a feature vector of 1*30. For each square region, the authors attempt to predict two target bounding boxes. Defining a bounding box needs four floating-point values: the center point coordinates (x, y) of the bounding box and the width and height (w, h) of the bounding box. The prediction of the bounding box also produces a confidence value, i.e., the probability of the bounding box representing an object. So the number of predicted values of each bounding box is $4 + 1 = 5$. Two bounding boxes require $5*2 = 10$ floating-point values. The remaining 20 floating-point numbers are used for prediction of class labels—20 categories in total since YOLO initially used PASCAL VOC for training. Thus, since each of the 7*7 squares generates $20 + 10 = 30$ floating-point numbers, a 7*7*30 matrix is generated by the network at the end.

The reader can change the number of regions for dividing the image, the number of bounding boxes for each region, and the number of categories to be predicted, based on the characteristics of the data and its applications. Assuming that the image is divided into S*S small regions, each region corresponds to B bounding boxes, and C classes need to be predicted, then the only work is to define the regression target of the neural network a matrix of $S*S*(B*5 + C)$ and retrain or

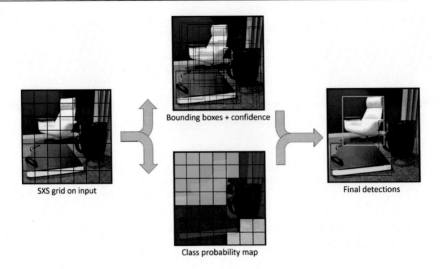

Fig. 6.22

The illustration of the Yolo model. The model divides the input image into small squares of S*S and predicts B bounding boxes for each small square, the confidence for each bounding box, as well as the probability for each category. All predictions can be encoded as a tensor of S*S*(B*5+C). Different colors in the class probability map represent different categories, which are also corresponding to the bounding boxes in the final detection result.

fine tune the network parameters. It should be noted here that a small square in the image corresponds to two bounding boxes, but the two bounding boxes share the same probability value of a particular category. This results in less satisfactory detection results of Yolo for close objects and small objects.

To improve the accuracy under the premise of high performance and to solve the problem of missing the detection of small and close objects, two newer versions of the Yolo network was developed. In a later version, the authors bind the predicted category probabilities to each bounding box. In YoloV2, the authors use a 19-layer Darknet network structure to extract features, and use a couple of techniques such as high-resolution classifier, batch normalization, convolutional with anchor boxes, dimension clusters, and multiscale training, to improve the efficiency and accuracy of the model. In YoloV3, the authors borrow the idea of the residual network, which is mentioned in the previous section, and set a shortcut structure on the 53-layer Darknet network to extract image features. Based on the concept of Feature Pyramid Networks, the authors further modify the network structure and adjust the input size to 416*416, and use feature maps in three scales (the image is divided in three ways 13*13, 26*26, 52*52, respectively). Fine-grained features and the residual network bring a higher level of abstraction, which improves the detection accuracy of YoloV3 for small objects and hence boosting its popularity in industrial practice.

6.3.3 Customized operator practice

Similar to the previous image classification practice, after obtaining the weight file and configuration file of the YoloV3 model from the official website[g] of the author Joseph, the first step is to convert the existing YoloV3 model into the .om format, which is supported by the Ascend AI processor. In this tutorial, the focus is on the process of developing customized operators, so the original implementation of the convolution operators is intentionally removed from the framework. Readers can get all the source code for this use case from the official website of Huawei's Ascend AI processor.[h] In the fifth chapter of this book, we explained how to implement a Reduction operator in the TBE domain-specific language. In this section, we will use the typical two-dimensional convolution operator as an example to illustrate the end-to-end process of customizing a convolution operator and integrating it into networks.

When the reader attempts to convert models from other frameworks into DaVinci offline models through the offline model generation commands mentioned in the image classification section, if there are undefined operators in the model, "operator unsupported" errors can be found in the log files for offline model generation. At this point, you may choose to implement a customized operator. It is notable that when the user redefines the operators that are already supported in the framework and the names are exactly the same (e.g., the two-dimensional convolution operator Conv2D has been defined in the framework, and the reader also implements a new Conv2D operator), the convertor will choose the user's new implementation.

To customize the TBE operator, you need to implement the logic for both Compute and Schedule. Compute describes the computational logic of the algorithm itself, and Schedule describes the scheduling mechanism of the algorithm on the hardware side, including the way to implement the computational logic such as network splitting and data stream. The split of Compute and Schedule resolves the problem of strong coupling of computational logic and hardware implementation, making computing independent from scheduling. Compute can be reused as a standard algorithm on different hardware platforms. After Compute is implemented, the hardware-related mechanism is designed based on the data stream of the computation. Furthermore, to make the customized operators visible to the framework, the customized operators need to be registered with plugins.

As shown in Fig. 6.23, the implementation of the operator logic (including Img2Col matrix expansion, MAD matrix multiplication, etc.) is decoupled from hardware. That is to say, the task scheduling of the operators on the processor side, such as data stream and memory management, is automatically generated by independent scheduling modules. After integration with computational logic and task scheduling, TBE generates cce codes. Then the cce codes are

---

[g] https://pjreddie.com/darknet/yolo/.

[h] https://www.huawei.com/minisite/ascend/cn/.

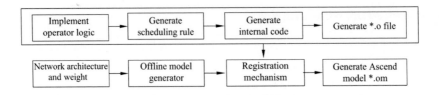

Fig. 6.23
The process of developing a customized operator.

compiled into executable files by the offline model generator through the plug-in mechanism. The .om model file supported by the Ascend AI processor is generated based on the original network weights and configuration files. When individual operators of the current model are not supported, users can develop customized operators in this way and enable the inference of customized models from end to end. Next, let's look at the implementation of the plugin module, operator logic module, and scheduling generation module step by step.

6.3.3.1 Development of plugin

The development of the plugin is similar to what has been described in the programming section. After the offline model generator is launched, the plugin mechanism is called first to notify the framework that the current operator is a user-defined TBE operator and then registers the operator into the framework. So before defining the operator, you need to complete the development of the plugin, so that the executable file which supports the new operator can be generated successfully in the subsequent model conversion.

Specifically, the primary function of the plugin is to establish the correspondence between the name of the DaVinci operator and that of the Caffe operator in the offline model generator, so that the offline model generator can find the dll (dynamic link library) file corresponding to the needed operator during conversion. The customized operator with the same name of the Caffe operator is registered and the executable file for the current operator is generated in a specified path. After conversion, the customized operator is packaged into the DaVinci model to form an .om file. Inference can be done by the offline model directly during the offline model execution phase. It should be noted here that the dll file compiled by the plugin is on the host side and it belongs to the preprocessing stage of model conversion.

The registration of the plugin requires the following items:

- The name of the operator: conv_layer, defined by the user;
- Type of framework: CAFFE (i.e., the framework on which the model trained);
- Operator name in the original framework (here we use Caffe): "Convolution," note that the operator name should be exactly the same as the name in the prototxt file for Caffe model;
- The method used to derive the shape and type of the output: For example, for InferShapeAndType_conv, its implementation can be referred to as the derivation of tensor

shape in the Caffe framework. For the activation function, the shape of the input and the output tensor is the same. Users may implement the functions in other ways as needed;

- Compilation method for the target files of the operator: for example, BuildTeBin_conv;
- Method for executing the operator parsing: TVM;
- Data format: DOMI_TENSOR_NC1HWC0;
- Arrangement of weights: DOMI_TENSOR_FRACTAL_Z;

This book has mentioned many times that when a matrix larger than 16*16 is used for computation, it is recommended to store the matrix in a specific data format in advance, and to read the data in specific tiles during the computation. The way of data arrangement specifies the way of data reading, which is represented by DOMI_TENSOR_FRACTAL_Z. In the next section about the implementation of operators, the details of the data arrangement and computations based on the tiling strategy will be further explained.

To sum up, the way to define a typical operator plugin is presented in Code 6.6:

6.3.3.2 Implementation of the operator

Different from the implementation of the CPU, the implementation of a convolution operator on the Ascend AI processor is more complicated. In order to make full use of the computing power of the Cube Unit, it is necessary to change the input data format in advance, such as arrangement, expansion, and dicing. This section will elaborate on how to implement the convolution operator on the AI Core with a given configuration.

Matrix operation based on Cube Unit

The most basic operations that can be performed by the Cube Unit on the Ascend AI processor are matrix multiplications with input size $M_{cube} \times K_{cube}$ and $K_{cube} \times N_{cube}$. The Cube Unit supports three data types: FP16, INT8, and UINT8. The value of M_{cube}, K_{cube}, and N_{cube} differs by data type, as illustrated in Table 6.5.

CODE 6.6 Example of the definition of a typical operator plugin.

```
REGISTER_CUSTOM_OP("conv_layer")  // Target operator name
   .FrameworkType(CAFFE)          // Source framework
   .OriginOpType("Convolution")   // Source operator name
   .InferShapeAndTypeFn(InferShapeAndType_conv) // Method to derive
shape and type of output
   .TEBinBuildFn(BuildTeBin_conv) // Method to generate target file
   .Formats(DOMI_TENSOR_NC1HWC0}  // Input data format (NC1HWCO 5D)
   .WeightFormats(DOMI_TENSOR_FRACTAL_Z); // Data arrangement
}
```

Table 6.5 M_{cube}, K_{cube}, N_{cube} for different data types.

Data type	M_{cube}	K_{cube}	N_{cube}
INT8	16	32	16
UINT8	16	32	16
FP16	16	16	16

In order to support matrix multiplication operations of any input size, e.g., matrix A of size $M \times K$ and matrix B of size $K \times N$, the input matrices need to be partitioned in advance. To be specific, you need to pad M to multiples of M_{cube}, K to multiples of K_{cube}, and N to multiples of N_{cube}, so that the matrix A can be partitioned into a block matrix of size $\lceil \frac{M}{M_{cube}} \rceil \times \lceil \frac{K}{K_{cube}} \rceil$ (each block is $M_{cube} \times K_{cube}$), and matrix B can be partitioned into a block matrix of size $\lceil \frac{K}{K_{cube}} \rceil \times \lceil \frac{N}{N_{cube}} \rceil$ (each block is $K_{cube} \times N_{cube}$). Then matrix multiplication is performed on each pair of blocks. For example, each multiplication is between two matrices with the size of $M_{cube} \times K_{cube}$ and $K_{cube} \times N_{cube}$, and each addition is between two matrices with the size of $M_{cube} \times N_{cube}$.

Definition of convolution operator parameters and data arrangement

A convolution operator takes an input feature map and a convolution kernel as input, and generates an output feature map.

As mentioned in Chapter 4, in deep learning framework, the feature map data of the convolutional operator is generally arranged in the format of *NHWC* or *NCHW*, where:

- N: The number of sample images in a batch of input data.
- H: The height of the feature map.
- W: The width of the feature map.
- C: The number of channels of the feature map.

On the CPU, the feature map data in the memory is generally arranged in the *NHWC* format. In order to facilitate the presentation, the shape of the input feature map is written as $NH_{in}W_{in}C_{in}$, and the output feature map shape is written as $NH_{out}W_{out}C_{out}$.

The shape of the convolution kernel is written as $C_{out}C_{in}H_kW_k$, where:

- C_{out}: The number of convolution kernels, which is equivalent to the number of channels in the output feature map.
- C_{in}: The number of weight matrices in each convolution kernel, which is equivalent to the number of channels in the input feature map.
- H_k: The height of the weight matrix in the convolution kernel.
- W_k: The width of the weight matrix in the convolution kernel.

In addition, the convolution operator generally has the following parameters:

- P_h: Padding size (one side) along the height of the feature map.
- P_w: Padding size (one side) along the width of the feature map.
- S_h: The stride size of the convolution along the height of the feature map.
- S_w: The stride of the convolution along the width of the feature map.

Accordingly, the height and width of the output feature map are obtained by the following formula:

$$H_{out} = \frac{H_{in} - H_k + 2 \times P_h}{S_h} + 1$$

$$W_{out} = \frac{W_{in} - W_k + 2 \times P_w}{S_w} + 1$$

Example of the Convolutional operator

In order to facilitate the explanation, we assume that the data type is FP16 and all the parameters mentioned above are represented with the following specific values:

- $N = 10$
- $C_{in} = 32$
- $C_{out} = 64$
- $H_{in} = W_{in} = H_{out} = W_{out} = 28$
- $H_k = W_k = 3$
- $P_h = P_w = 1$
- $S_h = S_w = 1$

In this case:

- The shape of input feature map $[N, H_{in}, W_{in}, C_{in}]$, i.e., $[10, 28, 28, 32]$.
- The shape of kernel weights $[C_{out}, C_{in} H_k, W_k]$, i.e., $[64, 32, 3, 3]$.
- The shape of the output feature map $[N, H_{out}, W_{out}, C_{out}]$, i.e., $[10, 28, 28, 64]$.

Format conversion of the input feature map

The format conversion of the input data involves the following steps:

Step 1.   The input data in the *NHWC* format is converted into the 5D format of NC_1HWC_0 defined under the DaVinci architecture.

Step 2.   The 5D format of NC_1HWC_0 is expanded into the 2D format of the input feature map matrix by the Img2Col method.

Step 3.   Based on the "small Z big Z" rule, the memory arrangement of the input feature map matrix is converted.

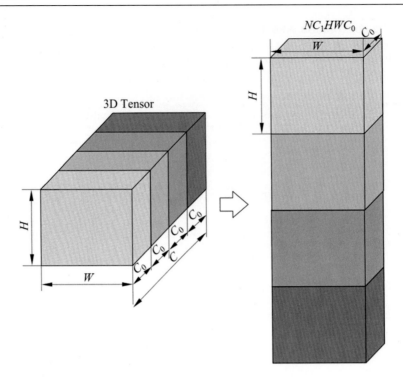

Fig. 6.24
Converting data to 5D NC_1HWC_0 format.

On the Ascend AI processor, the data is saved in the 5D format of NC_1HWC_0, where C_0 is related to the DaVinci architecture and is equal to K_{cube}, and C_1 is the quotient of C_{in} divided by C_0, which can be expressed as $\left\lceil \frac{C_{in}}{K_{cube}} \right\rceil$, as shown in Fig. 6.24. The specific conversion process is as follows:

Step 1. The C_{in} of the input feature map data $[N, H_{in}, W_{in}, C_{in}]$ is split based on K_{cube} to obtain $\left[N, H_{in}, W_{in}, \left\lceil \frac{C_{in}}{K_{cube}} \right\rceil, K_{cube}\right]$, i.e., $[10, 28, 28, 32]$ is split into $[10, 28, 28, 2, 16]$. If C_{in} is not a multiple of K_{cube}, you need to pad zeros to reach the multiple of K_{cube} and then split.

Step 2. Dimensional permutation of $\left[N, H_{in}, W_{in}, \left\lceil \frac{C_{in}}{K_{cube}} \right\rceil, K_{cube}\right]$ gives $\left[N, \left\lceil \frac{C_{in}}{K_{cube}} \right\rceil, H_{in}, W_{in}, K_{cube}\right]$, i.e., $[10, 28, 28, 2, 16]$ is further converted to $[10, 2, 28, 28, 16]$.

The illustration of the entire conversion process is shown in Fig. 6.25. This process takes place in two scenarios:

- The first layer of RGB image data needs to be converted.
- The output feature map data for each layer needs to be rearranged.

After converting the input feature map into the 5D NC_1HWC_0 format, according to the Img2Col algorithm, the data needs to be converted into a 2D format, namely the input feature map matrix. Based on the Img2Col algorithm described above, the shape of the final input feature map matrix is $[N, H_{out}W_{out}, H_kW_kC_{in}]$, where $H_{out}W_{out}$ the height is and $H_kW_kC_{in}$ is the width. As shown in Fig. 6.25, since the C_{in} dimension is split by the Ascend AI processor, the shape of the final input feature matrix is $\left[N, H_{out}W_{out}, \left\lceil \frac{C_{in}}{K_{cube}} \right\rceil H_kW_kK_{cube}\right]$, i.e., $[10, 28*28, 2*3*3*16]$, i.e., $[10, 784, 288]$.

After Img2Col conversion, the input feature map matrix needs to be further converted into the "small Z big Z" layout format, so further splitting and conversion of the axis are needed. Finally, the shape of the input feature map block format is $\left[N, \left\lceil \frac{H_{out}W_{out}}{M_{cube}} \right\rceil, \left\lceil \frac{C_{in}}{K_{cube}} \right\rceil H_kW_k, M_{cube}, K_{cube}\right]$, where $H_{out}W_{out}$ is padded to the multiple of M_{cube} and then split. Considering the example mentioned above, the output shape should be $[10, 49, 18, 16, 16]$. It can be seen that $[16, 16]$ are the height and width of the small matrix, respectively, so it is called the "small Z" arrangement. $[49, 18]$ are the height and width of the block format of the input feature map matrix, respectively. It is called the "big Z" arrangement.

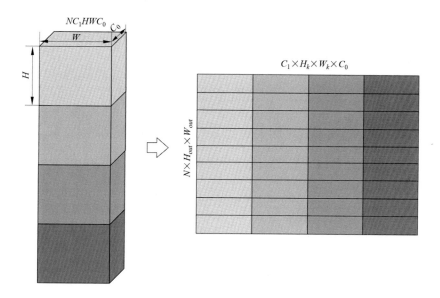

Fig. 6.25
Img2Col on the Ascend AI processor.

The two steps above are done by dedicated hardware in the AI Core. The implementation of the hardware is relatively complicated due to the need to complete all the conversions simultaneously. Fig. 6.26 shows the process of further conversion using the example for calculating the parameters for the convolution kernel given in the previous section, which includes the following steps:

Step 1.   Since the step sizes S_h and S_w are both 1, in order to obtain a small matrix at coordinate (0, 0) in the input feature map matrix (a total of 49*18 small matrices), it is necessary to sequentially read $16*16=256$ number of data in the input feature map, whose shape is $[M_{cube}, K_{cube}]$ and can be directly expanded into a small matrix. It is equivalent to unfolding the pixel points at (0, 0) for the $K_{cube}=16$ convolution kernels.

Step 2.   Continue to read 256 number of data, and a small matrix at coordinate (0,1) can be obtained, which is equivalent to expanding the pixel points at coordinate (0, 1) for the $K_{cube}=16$ convolution kernels. During the process of data reading, based on the different stride sizes, some data may be read multiple times and the hardware can use these data during the conversion process.

Step 3.   Continue to get a small matrix at coordinate (0,2), which is equivalent to expanding the pixels at coordinate (0,2) for the $K_{cube}=16$ convolution kernels.

Step 4.   After the first three steps, $W_k=3$ small matrices have been obtained along the width of the input feature graph matrix, and then the input feature map need to be expanded along with the other $H_k=3$ dimensions. Repeat step 1–3 to expand pixel points of (1,0), (1,1), (1,2), (2,0), (2,1), (2,2) for the $K_{cube}=16$ convolution kernels.

Step 5.   After Steps 1–4, $H_kW_k=9$ small matrices have been obtained along the width of the input feature map matrix. Next is to do a further expansion for $\left\lceil \frac{C_{in}}{K_{cube}} \right\rceil = 2$ dimensions by repeating Steps 1–4.

Step 6.   After Steps 1–5, all the $\left\lceil \frac{C_{in}}{K_{cube}} \right\rceil H_kW_k = 18$ small matrices have been obtained along the width of the input feature map. Then further expansion is done along with the height of the input feature map for $\left\lceil \frac{H_{out}W_{out}}{M_{cube}} \right\rceil = 49$ dimensions by repeating Step 1–5.

Step 7.   After Step 1–6, the last to do is do a further expansion for N dimensions (the batch size of the input feature map), and Step 1–6 is then repeated.

After all the steps above, we finally get $10*49*18=490*18$ small matrices and convert the input feature map into the input feature matrix with the format of "big Z small Z." The final shape of the data is $[10, 49, 18, 16, 16]$.

Format conversion of the weight data

The format conversion of weight data includes the following steps:

Step 1.   The weight data is also converted into the 5D format of NC_1HWC_0, and finally the data of the format $C_{out} \left\lceil \frac{C_{in}}{K_{cube}} \right\rceil H_kW_kK_{cube}$ is obtained.

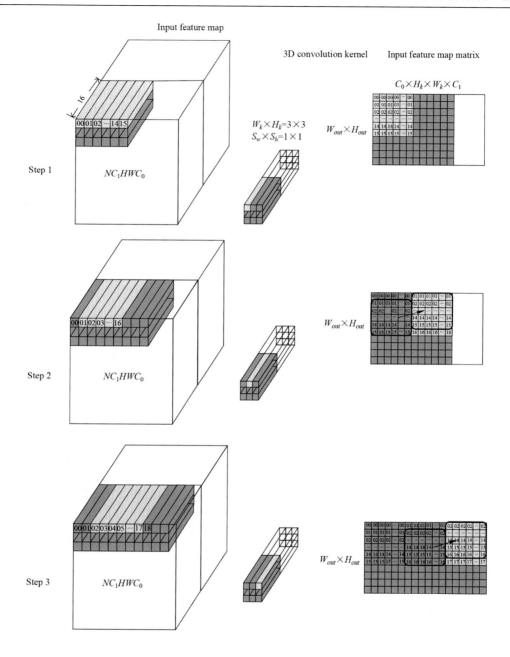

Fig. 6.26

Convert the input feature map data to the input feature matrix.

Step 2.　The 5D format of NC_1HWC_0 is expanded into a 2D format of the weight matrix.

Step 3.　The memory arrangement of the weight matrix is further converted based on "big Z small Z."

The steps above are completed offline by the offline model generator during the model conversion process, and the data can be directly loaded during inference on the Ascend AI processor.

The shape of the weight data is $[C_{out}, C_{in}, H_k, H_w]$, i.e., $[64, 32, 3, 3]$, and after converted to 5D format, the shape becomes $\left[C_{out}, \left\lceil \frac{C_{in}}{K_{cube}} \right\rceil, H_k, H_w, K_{cube}\right]$, i.e., $[64, 2, 3, 3, 16]$.

Since the data conversion is completed offline and the speed is not a concern, the 5D to 2D and the "big Z small N" conversion can be conducted separately. As shown in Fig. 6.27, the weight data needs to be converted into a weight matrix, which is relatively simple to implement. The convolution kernel data of each $K_{cube}(or\ C_0)$ channels are expanded into a column vector, and these column vectors are horizontally concatenated, forming a part of the weight matrix with the shape of $[H_kH_wK_{cube}, C_{out}]$, i.e., $[144, 64]$. After that, the operation is repeated along the height direction of the weight matrix for $\left\lceil \frac{C_{in}}{K_{cube}} \right\rceil = 2$ dimensions, and the final weight matrix $\left[\left\lceil \frac{C_{in}}{K_{cube}} \right\rceil H_kH_wK_{cube}, C_{out}\right]$ (i.e., $[288, 64]$) can be obtained.

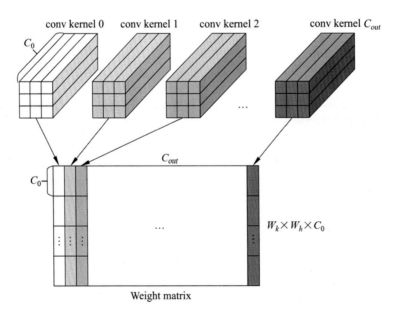

Fig. 6.27
Conversion of the weight data to the weight matrix.

After Img2Col conversion, the weight matrix needs to be further converted into a "big Z small N" layout format. Therefore, further splitting and conversion of the axis are needed. Finally, the shape of the weight matrix block format is $\left[\left[\left\lceil \frac{C_{in}}{K_{cube}} \right\rceil H_k W_k, \left\lceil \frac{C_{out}}{N_{cube}} \right\rceil \right], N_{cube}, K_{cube} \right]$ (i.e., $[18, 4, 16, 16]$ for the previous example), where C_{out} needs to be padded to the multiple of N_{cube}. It can be seen that $[16, 16]$ are the width and height of the small matrix, arranged based on the column-major, so it is called "small N" arrangement; $[18, 4]$ are the height and width of the weight matrix block format, arranged based on the row-major, so it is called "big Z" arrangement.

Based on the steps above, 18*4 small matrices are finally obtained, and the weight matrix is constructed based on the format of "big Z small N," and the final shape of the converted data is $[18, 4, 16, 16]$.

Format conversion of the output feature map

The shape of the input feature map matrix is $\left[N, \left\lceil \frac{H_{out} W_{out}}{M_{cube}} \right\rceil, \left\lceil \frac{C_{in}}{K_{cube}} \right\rceil H_k W_k, M_{cube}, K_{cube} \right]$, i.e., $[10, 49, 18, 16, 16]$; the weight matrix shape is $\left[\left[\left\lceil \frac{C_{in}}{K_{cube}} \right\rceil H_k H_w, \left\lceil \frac{C_{out}}{N_{cube}} \right\rceil \right], N_{cube}, K_{cube} \right]$, i.e., $[18, 4, 16, 16]$.

The multiplication of the two matrices is done in two steps:

Step (1) The small matrices are multiplied. In specific, two small matrices of size $M_{cube} \times K_{cube}$ and $K_{cube} \times N_{cube}$ are multiplied to obtain a small matrix of size $M_{cube} \times N_{cube}$. For the previous example, two small matrices of size 16×16 are multiplied to obtain a small matrix of size 16×16.

Step (2) The block matrix is multiplied, and the dimension N is placed in the width of the input feature map matrix, that is, block matrices of size $N \left\lceil \frac{H_{out} W_{out}}{M_{cube}} \right\rceil \times \left\lceil \frac{C_{in}}{K_{cube}} \right\rceil H_k W_k$ and $\left\lceil \frac{C_{in}}{K_{cube}} \right\rceil H_k H_w \times \left\lceil \frac{C_{out}}{N_{cube}} \right\rceil$ are multiplied to obtain a block matrix of size $N \left\lceil \frac{H_{out} W_{out}}{M_{cube}} \right\rceil \times \left\lceil \frac{C_{out}}{N_{cube}} \right\rceil$. Specifically, two-block matrices of size 490×18 and 18×4 are multiplied to obtain a block matrix of size 490×4.

AI Core's Cube Unit directly supports small matrix multiplication, which can be computed with one instruction. The resulting small matrix is stored in the format of row-major, i.e., "small Z" arrangement, and the shape is $[M_{cube}, N_{cube}]$, i.e., $[16, 16]$.

For the multiplication of block matrices, it is very similar to regular matrix multiplication. However, the AI Core uses the operation order as shown in Fig. 6.28. That is, the input feature map matrix traverses the small matrices in column-major, the weight matrix traverses the small matrices in row-major, and the output feature map stores the small matrices in column-major.

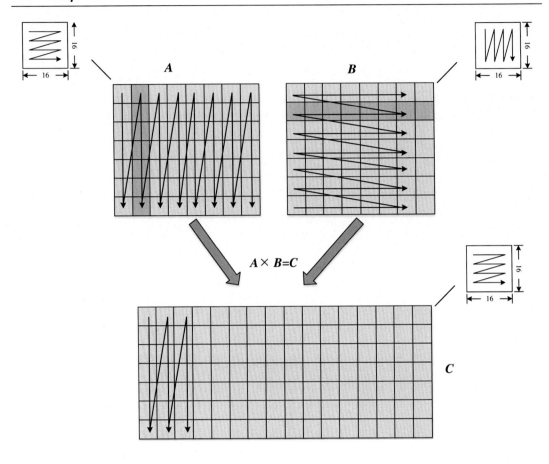

Fig. 6.28
Block matrix multiplication strategy on the Ascend AI processor.

Among the three dimensions of matrix multiplication, the loop numbers are $loop(M) = 490$, $loop(K) = 18$, $loop(N) = 4$. The strategy is to compute the loops from the outside to the inside, i.e., $op(K) \rightarrow loop(N) \rightarrow loop(M)$. So the small matrices of the final output feature map are stored in column-major, i.e., "big N" arrangement, and the data format is $\left[\left\lceil \frac{C_{out}}{N_{cube}} \right\rceil, N \left\lceil \frac{H_{out}W_{out}}{M_{cube}} \right\rceil \right]$, i.e., $[4, 490]$. The corresponding pseudo code is shown in Code 6.7. There are several points to note about such a loop strategy:

- Having the loop with the most iterations, i.e., $loop(M)$, as the innermost loop helps to improve the loop efficiency.
- Put $loop(K)$ as the outermost loop so that the partial accumulation results obtained in each loop and the partial results stored in the buffer, obtained by multiple loops can be accumulated into the final result.

CODE 6.7 Multiplication loop of the block matrix on the AI processor.

```
fp16 A[490][18][16][16], B[18][4][16][16];
fp32 C[4][490][16][16];
for (int k = 0; k < 18; k++) {      // Dimension K
    for (int n = 0; n < 4; n++) { // Dimension N
        for (int m = 0; m < 490; m++) { // Dimension M
        // Multiplication of small matrices
        C[n][m] += A[m][k] * B[k][n]);
        }
    }
}
```

After all the steps above, 490*4 small matrices are obtained, and the output feature map matrix is constructed in the format of "big N small Z," and the final shape is $[4, 490, 16, 16]$. The shape of the output feature map matrix is $\left[\left\lceil \frac{C_{out}}{N_{cube}} \right\rceil, N \left\lceil \frac{H_{out}W_{out}}{M_{cube}} \right\rceil, M_{cube}, N_{cube} \right]$, i.e., $[4, 490, 16, 16]$. In the process of data transfer, a specific reading strategy can be used to remove the redundancy caused by zero paddings, and the obtained data shape is $\left[\left\lceil \frac{C_{out}}{N_{cube}} \right\rceil, N, H_{out}, W_{out}, N_{cube} \right]$, i.e., $[4, 10, 28, 28, 16]$; then through the dimension conversion, we can get the 5D layout format of the output feature map data $\left[N, \left\lceil \frac{C_{out}}{N_{cube}} \right\rceil, H_{out}, W_{out}, N_{cube} \right]$, i.e., $[10, 4, 28, 28, 16]$. For the data type of FP16, $N_{cube} = K_{cube} = 16$, so the resulting output feature map shape is $\left[N, \left\lceil \frac{C_{out}}{K_{cube}} \right\rceil, H_{out}, W_{out}, K_{cube} \right]$, i.e., $[10, 4, 28, 28, 16]$, which is the 5D format of NC_1HWC_0 specified for the AI processor.

Furthermore, if the batch size dimension N of the feature map is placed in the outermost loop of Code 6.7, the shape of the output feature map matrix is $\left[N, \left\lceil \frac{C_{out}}{N_{cube}} \right\rceil, \left\lceil \frac{H_{out}W_{out}}{M_{cube}} \right\rceil, M_{cube}, N_{cube} \right]$. By removing the redundancies, it can be rearranged as $\left[N, \left\lceil \frac{C_{out}}{K_{cube}} \right\rceil, H_{out}, W_{out}, K_{cube} \right]$ (i.e., $[10, 4, 28, 28, 16]$) without performing dimension conversion. Both loop methods introduced above are used in practice and can be selected based on specific needs.

At this point, the whole process of using the Cube Unit for the convolutional operation on AI Core is completed. This operation can be implemented with the TVM primitives. The Ascend AI software stack has encapsulated the implementation of computing and scheduling into an interface te.lang. Cce.conv. Readers can refer to the TVM implementation provided in DDK if interested.

6.3.3.3 Performance analysis

Looking back at the beginning of this section, when the offline model generator generates the offline model yolov3.om, the error log shows there are unsupported operators.[i] At this point, since the reader has completed the development of the convolutional operator computing logic and plugins, the next step is just to copy the completed plugin codes to the installation folder of the ddk package, find the TOPDIR parameter in the corresponding makefile and modify it to the directory where the plugin is located, and compile the plugin.

Once the plugin has been successfully compiled, you can generate the .om model using the same commands at the beginning of this section. Here, the .om model is executed in the same way as the image recognition case. You can refer to the commands shown in Code 6.8.

The object detection results given by YoloV3 are shown in Fig. 6.29. Each image can contain multiple detection bounding boxes, and the category with the highest confidence is used as the detection result. Since the primary strength of YoloV3 is speed, this section focuses on the efficiency of YoloV3 and how the customized convolution operators implemented on the AI CPU and AI Core will affect the throughput of the YoloV3 model.

For the convolutional layers, the total number of operations required is assessed in a simple way. Assume that the number of convolution kernels in the current layer is C_{out} and the convolution kernel size is W_k*H_k, the input feature map channel number is C_{in}, the size of the output data in the horizontal direction is W_{out}, and the size of the output data in the vertical direction is H_{out}. The required number of operations for the current convolutional layer is (in GFLOPS, 1 TFLOPS $=10\,\hat{}\,3$ GFLOPS):

$$T=2*W_k*H_k*C_{out}*H_{out}*W_{out}*C_{in}$$

Based on this, the number of operations of the first 10 layers of YoloV3 can be analyzed as shown in Table 6.6. Following this method, it is not difficult to find that the total number of operations required for the 105 layers of the entire YoloV3 is 65.86 GFLOPS.

The core of the DaVinci architecture is the Cube Unit, which can perform the multiply-accumulate computation of two 16*16 FP16 matrices per instruction, that is, perform 4096

CODE 6.8 Example of generating the offline model for object detection with OMG.

```
$HOME/tools/che/ddk/ddk/uihost/bin/omg —model=yolov3.prototxt —
Weight= yolov3.caffemodel —framework=0 —output= yolov3
```

---

[i] The sample code of the customized operator can be downloaded from https://www.huawei.com/minisite/ascend/cn/.

Fig. 6.29

Example of the object detection result of YoloV3. *Image from https://upload.wikimedia.org/wikipedia/commons/7/79/Motorbike_rider_mono.jpg.*

Table 6.6 Number of operations for YoloV3.

#Layers	Operator	#Conv kernels	Conv kernel	Input shape ($H*W*C$)	Output shape ($H*W*C$)	#Operations (GFLOPs)
0	conv	32	3 * 3/1	416 * 416 * 3	416 * 416 * 32	0.299
1	conv	64	3 * 3/2	416 * 416 * 32	208 * 208 * 64	1.595
2	conv	32	1 * 1/1	208 * 208 * 64	208 * 208 * 32	0.177
3	conv	64	3 * 3/1	208 * 208 * 32	208 * 208 * 64	1.595
4	res	1		208 * 208 * 64	208 * 208 * 64	
5	conv	128	3 * 3/2	208 * 208 * 64	104 * 104 * 128	1.595
6	conv	64	1 * 1/1	104 * 104 * 128	104 * 104 * 64	0.177
7	conv	128	3 * 3/1	104 * 104 * 64	104 * 104 * 128	1.595
8	res	5		104 * 104 * 128	104 * 104 * 128	
9	conv	64	1 * 1/1	104 * 104 * 128	104 * 104 * 64	0.177
10	conv	128	3 * 3/1	104 * 104 * 64	104 * 104 * 128	1.595
...						
104	conv	256	3 * 3/1	52 * 52 * 128	52 * 52 * 256	1.595
105	conv	255	1 * 1/1	52 * 52 * 256	52 * 52 * 255	0.353
						65.862

multiply-accumulate operations. On a typical CPU, only one multiply-accumulate operation can be performed under each instruction. Assume that within the same period of time, the number of instructions that the CPU can execute is 4 times more than that of the AI Core. However, the execution efficiency of the CPU is a 1000 times worse than the AI Core.

Of course, the end-to-end throughput of the computing hardware does not entirely depend on its computing power. It is also affected by multiple factors, such as memory transfer and task scheduling. Assuming the computation time when the Cube Unit is fully loaded is Tc, and the task scheduling and data transfer time required on the AI CPU and the AI Core are similar and are represented by Td, the estimated time on the AI Core is:

$$Tc + Td$$

The time required on the AI CPU is:

$$1000 * Tc + Td$$

Furthermore, if assuming the time Tc of the full-load computation in the Cube Unit is to be p times larger than Td, with the ratio of the execution time on the AI Core and the AI CPU as the vertical axis R, curves can be drawn as shown in Fig. 6.30. In Fig. 6.30A, p ranges from 0.01 to 10 with a step size of 0.01; in Fig. 6.30B, p ranges from 0.0001 to 0.01 with a step size of 0.0001. It is easy to see that as the value of p increases, the advantage of the AI Core becomes increasingly significant, but the growth rate gradually slows down and eventually converges to the theoretical limit. When p is small, as shown in (Fig. 6.30B), which is also a more common situation in practice, the ratio R of the computational efficiency on the AI Core to the AI CPU can be approximated by a linear function.

For the implementation of the TBE operator, the Compute and Schedule are implemented separately, and it means the computation logic and the scheduling logic are separated. With the change of one single line of code, the convolutional operator can be implemented either on the AI CPU or AI Core.

The implementation of AI Core is:

```
sch = auto_schedule(tensor_list[-1])
```

The implementation on the AI CPU is:

```
sch = cpu_schedule(tensor_list[-1])
```

Taking the YoloV3, which has 65.86 GFLOPS as an example, the convolution operator is implemented on the AI CPU and the AI Core, respectively, and the ideal throughput ratio produced is as shown in the Fig. 6.31 (here Batch Size = 1). Of course, the specific implementation of the customized operator (especially the way of data segmentation) will also affect the resource utilization of the Cube Unit in the AI Core, thus affecting the computational efficiency. However, in general, when performing a large number of matrix multiplication operations, the operators will be arranged on the AI Core as much as possible; when the amount of computation is small, or the parallelization is difficult, the operators will be arranged on the AI CPU for better computational efficiency. In this case, since the Ascend 310 single processor

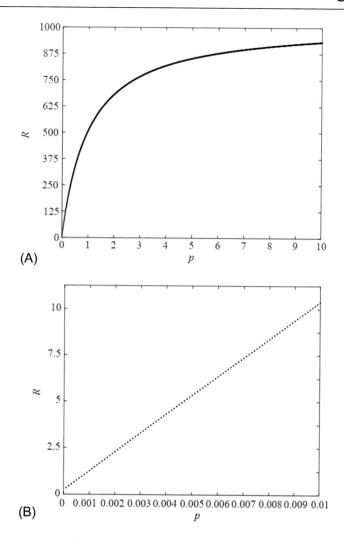

Fig. 6.30
Comparison of computational efficiency between AI CPU and AI Core. (A) p range: 0.01–10.
(B) p range: 0.0001–0.01.

has the computing power of 16 TOPS for INT8, if the model is quantized to INT8, the theoretical throughput limit is:

$$16\,\text{TOPS}/65.86\,\text{GFLOPS} = 242.94\,\text{frames/s}$$

In practice, it is also necessary to concern about the time of task scheduling and data transfer, and the utilization rate of the Cube Unit often cannot reach 100%. So, the measured running time will be negatively affected, which can only reach half of the theoretical limit.

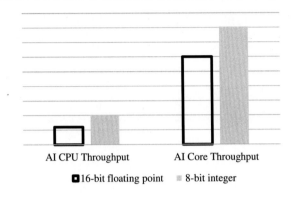

AI CPU Throughput   AI Core Throughput

■ 16-bit floating point   ▪ 8-bit integer

Fig. 6.31
Throughput of YoloV3's convolution operators implemented on AI CPU and AI Core.

Another factor that has a tremendous impact on throughput is the number of input images per batch (i.e., Batch Size, BS). Similar to other dedicated processors, for the Ascend AI processor, a larger Batch Size can often lead to better performance and can increase the gap between the performance for FP16 and INT8. Fig. 6.32 shows the throughput of the two commonly used image recognition networks VGG19 and ResNet50 with different Batch Sizes on the ImageNet dataset. It is easy to observe that for INT8, increasing the Batch Size from 1 to 8 doubles the performance of ResNet and triples the throughput for VGG19. Therefore, the user can choose the appropriate number of images per batch in practice to achieve an optimal balance between throughput and response time.

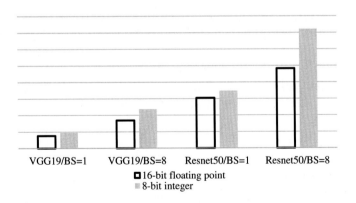

VGG19/BS=1   VGG19/BS=8   Resnet50/BS=1   Resnet50/BS=8

■ 16-bit floating point
▪ 8-bit integer

Fig. 6.32
Throughput between VGG19 and ResNet50 at Batch Size = 1/Batch Size = 8 on the ImageNet dataset.

6.3.3.4 Performance improvement tips

In summary, given the characteristics of the Ascend 310 processor, to improve the performance of the algorithm, it is necessary to maximize the utilization rate of the Cube and reduce the ratio of data transfer and Vector computation. In general, consider the following tips:

(1) Network structure selection

It is recommended to use mainstream network structures. For example, the image recognition networks can be selected from the built-in networks such as ResNet and MobileNet, as the performance of these networks has been optimized. For object detection, similarly, it is recommended to use mainstream detection networks, such as FasterRCNN, SSD, etc., as their performance has been optimized.

It is not recommended to use obsolete network structures, such as VGG, AlexNet, etc., because the model sizes of these networks are enormous, the bandwidth pressure is high, and the accuracy of these models is lower than that of the ResNet.

As shown in Fig. 6.33, the M, K, N in the matrix multiplication should be taken as multiples of 16. The algorithm should consider increasing the number of channels as appropriate, rather than reducing the number of channels by grouping.

Increasing data reuse rate: more times of a parameter is used, lower bandwidth utilization rate will be. Therefore, the algorithm should consider increasing the number of times for reusing the convolution kernels, such as increasing the feature map sizes or avoiding large stride sizes.

(2) Convolution (Conv) operator

In FP16 mode, the number of input and output channels of the convolution operator is recommended to be a multiple of 16.

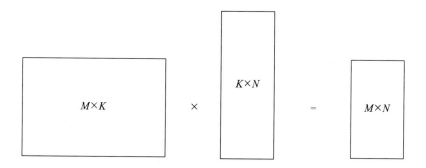

Fig. 6.33

Illustration of matrix multiplication (left matrix size $M*K$, right matrix size $K*N$, output matrix size $M*N$).

In INT8 mode, the number of input and output channels of the convolution operator is recommended to be a multiple of 32.

In INT8 mode, between multiple convolution operators, it is recommended to insert as few pooling operators as possible.

(3) Fully connected (FC) operator

When there is a fully connected operator in the network, try to perform inference with more images in a batch.

(4) Concatenation (Concat) operator

In FP16 mode, the channel number of the input tensor of the concatenation operator is recommended to be a multiple of 16.

In INT8 mode, the channel number of the input tensor of the concatenation operator is recommended to be a multiple of 32.

(5) Operator fusion

It is recommended to use a combination of Conv+BatchNorm+Scale+ReLU, whose performance has been optimized.

(6) Normalized operator

It is recommended to use the BatchNorm operator and use pretrained normalization parameters.

It is not recommended to use operators that need to calculate normalized parameters online, such as LRN [20].

(7) Techniques for optimizing the performance of typical operators

The performance of Conv+(BatchNorm+Scale)+ReLU is better than the performance of Conv+(BatchNorm+Scale)+tanh. As shown in Fig. 6.34, complex activation functions should be avoided.

When the concatenation operator is used on the channel (C) dimension, the performance is better when the number of channels of the input tensor is a multiple of 16.

The fully connected operator performs better when the batch size is a multiple of 16.

Continuous convolution operators perform better; if more Vector operators (such as Pooling) are inserted between convolutional layers, the performance will go down. This is especially obvious for the INT8 model.

In earlier convolutional networks such as AlexNet and GoogleNet, LRN was used as the normalization operator. The computation of this operator is very complicated. During the evolution of the algorithms, it was gradually replaced with other implementation methods such as BatchNorm. In the current mainstream network structures such as ResNet and Inception, LRN is not used anymore. If you want to maximize the performance on the Ascend AI processor, it is recommended to replace the LRN operator with BatchNorm in the network.

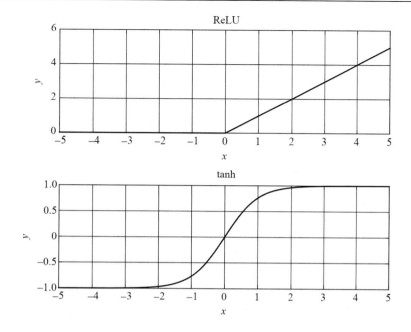

Fig. 6.34

Illustration of the typical activation functions. The computational complexity of the ReLU operator (upper) is significantly lower.

References

[1] F. Yu, V. Koltun, Multi-scale context aggregation by dilated convolutions, arXiv preprint arXiv:1511.07122 (2015).

[2] J. Dai, et al., Deformable convolutional networks, in: Proceedings of the IEEE International Conference on Computer Vision, 2017, pp. 764–773.

[3] A.G. Howard, et al., Mobilenets: efficient convolutional neural networks for mobile vision applications, arXiv preprint arXiv:1704.04861 (2017).

[4] X. Zhang, X. Zhou, M. Lin, J. Sun, Shufflenet: an extremely efficient convolutional neural network for mobile devices, in: Proceedings of the IEEE Conference on Computer Vision and Pattern Recognition, 2018, pp. 6848–6856.

[5] I. Goodfellow, Y. Bengio, A. Courville, Deep Learning, MIT Press, 2016.

[6] COCO Dataset. http://cocodataset.org/#home (Accessed).

[7] Imagenet. http://www.image-net.org/ (Accessed).

[8] O. Russakovsky, et al., Imagenet large scale visual recognition challenge, Int. J. Comput. Vis. 115 (3) (2015) 211–252.

[9] M. Everingham, S.A. Eslami, L. Van Gool, C.K. Williams, J. Winn, A. Zisserman, The pascal visual object classes challenge: a retrospective, Int. J. Comput. Vis. 111 (1) (2015) 98–136.

[10] K. He, X. Zhang, S. Ren, J. Sun, Deep residual learning for image recognition, in: Proceedings of the IEEE Conference on Computer Vision and Pattern Recognition, 2016, pp. 770–778.

[11] Resnet Tensorflow Implementation. https://github.com/tensorflow/models/tree/master/official/resnet (Accessed).

[12] K. He, X. Zhang, S. Ren, J. Sun, Identity mappings in deep residual networks, in: European Conference on Computer Vision, Springer, 2016, pp. 630–645.

[13] R. Girshick, J. Donahue, T. Darrell, J. Malik, Rich feature hierarchies for accurate object detection and semantic segmentation, in: Proceedings of the IEEE Conference on Computer Vision and Pattern Recognition, 2014, pp. 580–587.

[14] R. Girshick, Fast r-cnn, in: Proceedings of the IEEE International Conference on Computer Vision, 2015, pp. 1440–1448.

[15] W. Liu, et al., Ssd: single shot multibox detector, in: European Conference on Computer Vision, Springer, 2016, pp. 21–37.

[16] T.-Y. Lin, P. Goyal, R. Girshick, K. He, P. Dollár, Focal loss for dense object detection, in: Proceedings of the IEEE International Conference on Computer Vision, 2017, pp. 2980–2988.

[17] N. Dalal, B. Triggs, Histograms of oriented gradients for human detection, in: 2005 IEEE Computer Society Conference on Computer Vision and Pattern Recognition (CVPR'05), vol. 1, IEEE, 2005, pp. 886–893.

[18] P.F. Felzenszwalb, R.B. Girshick, D. McAllester, D. Ramanan, Object detection with discriminatively trained part-based models, IEEE Trans. Pattern Anal. Mach. Intell. 32 (9) (2009) 1627–1645.

[19] J.R. Uijlings, K.E. Van De Sande, T. Gevers, A.W. Smeulders, Selective search for object recognition, Int. J. Comput. Vis. 104 (2) (2013) 154–171.

[20] A. Krizhevsky, I. Sutskever, G.E. Hinton, Imagenet classification with deep convolutional neural networks, in: NIPS 2012.

Index

Note: Page numbers followed by *f* indicate figures, *t* indicate tables, and *b* indicate boxes.

Printed in the United States
By Bookmasters